DEFINING MOMENTS
THE KOREAN WAR

DEFINING MOMENTS
THE KOREAN WAR

Leif A. Gruenberg

Omnigraphics

615 Griswold, Detroit MI 48226

Omnigraphics, Inc.

Kevin Hillstrom, *Series Editor*
Cherie D. Abbey, *Managing Editor*
Barry Puckett, *Librarian*
Liz Barbour, *Permissions Associate*

Matthew P. Barbour, *Senior Vice President*
Kay Gill, *Vice President – Directories*
Kevin Hayes, *Operations Manager*
Leif A. Gruenberg, *Development Manager*
David P. Bianco, *Marketing Director*

Peter E. Ruffner, *Publisher*
Frederick G. Ruffner, *Chairman*

Library of Congress Cataloging-in-Publication Data

The Korean War/ by Leif A. Gruenberg
   p. cm. -- (Defining moments)
   Includes bibliographical references and index.
   ISBN 0-7808-0766-9 (hardcover : alk. paper)
   1. Korean War, 1950-1953. 2. Korean War, 1950-1953--Participation, American. 1.
Gruenberg, Leif A., 1959- II. Series.
    DS918.K556 2004
    951.904'2--dc22

        2004020793

TABLE OF CONTENTS

NARRATIVE OVERVIEW

BIOGRAPHIES

PRIMARY SOURCES

PREFACE

Throughout the course of America's existence, its people, culture, and institutions have been periodically challenged—and in many cases transformed—by profound historical events. Some of these momentous events, such as women's suffrage, the civil rights movement, and U.S. involvement in World War II, have invigorated the nation and strengthened American confidence and capabilities. Others, such as the McCarthy era, the Vietnam War, and Watergate, have prompted troubled assessments and heated debates about the country's core beliefs and character.

Some of these defining moments in American history were years or even decades in the making. The Harlem Renaissance and the New Deal, for example, unfurled over the span of several years, while the American labor movement and the Cold War evolved over the course of decades. Other defining moments, such as the Cuban missile crisis and the terrorist attacks of September 11, 2001, transpired over a matter of days or weeks.

But although significant differences exist among these events in terms of their duration and their place in the timeline of American history, all share the same basic characteristic: they transformed the United States' political, cultural, and social landscape for future generations of Americans.

Taking heed of this fundamental reality, American citizens, schools, and other institutions are increasingly emphasizing the importance of understanding our nation's history. Omnigraphics' new *Defining Moments* series was created for the express purpose of meeting this growing appetite for authoritative, useful historical resources. This new series, which focuses on the most pivotal events in U.S. history from the 20th century forward, will be of enduring value to anyone interested in learning more about America's past—and in understanding how those historical events continue to reverberate in the 21st century.

Each individual volume of *Defining Moments* provides a valuable resource for readers interested in learning about the most profound events in our nation's history. Each volume is organized into three distinct sections—Narrative Overview, Biographies, and Primary Sources.

- The **Narrative Overview** provides readers with a detailed, factual account of the origins and progression of the "defining moment" being examined. It also explores the event's lasting impact on America's political and cultural landscape.

- The **Biographies** section provides valuable biographical background on leading figures associated with the event in question. Each biography concludes with a list of sources for further information on the profiled individual.

- The **Primary Sources** section collects a wide variety of pertinent primary source materials from the era under discussion, including official documents, papers and resolutions, letters, oral histories, memoirs, editorials, and other important works.

Individually, each of these sections is a rich resource for users. Together, they comprise an authoritative, balanced, and absorbing examination of some of the most significant events in U.S. history.

Other notable features contained within each volume in the series include a glossary of important individuals, places, and terms; a detailed chronology featuring page references to relevant sections of the narrative; an annotated bibliography of sources for further study; an extensive general bibliography that reflects the wide range of historical sources consulted by the author; and a subject index.

Acknowledgements

This series was developed in consultation with a distinguished Advisory Board comprised of public librarians, school librarians, and educators. They evaluated the series as it developed, and their comments and suggestions were invaluable throughout the production process. Any errors in this and other volumes in the series are ours alone. Following is a list of board members who contributed to the *Defining Moments* series:

Gail Beaver, M.A., M.A.L.S.
Adjunct Lecturer, University of Michigan
Ann Arbor, MI

Melissa C. Bergin, L.M.S., NBCT
Niskayuna High School
Niskayuna, NY

Rose Davenport, M.S.L.S., Ed.Specialist
Library Media Specialist
Pershing High School Library
Detroit, MI

Karen Imarisio, A.M.L.S.
Assistant Head of Adult Services
Bloomfield Twp. Public Library
Bloomfield Hills, MI

Nancy Larsen, M.L.S., M.S. Ed.
Library Media Specialist
Clarkston High School
Clarkston, MI

Marilyn Mast, M.I.L.S.
Kingswood Campus Librarian
Cranbrook Kingswood Upper School
Bloomfield Hills, MI

Rosemary Orlando, M.L.I.S.
Assistant Director
St. Clair Shores Public Library
St. Clair Shores, MI

Comments and Suggestions

We welcome your comments on *Defining Moments: The Korean War* and suggestions for other events in U.S. history that warrant treatment in the *Defining Moments* series. Correspondence should be addressed to:

Editor, *Defining Moments*
Omnigraphics, Inc.
615 Griswold
Detroit, MI 48226
E-mail: editorial@omnigraphics.com

HOW TO USE THIS BOOK

Defining Moments: The Korean War provides users with a detailed and authoritative overview of the conflict, as well as the principal figures involved in this pivotal event in U.S. history. The preparation and arrangement of this volume—and all other books in the *Defining Moments* series—reflect an emphasis on providing a thorough and objective account of events that shaped our nation, presented in an easy-to-use reference work.

Defining Moments: The Korean War is divided into three primary sections. The first of these sections, the **Narrative Overview**, provides a detailed, factual account of the Korean War, exploring pivotal events such as the invasion at Inchon, the surprise entrance of the Chinese into the conflict, and the Cold War ramifications of the war. It also explores the conflict's lasting impact on America's political landscape and military strategies.

The second section, **Biographies**, provides valuable biographical background on leading figures involved in the conflict, including President Harry S. Truman, General Douglas MacArthur, South Korean President Syngman Rhee, and North Korean President Kim Il Sung. Each biography concludes with a list of sources for further information on the profiled individual.

The third section, **Primary Sources**, collects crucial and enlightening documents from the Korean War, from President Harry Truman's condemnation of the North Korean invasion of South Korea to an American serviceman's account of his experiences as a POW. Other primary sources featured in *Defining Moments: The Korean War* include excerpts from official documents, papers and resolutions, speeches, letters, memoirs, editorials, and other important works.

Defining Moments: The Korean War also includes the following valuable features:

- Attribution and referencing of primary sources and other quoted material to help guide users to other valuable historical research resources.

- Glossary of Important People, Places, and Terms.

- Detailed Chronology of events with a *see reference feature.* Under this arrangement, events listed in the chronology include a reference to page numbers within the Narrative Overview wherein users can find additional information on the event in question.

- Photographs of the leading figures and major events of the Korean War.

- Sources for Further Study, an annotated list of noteworthy Korean War-related works.

- Extensive bibliography of works consulted in the creation of this book, including books, periodicals, Internet sites, and videotape materials.

- A Subject Index.

IMPORTANT PEOPLE, PLACES, AND TERMS

Note on personal names and alphabetization: Traditionally, Korean, Chinese, and other Asian names are listed with the family name first and the given name last, as in Kim Il Sung. In an alphabetical list, the elements of these Korean names are not reversed and they are alphabetized under the family name—the first element (Kim). Some Koreans choose to use a Westernized form of their name, placing the family name as the last element, as in Syngman Rhee. These names, in an alphabetical list, are treated like Western names—the elements of the names are reversed and separated by a comma (Rhee, Syngman). For Chinese names, the pinyin spelling system has been used (Mao Zedong), except when a different form would be more easily recognized (Chiang Kai-shek).

Acheson, Dean
Secretary of State under President Truman

Allied powers
During World War II, a group of countries (including France, Great Britain, the Soviet Union, the United States, Canada, Australia, most of Europe, and other nations) that fought against the Axis powers

Almond, Edward (Ned)
Commander of X Corps in Korea (August 1950-July 1951)

Armistice agreement
Agreement between UN and Communist forces that concluded the Korean War, signed July 27, 1953

Axis powers
During World War II, a group of countries (primarily Germany, Italy, and Japan) that fought against the Allied powers

CCF
Chinese Communist Forces—armed forces from the People's Republic of China

Chiang Kai-shek
Leader of the Nationalist government of the Republic of China in Taiwan (Formosa)

Clark, Mark W.
Commander of UN forces in East Asia from May 1952 to signing of armistice

Collins, Joseph Lawton
Army Chief of Staff under President Truman

Dean, William F.
U.S. Army General and the highest-ranking POW of the war, captured in the opening days of the conflict

Democratic People's Republic of Korea
North Korea

Eighth Army
Main U.S. combat force in Korea under UN command

Eisenhower, Dwight D.
President of the United States (1953-1961) at the end of the Korean War

Inchon
Port west of Seoul, where the U.S. staged a major amphibious assault in September 1950

Joint Chiefs of Staff (JCS)
Advisory group made up of the highest-ranking officer in each branch of the U.S. Armed Forces, led by a JCS chairman from the military ranks

Kim Il Sung
Premier of the Democratic People's Republic of Korea (North Korea)

MacArthur, Douglas
Supreme Commander of UN forces in East Asia (July 1950-April 1951)

Mao Zedong (also spelled Mao Tse-tung)
Premier of the People's Republic of China (Communist China)

NKPA
North Korean People's Army

No Gun Ri
Site of the alleged massacre of numerous South Korean civilians by U.S. forces

Paik Sun Yup
ROK general and commander of South Korean forces

People's Republic of China
Communist China

POW
Prisoner of war

Pusan
Port city in South Korea that was vital link in U.S. military supply line

Pusan Perimeter
Defensive line behind which U.S. and ROK forces retreated during North Korea's initial push south

Pyongyang
Capital of North Korea

Republic of Korea
South Korea

Rhee, Syngman
President of the Republic of Korea (South Korea)

Ridgway, Matthew B.
Commander of the Eighth Army in Korea (December 1950-April 1951), Commander of UN forces in Korea (April 1951-May 1952) after MacArthur was removed

ROK
Republic of Korea (South Korea)

Seoul
Capital of South Korea

Soviet Union
The Union of Soviet Socialist Republics (USSR), a confederation of 15 republics, including Russia

Stalin, Joseph
Premier of the Union of Soviet Socialist Republics (USSR)

T-34
Soviet-built tank that was a cornerstone of North Korea's military forces

Taylor, Maxwell D.
Commander of the Eighth Army in Korea from February 1953 to signing of armistice

Truman, Harry S.
President of the United States (1945-1953) at the beginning of the Korean War

UN
United Nations

USSR
The Union of Soviet Socialist Republics, or Soviet Union, a confederation of 15 republics, including Russia

Van Fleet, James A.
Commander of the Eighth Army in Korea (April 1951-February 1953)

Walker, Walton H. (Johnnie)
Commander of the Eighth Army in Korea (June 1950-December 1950)

X Corps
UN force created in August 1950 specifically for the Inchon invasion

CHRONOLOGY

1910

Japan annexes Korea, and Korean citizens become subjects of Japan's emperor. *See p. 11.*

1941

Korean nationals forced to serve in Japan's military in World War II. *See p. 12.*

1945

August 6, 1945—The United States drops an atomic bomb on Hiroshima, Japan; three days later, the U.S. drops a second bomb on Nagasaki. *See p. 17.*

August 8, 1945—The Soviet Union declares war on Japan, marches into Japanese-controlled Manchuria (China) and Korea. *See p. 17.*

August 15, 1945—Japan surrenders unconditionally to the United States, releasing its claim on the Korean peninsula. The Soviet Union is to accept the surrender north of the 38th parallel, and the United States will accept the surrender to the south. *See p. 17.*

August-September 1945—U.S. and Soviet troops occupy Korea. *See p. 17.*

September 2, 1945—Japan signs the formal surrender document and relinquishes control over all colonial holdings, including Korea. *See p. 17.*

1946-47

The United States and the Soviet Union hold talks but fail to agree on particulars of a joint trusteeship that will result in the unification of the Korean peninsula. *See p. 20.*

1948

May 10, 1948—A national election is held in Korea under United Nations supervision, but North Korea refuses to participate. Syngman Rhee is elected president of the Republic of Korea (South Korea). *See p. 21.*

September 9, 1948—With Soviet sponsorship, the Democratic People's Republic of Korea (North Korea) is established, with Kim Il Sung as its premier. *See p. 21.*

November-December 1948—Both the United States and the Soviet Union withdraw troops from the Korean peninsula, leaving only advisory forces in place. *See p. 21.*

1950

June 24-25, 1950—Troops from the North Korean People's Army (NKPA) cross the 38th parallel and invade South Korea (ROK). The unprepared ROK troops are overrun. *See p. 29.*

June 25, 1950—The United Nations (UN) Security Council meets in its first-ever emergency session; the Council issues a U.S.-sponsored resolution condemning the NKPA attack and calling for an immediate cessation of hostilities and withdrawal of NKPA troops to the north of the 38th parallel. *See p. 33.*

June 27, 1950—The UN Security Council passes a resolution declaring the North Korean invasion a breach of world peace and calling for UN members to assist the ROK in its resistance against the NKPA. U.S. President Harry S. Truman authorizes air and naval support of the ROK south of the 38th parallel. *See p. 34.*

June 27, 1950—Seoul, the capital of South Korea, falls to the NKPA. *See p. 34.*

June 30, 1950—President Truman authorizes the use of ground troops in North Korea under the command of General Douglas MacArthur. Truman's authorization of the use of ground troops is done without the approval of Congress. *See p. 37.*

July 5, 1950—Task Force Smith, the first U.S. contingent of ground forces, engages the NKPA near Osan. The superior numbers and armor of the NKPA shatter the small U.S. force. *See p. 43.*

July 7, 1950—The UN asks the United States to oversee UN military efforts in Korea. *See p. 47.*

July 8, 1950—President Truman names General MacArthur to command UN forces in Korea. *See p. 47.*

July 20, 1950—Taejon falls to the NKPA. *See p. 48.*

July 29, 1950—General Walton "Johnnie" Walker, commander of the Eighth Army, gives his famous "Stand or Die" speech. *See p. 49.*

August 1-3, 1950—Pusan Perimeter established. *See p. 50.*

September 15, 1950—UN forces launch the pivotal invasion at Inchon. *See p. 59.*

September 16-22, 1950—The Eighth Army breaks out of Pusan Perimeter. *See p. 61.*

September 27-28, 1950—Seoul recaptured by UN forces; Truman authorizes operations north of 38th parallel. *See p. 65.*

September 29, 1950—General Douglas MacArthur officially "delivers" Seoul to South Korean president Syngman Rhee. *See p. 66.*

October 7, 1950—The UN passes a resolution officially authorizing UN troops to take action north of the 38th parallel, stating the new goal of unification of the Korean peninsula. *See p. 68.*

October 15, 1950—President Truman and General MacArthur meet at Wake Island. *See p. 72.*

October 20, 1950—UN forces capture Pyongyang, abandoned by retreating NKPA. *See p. 73.*

October 25-November 2, 1950—First Chinese offensive begins; Chinese Communist Forces (CCF) attack at Unsan; elements of U.S. Eighth Army encounter CCF for the first time. *See p. 76.*

November 24, 1950—The Eighth Army begins its "Home by Christmas" offensive. *See p. 80.*

November 25-27, 1950—Second Chinese offensive begins; CCF attack Eighth Army to the west and X Corps at the Chosin Reservoir. *See p. 81.*

November 28, 1950—General withdrawal of UN forces begins. *See p. 83.*

December 11, 1950—Beginning of massive two-week evacuation of UN forces from North Korea, via port of Hungnam. *See p. 85.*

December 23, 1950—Eighth Army commander General "Johnnie" Walker killed in a jeep accident. General Matthew B. Ridgway named to replace him. *See p. 88.*

December 31, 1950—Third Chinese offensive begins; the CCF invade South Korea and attacks UN positions near the 38th parallel. *See p. 90.*

1951

January 4, 1951—Seoul recaptured by NKPA and CCF. *See p. 90.*

January 4-February 11, 1951—Patrols sent out by Ridgway to search out the CCF encounter little action. *See p. 93.*

February 11, 1951—Fourth Chinese offensive begins; CCF attack UN forces near Chipyong, southeast of Seoul; UN forces follow Ridgway's order to stand rather than retreat, resulting in many Communist casualties. *See p. 93.*

March 14-15, 1951—UN forces regain control of Seoul. *See p. 96.*

April 11, 1951—President Truman relieves General MacArthur of command of UN forces in Korea and Far East; General Ridgway replaces MacArthur; General James Van Fleet replaces Ridgway as commander of Eighth Army. *See p. 97.*

April 22, 1951— Fifth Chinese offensive begins. *See p. 99.*

May 16, 1951—Sixth Chinese offensive begins. *See p. 99.*

June 23, 1951—Soviet ambassador to the UN Jacob Malik broadcasts statement of support for "peace in Asia." *See p. 100.*

June 30, 1951—U.S. broadcasts message to Communist leaders expressing willingness to discuss a cease-fire. *See p. 100.*

July 2, 1951—China and North Korea signal willingness to begin negotiations. *See p. 100.*

July 10, 1951—First armistice talks begin in Kaesong. *See p. 100.*

August 18, 1951—Battle for Bloody Ridge begins, in the area known as the Punchbowl. *See p. 102.*

August 22, 1951—Peace talks suspended amid allegations that the U.S. is using chemical or biological weapons. *See p. 102.*

September 13—Battle for Heartbreak Ridge begins, in the area known as the Punchbowl. *See p. 104.*

October 25, 1951—Diplomatic negotiations resume at Panmunjom. *See p. 104.*

November 27, 1951—Agreement ratified on a dividing line between North and South Korea, also creating the Demilitarized Zone (DMZ). *See p. 106.*

1952

May 12, 1952—General Matthew Ridgway assumes command of NATO forces in Europe, replacing Dwight D. Eisenhower; General Mark Clark replaces Ridgway as UN Commander of forces in Korea. *See p. 108.*

November 4, 1952—Republican presidential nominee Dwight D. Eisenhower defeats Democratic nominee Adlai Stevenson to become the 34th president of the United States. *See p. 108.*

December 1952—President-elect Eisenhower visits American troops in Korea. *See p. 108.*

1953

March 5, 1953—Soviet Premier Joseph Stalin dies; Georgy Malenkov replaces him and makes speech expressing desire for peace in Asia. *See p. 109.*

April 20-May 3, 1953—Operation "Little Switch," an exchange of wounded and sick POWs between UN and Communist forces. *See p. 110.*

July 27, 1953—Armistice signed at Panmunjom, bringing an end to three years of fighting. *See p. 111.*

August 5-December 23, 1953—Operation "Big Switch," the final exchange of POWs on both sides. *See p. 111.*

NARRATIVE OVERVIEW

PROLOGUE

U.S. Army Captain Joseph R. Darrigo went to bed on the night of June 24, 1950, feeling strangely lonesome. He had been sharing a house near the dividing line between North and South Korea with a young, recently arrived lieutenant. The lieutenant had left earlier that day, headed south to Seoul, the capital of South Korea, and was gone for the night. Both officers were part of a military advisory group from the United States that was helping the South Korean army prepare for any potential conflict with North Korea, a Communist nation supported by both China and the Soviet Union. As he drifted off to sleep, he realized that his loneliness stemmed from the fact that he was the only American Army officer at the border.

Darrigo awoke at 3:30 a.m. on Sunday, June 25, to the thundering crash of close artillery fire. His first thought was that the South Korean army was firing at North Korean positions across the border. But when he ran outside the house, he could see the continuous flash of artillery lighting the underside of clouds to the north. Clearly, North Korea was firing on South Korea. Then, in brief lulls between the percussive roar of exploding shells, Darrigo could hear the staccato firing of small arms fire. Some bullets were even hitting his house, which meant that foot soldiers were advancing on his position.

South Korea was being invaded.

In the preceding weeks, Captain Darrigo had become increasingly concerned about strange activity across the border. As part of his assignment, Darrigo had been observing and reporting the activity of the North Koreans, much of which he could see through binoculars.

The 30-year-old Darrigo had been stationed in Korea as an adviser for only six months. Despite his short tour in Korea, however, he was already familiar with the two nations' uneasy coexistence at the border. Since taking up his duties at the border, he had witnessed repeated clashes between North and South Korean troops. These skirmishes were considered typical border harassment, minor enough not to warrant much concern.

In May 1950, though, Darrigo felt a perceptible and alarming change in the atmosphere along the border. The skirmishes initiated by the North suddenly ceased. North Korean civilians near the border were evacuated. Radio broadcasts from Pyongyang, the North Korean capital, spoke of peaceful reunification, which seemed to lull some South Korean border troops into complacency. Finally, the North Korean army had for mysterious reasons removed the railroad tracks that led from Pyongyang to Kaesong, a South Korean city perched on the border dividing North and South Korea.

To Darrigo, these were all signs that an invasion from the North was imminent. He felt that the army had pulled back from the border to prepare for attack, that the removal of civilians was intended to protect them from the impending conflict, and that the radio broadcasts were simply propaganda. The reason for the removal of the railroad tracks, however, remained a puzzle to him.

Darrigo took his concerns to the commanders of the South Korean border forces, but his warnings went unheeded. Even worse, the commanders permitted about half of the South Korean forces normally deployed in the area to go on leave, which left South Korea's border defenses even more vulnerable. Now, they were being overrun by a North Korean army intent on taking full advantage of its enemy's stunned confusion.

Clay Blair, author of *The Forgotten War*, described Captain Joseph Darrigo's experience as he left his house in the early morning hours of June 25, 1950:

> Darrigo grabbed his shirt and shoes and jumped into his jeep, his Korean houseboys on his heels. Still shirtless and shoeless, he drove the jeep down twisting, dusty roads, south toward downtown Kaesong. In the middle of town at a traffic circle, he stopped suddenly, mouth agape. Pulling into the railroad station was a 15-car North Korean train, jammed with infantry—some hanging on the sides. Sometime during the evening the NKPA [North Korean People's Army] had re-laid the railroad tracks!

When the North Korean soldiers spotted Darrigo in his open jeep, they immediately opened fire on him with their Russian-made rifles. Dodging bullets, he sped out of town. He could not go back to his post on the border, as by now it was surely swarming with North Korean soldiers. Instead he drove toward the headquarters of the South Korean army. When he arrived, he was unable to awaken the sleeping guards at headquarters, so he used the jeep to get their attention, ramming it repeatedly against the compound's wooden gate until he was able to rouse them.

The unpreparedness of the defending South Koreans and the chaotic events of that morning would prove to be emblematic of the entire conflict known as the Korean War.

Chapter 1

"LAND OF THE MORNING CALM"

—◁◉▷—

Unlike the terrain, the people of Korea are thoroughly hospitable, a docile, gentle folk for the most part, potentially fine soldiers when properly trained, thrifty farmers, and fierce patriots who harbor a century-old hatred for the Japanese, whose brutal police force they well remember.

—U.S. General Matthew B. Ridgway

The causes and effects of the Korean War are rooted in the history and geography of the country that was once called "The Land of the Morning Calm." Indeed, the cultural background of the people of Korea and the geographical characteristics of the land in which they lived influenced why and how the Korean War was fought.

Geography

The Korean peninsula is about 600 miles long, north to south, and varies from 100 to 200 miles wide, east to west. It is surrounded by water on three sides, with the Sea of Japan to the east, the Yellow Sea (including Korea Bay) to the west, and the East China Sea to the south. To the north, Korea shares an 850-mile jagged border with China. It also shares an 11-mile border at the northeastern edge of the peninsula with what was—at the time of the Korean War—the Soviet Union (the Union of Soviet Socialist Republics, or USSR). Korea's other closest neighbor is Japan, to the east on the other side of the Sea of Japan.

In many ways, the Korean peninsula is a place of physical extremes. Located between the sub-arctic Sea of Japan and the tropical Yellow Sea, the country

The Korean Peninsula in the Far East after World War II.

is subject to a wide range of weather conditions throughout the year. The Korean peninsula lies in what is normally a temperate zone. But weather conditions include long bitter winters in which temperatures sometimes plunge to -50° Fahrenheit and short, oppressively muggy summers that include mud-soaked typhoons. Spring and fall are more pleasant but brief.

Mountains cover much of Korea. The Hamgyong Range runs north to south near the eastern shore of the northern half of the peninsula, and the Taebaek Range runs north to south near the eastern shore of the southern half of the peninsula. The Nangnin Mountains runs north to south in the center of North Korea, and the smaller Sobaek Mountains rise in the center of South Korea.

The southern part of the peninsula contains the richer farmland. Here the region's two main food staples, rice and cabbage, have been cultivated in wide green fields for generations. "The country, as a whole, viewed from the air, or while walking in peace among its hills or on its seashores, seems especially blessed with beauty," remarked General Matthew B. Ridgway, who served in the Korean War. Populated areas, however, offered a less pleasant environment, as Ridgway also noted in his book *The Korean War*:

> In the lowlands of the south, its natural cover, the grasses and trees, have long ago been cropped for fuel, food, and fodder, and now the chief growth there is a gnarled and scrubby brush that offers almost no concealment, little fuel, and a minimum of shelter and greenery. Villagers in the south scratch the earth with sticks to collect every last bit of burnable substance to feed their fires. Roots, twigs, straw, rags, trash of every sort are patiently scraped up and stored to keep the stoves going. In the villages the gutters are open sewers and contribute their own savor to the universal stench. Pigs, the chief livestock, roam in indescribable filth.

"A Shrimp between Whales"

When discussing Korean history, many historians find an apt analogy for its past in a Korean proverb that roughly translates to "The shrimp is broken when it's between colliding whales." At the time of North Korea's invasion, two of its closest neighbors were China and the Soviet Union. Both countries were formidable military and economic powers. In addition, they both featured governments determined to exert their will on the Korean peninsula and other places far beyond their borders. But external interference in Korean affairs was nothing new. The tiny nation had been a pawn in the struggles of surrounding empires in many previous centuries.

Early historical evidence indicates that Korea had originally established itself as a nation called Choson in about 2333 B.C.E.. (B.C.E. means "Before the Common Era" and corresponds to BC, while C.E. means "Common Era" and corresponds to AD). Choson was invaded by the Chinese in about 108 B.C.E.. For the next 400 years, parts of Choson were essentially colonies of China. Korea paid tribute, in the form of goods and services, to the Han dynasty of China. This state of affairs led Koreans to pattern much of their civilization after the Chinese.

At the same time, though, three separate Korean states had formed on the peninsula during the last century B.C.E. and had begun to fight for con-

Korean Religious Identity and Nationalism

Japan dominated Korea economically and militarily for nearly half a century. But Korean nationalism thrived, in part due to the religious and national identity that its people had forged over previous centuries.

At the outset of the Three Kingdoms period, which began in about 668 C.E., Korea freed itself from China's grip and re-established itself as an independent kingdom. But some elements of Chinese society remained rooted in Korean culture. One such element was the religion of Buddhism, which had been introduced in Korea by the Chinese. Buddhism became the chief religion in Korea and has remained an important religious, philosophical, and cultural influence on the Korean peninsula for 15 centuries. During the Choson dynasty (1392-1910), which brought the Three Kingdoms period to a close, the teachings of the Chinese philosopher Confucius also became very influential in Korea. In Confucianism, which stresses morality in both personal and public conduct, poetry was held to be the highest of the arts, and men who could not write poetry were not allowed to serve in government positions. Common themes in Korean poetry of the era were the beauty of nature, philosophical contemplation, purity, and serenity. A representative example of the treatment of these themes can be found in this short poem written by an unknown poet of the time:

trol. These three states, called Koguryo, Paekche, and Silla, were also known as the Three Kingdoms. In 313 C.E., Koguryo conquered much of the northern half of the Korean peninsula, wresting control from the Chinese. Still, Chinese influence on the peninsula continued, as Buddhism became the dominant religion in the region in the 300s and 400s. The 500s and 600s were marked by tribal rivalries and divisions, as the Three Kingdoms continued their struggle for control of the peninsula. By 668 C.E., Silla had conquered the other two, unified the Korean peninsula, and established independence from China. The Silla dynasty ruled from about 668 until about 918. The Silla dynasty was replaced by the Koryo (Koguryo) dynasty (the English

Do not enter, snowy heron,
in the valley where the crows are quarreling.
Such angry crows are envious of your whiteness,
And I fear that they will soil the body you have
Washed in the pure stream.

Korean society under Confucianism emphasized classical education over commerce and the arts of war. As a result, when the industrially ambitious and militarily aggressive Japanese annexed Korea in 1910, the clash of societal values was intense. The Japanese attempt to colonize Korea extended not only to industry, agriculture, and education, but also to religious life. Buddhist temples and Confucian shrines were torn down in favor of Shinto shrines. Shintoism, which was distinctly Japanese, emphasized devotion to the gods of natural forces and the divinity of Japan's emperor. Shintoism taught that the emperor was a direct descendant of the sun goddess. At one point during Japan's rule of Korea, worship at Shinto shrines even became mandatory.

But the Japanese failed in their efforts to change Koreans' religious beliefs. Instead, Koreans maintained their traditional beliefs in Buddhism and Confucianism. These religious and philosophical movements became a central force in the struggle against the Japanese occupation and in the development of a nationalist movement, as Koreans turned to these traditional beliefs to help solidify their sense of national identity and to strengthen their desire for independence from Japan.

word "Korea" comes from "Koryo"). The Koryo dynasty was replaced in 1392 by the Choson dynasty, which ruled until 1910.

By the late 1700s, during the Choson dynasty, expanding trade and evangelical missionaries had begun to spread Western ideas through much of Asia. Great Britain, France, and the United States all made efforts to develop international trade with Korea. But the Choson rulers objected to the Catholic ban of Buddhist ancestor worship, and their suspicion of Western learning and religious practices led them to reject Western contact altogether. In fact, their distrust was so great that the Choson regime tightly sealed

11

Communist Kim Il Sung emerged as a major guerrilla leader against Japan.

Korea's borders and shores against any Western trade overtures. This action earned Korea the name "The Hermit Kingdom."

Korea isolated itself from foreign influence for more than half a century. Neighboring Japan, however, had begun trading with countries like the United States as early as 1834. This enabled Japan to expand its economic and military power. In 1876 it used this power to bend Korea to its will. That year, Japan forced Korea to accept an unequal treaty that opened the peninsula's ports to foreign trade.

During the final decades of the 1800s, both China and Russia exhibited strong interest in the Korean peninsula. They were intrigued by Korea's bountiful natural resources and its strategic military location. But China and Russia both remained on the sidelines when Japan forcibly annexed Korea in 1910.

Life under the Japanese Flag

With annexation, Koreans became subjects of the Japanese emperor. Japan brought economic and technological growth to Korea, especially in the north. But the Japanese government treated Korea as a conquered nation. When Japan declared war against China in the Second Sino-Japanese War (1937-45), Japan used Korea as a major staging ground against the massive Chinese ground forces. Korean youths were drafted into the Japanese army during this time, and the country's limited resources were diverted to fighting Japan's war with China. In 1941, about a half million Korean men were drafted into Japan's army to fight in World War II.

In addition, Japan developed industries in Korea through Japanese-owned companies and then removed the profits from the peninsula. It also appropriated Korea's natural resources for its own use. Much of Korea's production of rice in the south, for example, went to feed the growing Japanese population.

Japan even went so far as to try to wipe out the Korean language. In 1937, the Japanese governor of Korea ordered all schools to use the Japanese language and forbade Korean students from speaking their native tongue either inside or outside of school. Korean-language newspapers and magazines were closed, and people were pressured to view themselves as Japanese, rather than Korean. Despite the oppressive Japanese rule, however, Korean nationalism did not subside. As early as 1919, Korean nationalists and students displayed organized resistance to Japanese authority (see "Korean Religious Identity and Nationalism," p. 10).

Two Korean leaders emerged as particularly notable figures in the resistance against Japan. Kim Il Sung, who was deeply influenced by Chinese Communist teachings, led a guerrilla military resistance movement in the North. He was supported in these anti-Japanese activities by the Chinese government (see Kim Il Sung biography, p. 143).

Syngman Rhee, meanwhile, led the resistance movement in the South. Educated in the United States, he spent 14 years in the U.S. and graduated from Princeton University. He believed in capitalism and a democratic, independent Korea. He promoted Korean independence while in exile in Shanghai, China (see Syngman Rhee biography, p. 154).

Japan's annexation of Korea lasted until the final days of World War II. In August 1945, the Soviet Union, which was allied with the United States and others, declared war on Japan and launched an invasion of Korea. The superpowers that emerged victorious from World War II would soon be deciding the future of the tiny Korean peninsula—a shrimp caught between whales.

Chapter 2

THE AFTERMATH OF WORLD WAR II

⊷⦿⊶

We, acting by command of and in behalf of the Emperor of Japan ... hereby proclaim the unconditional surrender to the Allied powers of all the Japanese Imperial General Head-quarters and of all Japanese armed forces and all armed forces under Japanese control wherever situated.

—Excerpt from Japanese surrender document,
September 2, 1945

By the beginning of World War II, Japan had become a major power in Asia. Over the previous century, Japan had expanded its empire and its power far beyond the confines of its island in the western Pacific. In Asia, Japan had assumed control over the region of Manchuria and parts of eastern China, Burma, Thailand, Malaya, the Philippines, and dozens of other South Pacific island nations. And, of course, Korea had been a Japanese colony since 1910.

The Defeat of Japan

In 1945 the Second World War was drawing to a close, bringing an end to the fighting between the Allies (primarily France, Great Britain, the Soviet Union, and the United States), and the Axis powers (primarily Germany, Italy, and Japan). Allied forces had defeated Germany and Italy, two of the three primary Axis powers. But Allied forces had not yet defeated Japan, the third Axis power.

The leaders of the three most powerful Allied powers were U.S. President Franklin D. Roosevelt, Great Britain's Prime Minister Winston Churchill, and

British Prime Minister Winston Churchill (left), U.S. President Franklin D. Roosevelt (center), and Soviet Premier Joseph Stalin (right) at Yalta.

Soviet Premier Joseph Stalin. As the war progressed, these leaders periodically discussed what to do with the territories occupied by the Axis powers in the event of their defeat. At meetings in 1943 in Cairo, Egypt, for example, the "Big Three" leaders discussed the fate of Korea should the Allies defeat Japan. During that conference, Roosevelt endorsed a policy that would ensure a "free and independent Korea," but there were no details as to how that would come about.

In February 1945, Roosevelt, Churchill, and Stalin held their historic conference at Yalta, a town in the Soviet republic of Ukraine. During this meeting they refined their intentions for Korea. They agreed that once Japan was defeated, Korea would become an Allied "trusteeship," whose gradual independence would be overseen by the United States, Great Britain, the Soviet Union, and China.

Just two months later, in April 1945, President Roosevelt died and was succeeded by his vice president, Harry S. Truman (see Harry S. Truman biography, p. 163). In late July 1945, Truman and Stalin discussed the topic of Korea's trusteeship at a conference in Potsdam, The Netherlands. But again, no concrete plans were drawn up for how the trusteeship would be administered.

A short time later, Japan finally succumbed. On August 6, 1945, the United States dropped an atomic bomb on Hiroshima, destroying the city, killing some 66,000 people instantly, and exposing another 69,000 to radiation that would cause illness and death for many. On August 8, the Soviet Union declared war on Japan and invaded Korea and Manchuria, the Chinese region occupied by Japan. The United States warned Japan that unless they surrendered they could "expect a rain of ruin from the air." But Japan would not surrender.

On August 9, 1945, the United States dropped a second atomic bomb on the Japanese city of Nagasaki, killing 39,000 people and exposing 25,000 more to radiation. The carnage caused by the atomic bombs, combined with the Soviet military offensive, sent the Japanese empire reeling. The Japanese government agreed to an unconditional surrender on August 15. Japanese Emperor Hirohito formally signed the surrender document aboard the ship the USS *Missouri* in Tokyo Bay on September 2, 1945, with U.S. General Douglas MacArthur presiding.

Korea Divided

While the United States was celebrating the victory over Japan, Soviet forces made a rapid advance into North Korea. There was a good deal of concern over any expansion of Communism, so the eagerness with which the Soviets entered Korea caused some alarm (see "The Emergence of Communism," p. 22). While no formal treaty had been struck on the trusteeship of Korea, the United States acted quickly to assure that the Soviets would not occupy the entire Korean peninsula, as historian Clay Blair wrote in *The Forgotten War*:

> The swift movement of Soviet troops into northern Korea raised the possibility that Moscow intended to seize control of the whole peninsula. Confronting that unwanted possibility, the Pentagon hurriedly produced a plan to rush American troops into southern Korea to block the Soviet advance. A Pen-

U.S. General Douglas MacArthur accepted the Japanese surrender aboard the USS *Missouri* on September 2, 1945.

tagon Army colonel looked at a school map for "30 minutes" and with complete disdain for terrain or established lines of communication or trade or indigenous political institutions and jurisdictions or property ownership, proposed slicing the Korean peninsula in half at the 38th parallel. Moscow accepted the partition without objection.

The 38th parallel (38 degrees longitude north of the equator) was merely an identifiable imaginary line. It happened to fall in the midsection of the Korean Peninsula, crossing the mountains and valleys of the Taebaek Range and Nangnin Mountains. It also sliced through rivers and other geographic features that would have served as natural boundaries. In dividing the country in half along an east-west axis, the more industrialized north was isolated from the southern half, where agriculture was the primary economic activity. That distribution of assets hurt both regions, as it became clear that both agricultural and industrial resources were vital to a nation's economic success in the post-World War II era.

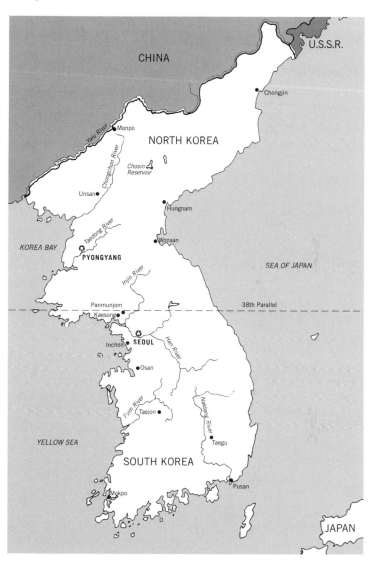

North and South Korea after World War II.

The United Nations

U.S. President Franklin Roosevelt first coined the term "United Nations" in 1942 during World War II, when 26 nations pledged to continue fighting against the Axis powers. Three years later, after the surrender of Germany to Allied forces, the representatives of 50 nations gathered in June 1945 in San Francisco. There, they forged the charter, or mission, of the United Nations, which formally came into existence on October 24, 1945. The preamble to the United Nations charter states the purpose of the international organization's existence:

WE THE PEOPLES OF THE UNITED NATIONS DETERMINED

- to save succeeding generations from the scourge of war, which twice in our lifetime has brought untold sorrow to mankind, and

- to reaffirm faith in fundamental human rights, in the dignity and worth of the human person, in the equal rights of men and women and of nations large and small, and

- to establish conditions under which justice and respect for the obligations arising from treaties and other sources of international law can be maintained, and

- to promote social progress and better standards of life in larger freedom,

The agreement on the dividing line between North and South Korea came relatively easily to the United States and the Soviet Union. The two superpowers, however, were never able to agree on how the trusteeship arrangement would evolve into an independent, unified Korea. Even when the U.S. and Soviet Union held talks in 1946-1947, they failed to approve a joint trusteeship. The United States, which was preoccupied with rebuilding conquered Axis territories, turned the problem over to the newly formed United Nations, or UN (see "The United Nations," p. 20). The Soviets saw this as a betrayal of the original agreement. When the UN tried to initiate free elections for a new Korean government in the North and the South, the Soviets refused to participate. The Soviets and North Korea effectively denied the authority of the UN to make such arrangements.

AND FOR THESE ENDS

- to practice tolerance and live together in peace with one another as good neighbors, and

- to unite our strength to maintain international peace and security, and

- to ensure, by the acceptance of principles and the institution of methods, that armed force shall not be used, save in the common interest, and

- to employ international machinery for the promotion of the economic and social advancement of all peoples,

HAVE RESOLVED TO COMBINE OUR EFFORTS TO ACCOMPLISH THESE AIMS

Accordingly, our respective Governments, through representatives assembled in the city of San Francisco, who have exhibited their full powers found to be in good and due form, have agreed to the present Charter of the United Nations and do hereby establish an international organization to be known as the United Nations.

On May 10, 1948, a UN-sponsored election took place in South Korea only. This election marked the formal beginning of the Republic of Korea (ROK). A national assembly was created, Syngman Rhee was inaugurated as president of the ROK, and the country's capital was established in Seoul. The Soviets countered on September 9, 1948, by sponsoring the creation of a Communist regime in North Korea—the Democratic People's Republic of Korea. Kim Il Sung became its premier, and the North Korean capital was established in Pyongyang.

Military Imbalance in Korea

Late in 1948, the United States began to withdraw its military forces

The Emergence of Communism

Communism is a political and economic system based on the idea that all people in a country should share equally in its property and resources. Communism eliminates most private property and gives it to the government to distribute as it sees fit; it also eliminates personal gain. Under Communism, the community or state as a whole—rather than individuals—owns all the resources, and goods and services are distributed to all as needed. Communism also places severe restrictions on individual rights and allows the government to control the educations, careers, and cultural experiences of the people. For example, freedom of speech, freedom of the press, freedom of religious expression, and political dissent—all of which are hallmarks of democratic societies—are suppressed under Communist forms of government. Capitalism, on the other hand, is a system whereby individuals own property and business, and a free market determines the cost and distribution of goods and services.

The Communist ideology, or system of political thought, was first introduced by Karl Marx and Friedrich Engels in 1848 in their book *The Communist Manifesto*. Communism became the central doctrine of the Russian Revolution, in which the Bolsheviks, led by Vladimir Lenin, violently overthrew the monarchy in Russia in 1917. The eventual result was the establishment of the Soviet Union, also called the Union of Soviet Socialist Republics (USSR), a confederation of 15 republics working toward a common Communist empire. In China, the Communist party was established just a few years later, in 1921. By the end of World War II, the Chinese Communist Party represented a political alliance among peasants, workers, and the middle class. In 1949 the Communists, led by Mao Zedong, formed the People's Republic of China, and Communism became the ruling government.

from Korea, perhaps naively, as pointed out later by General Matthew Ridgway in his memoir *The Korean War*:

> The difference between our approach to the Korean Problem and the Soviet approach is that we had no real goal to aim for

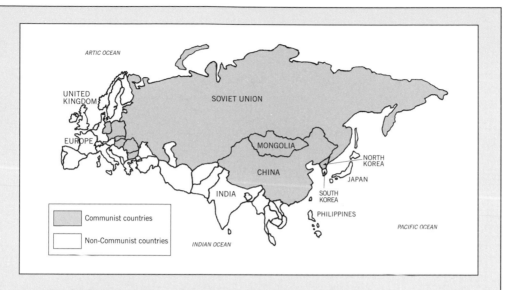

Communist Nations in Europe and Asia during the Cold War.

The Soviet Union and China developed an uneasy alliance during this era. In fact, part of the agreement that was drawn up at the super-powers' conference in Yalta in February 1945 stated: "For its part, the Soviet Union expresses its readiness to conclude with the National Government of China a pact of friendship and alliance between the U.S.S.R. and China in order to render assistance to China with its armed forces for the purpose of liberating China from the Japanese yoke." While this statement seemed reasonable in the context of the war against Japan, it also signaled a pact of Communist solidarity between these two huge nations. Their alliance would ultimately seem threatening to the West, and particularly to the United States, reinforcing many Americans' fears about the expansion of Communism.

beyond a rather dimly visualized "independence" that would leave us free to hasten home and pick up the threads of our domestic concerns. The Soviets, by contrast, visualized from the very beginning an "independence" that would leave the Korean peninsula independent of all nations but Russia.

Both the United States and the Soviet Union completed military withdrawals by the end of 1948. But when they departed, huge differences existed between North and South Korea in their readiness for future military action and the condition, quality, and quantity of their military equipment.

The U.S. withdrawal was colored by its concern about Syngman Rhee, the president of South Korea (ROK). Rhee had made statements about unifying the Korean peninsula by invading the North, which the United States strongly opposed. Hoping to avoid conflict with Soviet-sponsored North Korea, the United States decided to limit Rhee's capacity to conduct such an invasion. As a result, South Korea was outfitted with a "constabulary," essentially a police force, of about 50,000 men. They were supplied with World War II-issue small arms (pistols and rifles), machine guns, ammunition, jeeps, trucks, mortars, and some obsolete anti-tank guns. The South Korean military possessed no tanks, no heavy artillery, and no air force. The United States also provided South Korea with about 500 military advisers, called the Korean Military Advisers Group, or KMAG.

By contrast, when the Soviets withdrew from the North, they left behind a much larger and better equipped fighting force. The North Koreans had a true army, the North Korean People's Army (NKPA), of about 135,000 men. And even after withdrawing its troops, the Soviet Union continued to supply the NKPA with hardware. This included its state-of-the-art T-34 tanks, large quantities of modern arms, automatic weapons, heavy artillery, mortars, trucks, and 180 new aircraft, both fighters and bombers. With this kind of equipment, North Korea clearly held a pronounced military advantage over its southern counterpart.

Growing Tension in the United States: The Cold War

At the same time, there were several factors at work in the United States that affected American policy in South Korea. The greatest issue was the beginning of the Cold War, a period of hostility between the United States and its allies and the Soviet Union and its allies. The Cold War was defined not by open warfare, but by escalating hostilities between the two camps and the division of the major world governments into pro-U.S. and pro-Soviet nations. It was also defined by mutual distrust, suspicion, hostility, and the constant underlying fear that tensions between the two sides might someday erupt into a third world war capable of destroying humanity.

World War II had had a tremendous effect on the balance of power around the world, which American policy makers as well as American citizens were still struggling to understand. Much of the world had been decimated by the war—over 50 million people had been killed, and much of the infrastructure in Europe and Asia had been destroyed. The United States, on the other hand, emerged largely intact. The United States suffered many casualties during the conflict, but at war's end its economic and military power was unmatched, and American faith in and loyalty to the nation's democratic ideals was great.

This confidence was tested, however, by the actions of the Soviet Union and other Communist nations in the postwar era. Following World War II, the Soviet Union occupied many nations in Eastern Europe that it had liberated from the Nazis, including Albania, Bulgaria, Czechoslovakia, East Germany, Hungary, Poland, and Romania. The Soviets then cut off all contact between these nations and the West and installed Communist governments. These countries, collectively known as the Eastern Bloc, became satellites of the Soviet Union. They also formed a protective ring around the Soviet Union.

Western political leaders watched these developments with mounting dismay. Winston Churchill, the former Prime Minister of Great Britain, warned that "an iron curtain has descended across the Continent." Today, historians acknowledge that the Soviet Union's creation of a zone of protection could be construed in part as a defensive measure aimed at self-preservation. But many observers, then and now, interpreted the actions of the Soviets in Eastern Europe as an effort to spread Communism, perhaps as the first step to world domination.

President Truman responded to the emergence of the "Iron Curtain" with a firm argument for a policy of containment and an offer to help any free nation resist Communist aggression. This policy of Communist containment immediately became a bedrock principle of American foreign policy.

The Truman Doctrine

The containment policy was formally articulated for the first time in 1947, when both Greece and Turkey appeared to be on the verge of a Communist takeover. On March 12, 1947, Truman appeared before a joint session of Congress to request $400 million in economic aid to stop the spread of Communism. His speech laid out a new policy, now known as the Truman

Doctrine, which argued for U.S. global leadership in the post-war world and an end to the country's policy of isolationism. The Truman Doctrine guided U.S. foreign policy for the next 40 years (see "The Truman Doctrine," p. 171).

The following year, 1948, saw another escalation in international tensions. Germany had been divided after World War II into four occupation zones administered by the United States, France, Great Britain, and the Soviet Union. The three Western nations consolidated their occupation zones and formed West Germany, with a democratic form of government. The Soviet Union formed East Germany with a Communist form of government. The capital city, Berlin, was similarly divided into zones, with a democratic portion of the city, West Berlin, as the capital of West Germany and a Communist portion of the city, East Berlin, as the capital of East Germany. But Berlin was located inside East Germany, and the Soviets objected to a democratic region there.

In June 1948 the Soviets decided to blockade the city, preventing any goods from reaching West Berlin, with the hope that the West would leave the city rather than risk a war. Instead, the Western powers set up an airlift and shipped food, fuel, medicine, and all other supplies into West Berlin by air. The airlift lasted more than a year. Although the Soviets ultimately backed down, the blockade of Berlin showed their willingness to risk open confrontation.

"An Iron Curtain has descended across the continent," warned Winston Churchill.

Two events in 1949 further fueled international tensions. On August 29, 1949, the Soviet Union detonated its first atomic bomb, marking the beginning of the nuclear arms race. Until that point, only the United States had possessed the technology and scientific knowledge to build an atomic bomb. In fact, the U.S. defense policy relied heavily on the atomic bomb, which had served as a deterrent to outside aggression. Now, the Soviets' ability to match American weaponry altered the strategic landscape and increased the likelihood of global war. To many Americans, it also confirmed their belief that the Soviet Union intended to take over the world and enslave everyone under Communism.

The year 1949 also marked the conclusion of the revolutionary war in China. Mao Zedong and his Communist Party forces ousted Nationalist leader Chiang Kai-shek, who fled to Formosa (now Taiwan). With the People's Republic of China now a Communist country, more than one-quarter of the world's people—including about 500 million Chinese and 200 million Soviets—lived under a Communist form of government.

Taken together, these events created a climate of tension and fear in the United States. Americans increasingly worried that Communists from the Soviet Union and China were intent on destroying American democracy and the American way of life. It was in this environment of anxiety and dread that North Korea invaded South Korea and the United States grappled to find an appropriate response.

Chapter 3

INVASION AND UNITED NATIONS RESPONSE

<figure>✦</figure>

Immediately make a decision when things are put up to you, and you don't want to tell anybody that you've made the decision, but you want to get all the facts and try not to get those facts to support what you think you're going to do. Get all those facts and you put them together and, in the long run, if you're heart's right and you know the history and the background of these things it'll be right.

—President Harry S. Truman

On June 24, 1950, United States President Harry Truman was visiting his hometown of Independence, Missouri. At 9:20 p.m., he received a phone call from Secretary of State Dean Acheson informing him that he had received a wire report that the North Korean People's Army (NKPA) had invaded South Korea. Acheson told him that details were sketchy, but it appeared that the situation was "serious," and that Truman should immediately return to Washington, D.C.

The news that the NKPA had crossed the 38th parallel may well have been more shocking to the leadership in Washington than it was to Captain Joe Darrigo, the U.S. Army captain who witnessed the early morning attack. (Though the attack took place on June 25 on the Korean side of the international dateline, it was still June 24 when the United States learned of the invasion.)

The startling news of the invasion held serious implications for the post-World War II world. There was an assumption in the Truman administration that the only way North Korea would attack the South would be on the direct orders of Joseph Stalin of the Soviet Union. There also was great fear that this

Pressure on the Home Front

The fear of the Communist threat was not restricted to the spread of Communism in Europe and Asia after the end of World War II. In fact, as early as 1938, the U.S. House of Representatives created the House Committee on Un-American Activities (HUAC). The stated purpose of this committee was to identify and stop Communist agents attempting to infiltrate the American political system. The committee proclaimed that labor unions, the movie industry, and even some government agencies had been infiltrated by agents (so-called "reds") from the Soviet Union who were putting out Communist propaganda—this was known as the "Red Scare."

The Red Scare subsided when the country united with other democratic nations to defeat the Axis powers in World War II. However, in the aftermath of the war, some politicians felt that U.S. negotiators were too generous when they divided occupied territories with the Soviet Union. Their claims fed Americans' fears that the threat of Communism could include spies and saboteurs within the U.S. government. One of the most outspoken critics of U.S. policy was Senator Joseph McCarthy, a Wisconsin Republican.

On February 9, 1950, McCarthy made a speech at a Republican Women's Club in West Virginia in which he proclaimed that he had a list of

could be the beginning of a larger, worldwide initiative by Communists to spread their ideology by force, and that Korea might prove to be just one front among many in other parts of the world, including Eastern Europe, the Middle East, and Africa.

Foremost in the minds of political and military leaders in Washington was this question: Was the invasion of South Korea the beginning of a showdown between Communism and the free world that might degenerate into a World War III showdown with nuclear weapons?

U.S. Reaction to the Invasion

Truman was certainly aware of the lessons of World War II. Many historians had pondered how events might have unfolded differently if the democ-

205 members of the Communist Party who worked in the State Department as spies. In the ensuing months, in official hearings in the U.S. Senate, McCarthy indicated that he had evidence that Communists had infiltrated the highest levels of government, including the State Department, the U.S. Army, and even the White House. He repeatedly accused President Truman of being "soft on Communism," and his rhetoric swayed public opinion to a large degree. The Senate investigated hundreds of politicians, military leaders, writers, actors, film directors, and producers, ruining the lives and careers of many innocent people in the process. In the end, not one person who was accused by McCarthy of being a Communist infiltrator was proven to actually be one.

Wisconsin Senator Joseph McCarthy.

Nevertheless, the rhetoric of McCarthyism put additional pressure on the Truman administration to draw the line in Korea and repel the Communist takeover of the peninsula.

racies of Europe and North America had banded together earlier to stop Adolf Hitler. They raised the possibility that while an earlier alliance against Hitler's Germany might not have prevented armed conflict, it might have been sufficient to steer the planet clear of a second world war. If North Korea (with Soviet backing) was acting as an aggressor, as Germany had in World War II, maybe its invasion of South Korea was just the first step toward a wider war. When viewed from that perspective, it was imperative to stop the North Korean aggression in its tracks.

On the trip back to Washington, D.C., from Independence, Truman had some time to think and to consult with the few staff members that were flying back with him. "I was sure that they [the Russians] had trained the North Koreans in order to create a Communist state in Korea as a whole and that their intention was to overthrow the Republic of Korea [South Korea], which had been set up by the United Nations with the Russians' approval," Truman wrote in his memoirs. "The conclusion that I had come to was that force was the only language that the Russian dictatorship could understand. We had to meet them on that basis."

Once he arrived back in Washington, D.C., on June 25, President Truman met with his top military and foreign policy advisers, including Secretary of State Dean Acheson, Secretary of Defense Joseph Collins, Secretary of the Army Frank Pace, Jr., and the Chairman of the Joint Chiefs of Staff, General Omar Bradley. (The Joint Chiefs of Staff, or JCS, is a group made up of the highest-ranking officer in each branch of the U.S. Armed Forces. The JCS is the top military advisory group to the president.) General Bradley wrote in his memoir, *A General's Life*, of the consensus of the group that met that day:

> When you see a force the size of the North Korean army launching an attack … of this size, you knew they had to be backed by Russian equipment. We were not sure for a long time whether or not any Russians were actually in the fighting forces.… And, of course, we had to take into consideration whether or not this would bring on total war. Some of us felt that Russia did not want to go into a world war at this time but was using this as one of those small … aggressive movements to further Communism, more or less piecemeal. And, of course, we never knew whether or not Russia would have gone to war under certain circumstances, but we didn't think she would.

Secretary of the Army Frank Pace Jr., added his perspective as well. "I told [Truman] this was more than just a matter of Korea, that the Russians were testing, and if we allowed this test to go unchecked that they would undoubtedly take bigger steps and this would involve us in bigger problems" he recalled (see "Secretary Pace Recalls the Korean War," p. 183). After consulting with his top aides and his own conscience, President Truman formally asked the United Nations Security Council to issue a resolution denouncing the North Korean aggression.

Meanwhile, the North Korean People's Army continued to advance, routinely overrunning ROK army positions. The main offensive of the NKPA was at the Uijongbu Corridor, a wide valley on the western side of the Taebaek

Range that stood as a sort of gateway to Seoul, the capital of South Korea. It was spearheaded by 40 Russian-built T-34 tanks, each of which weighed 35 tons, had a huge 85-millimeter gun, and could reach speeds of up to 35 miles an hour. In his memoir *From Pusan to Panmunjom*, ROK General Paik Sun Yup, who commanded South Korean forces during the first days of the invasion, wrote that some of his soldiers made valiant attempts to turn back the armored behemoths: "The more courageous soldiers ... overcame their fears. Acting without orders from their officers, a number of them broke into suicide teams and charged T-34s clutching explosives and grenades. They clambered up onto the monsters before touching off the charges."

President Harry S. Truman (left) and Secretary of State Dean Acheson (right) agreed that North Korea's invasion demanded a strong U.S. response.

About 90 ROK soldiers died in this way, slowing but not stopping the advance of the NKPA toward Seoul. By the time the NKPA reached the outskirts of the capital, the city was in chaos. The bridge over the Han River, which cuts through the center of the city, became the main escape route for the city's inhabitants. But panicked ROK troops blew the bridge up—with more than 500 people on it—before they had even completed their retreat. On June 27, Seoul fell to the North Koreans, as thousands of ROK soldiers, refugees, and government officials hastily retreated toward the south.

UN Resolutions and President Truman's Statements

In the first emergency meeting ever of the United Nations Security Council, held on June 25, 1950, the recommendations of the Truman administration were followed. The Security Council issued a resolution, which was unanimously approved (although the Russian delegate did not vote, as he had walked out of the United Nations weeks earlier when the UN refused to admit China as a member). This resolution was the first significant action by the United

Nations, and it effectively paved the way for armed intervention for the first time in its history. It called for an "immediate cessation of hostilities" and for the withdrawal of North Korean forces back to a position north of the 38th parallel (see "United Nations Security Council Resolution, June 25, 1950," p. 178).

The next day, June 26, President Truman issued a brief statement supporting the UN resolution and strongly hinting at the willingness of the U.S. to use its military to assist South Korea: "Our concern over the lawless action taken by the forces from North Korea, and our sympathy and support for the people of Korea in this situation, are being demonstrated by the cooperative action of American personnel in Korea."

The "American personnel in Korea" mentioned in the president's statement, however, referred only to the 500 or so military advisers, who could do little to support the weak ROK Army in the face of superior forces. As the NKPA continued its relentless advance upon Seoul, ROK President Syngman Rhee issued impassioned pleas for military assistance to the United Nations and the United States.

On June 27, the same day that Seoul fell, both the UN and the United States responded. The UN Security Council issued a second resolution stating that "urgent military measures are required to restore international peace and security" and calling upon UN members to "furnish such assistance" (see "United Nations Security Council Resolution, June 27, 1950," p. 180). On the same day, President Truman issued a statement in support of the UN resolution. He also reported that he had ordered the U.S. armed forces to provide air and naval support to the ROK resistance to the NKPA attack (see "Statement by President Harry S. Truman, June 27, 1950," p. 181). Further, he made this broader political statement:

> The attack upon Korea makes it plain beyond all doubt that Communism has passed beyond the use of subversion to conquer independent nations and will now use armed invasion and war. It has defied the orders of the Security Council of the United Nations issued to preserve international peace and security.

In framing his statement of the U.S. response to the UN resolution in these terms, President Truman made it official that this looming conflict was not just about a civil war in a small, distant country—it was a battle between Communism and the free world.

South Korean armed forces were overrun by the ferocious North Korean incursion.

President Truman's quick decision to commit U.S. military forces to support South Korea reflected widely held fears in Washington, D.C., that Communism would engulf the world if it were not contained. As Brigadier General S.L.A. Marshall later wrote, "the future of collective security was at stake, and aggression left unchecked would soon ring the world with fire" (see "'Our Mistakes in Korea' by Brigadier General S.L.A. Marshall," p. 241).

U.S. Military Mobilization Begins

Truman's commitment of air and sea forces to the ROK resistance was just the beginning of the U.S. involvement. The gravity of this commitment

World War II hero Douglas MacArthur was selected to command UN forces in Korea.

escaped many, however, as General Matthew Ridgway acknowledged in his book, *The Korean War*:

The impact of these decisions was not immediately felt in the United States. I believe the majority of our citizens, convinced by press and politician, and by the promptings of their own deepest desires, thought of the Korean outbreak as hardly more than a bonfire that would be extinguished soon enough by the people we had left in charge of such matters. But soldiers everywhere received the news with deep misgivings.... We were not prepared for war, and most of us who first heard this ominous message ... told ourselves that World War III had begun.

The celebrated World War II hero General Douglas MacArthur, who had been serving in Japan as Supreme Commander of the Allied forces in the Pacific, was named Commander of U.S. forces in Korea (see MacArthur biography, p. 148). The Joint Chiefs of Staff (JCS) directive to MacArthur was to observe the situation and assess what assistance the U.S. should supply the ROK in terms of air and naval support. MacArthur wasted no time; on June 29, he flew from his headquarters in Tokyo to Suwon, where ROK president Syngman Rhee had established his government after fleeing from Seoul. As soon as the general arrived, Rhee bluntly told MacArthur, "We are in a hell of a mess."

MacArthur spent a total of eight hours in Korea. He then sent a report to the JCS in which he described the ROK army as being "in confusion." He also declared that the ROK "lacked leadership" and that it had "absolutely no system of communications." He dramatically stated that if the NKPA continued to advance farther south, it would "seriously threaten the fall of the republic." The force of his report was summed up in this paragraph:

> The only assurance for the holding of the present line, and the ability to regain later lost ground, is through the introduction of U.S. ground combat forces into the Korean battle area. To continue to utilize the forces of our Army and Navy without an effective ground element cannot be decisive.... Unless provision is made for the full utilization of the Army-Navy-Air team in this shattered area our mission will at best be needlessly costly in life, money and prestige. At worst it might even be doomed to failure.

U.S. Army Chief of Staff Joe Collins raised no objections to MacArthur's recommendation that the United States immediately commit ground forces to Korea, but he told MacArthur that the plan would take "several hours" to discuss with the president and his aides. Not satisfied, MacArthur shot back a message saying, "Time is of the essence and a clear-cut decision without delay is imperative." Collins responded by immediately sending Frank Pace, Jr., Secretary of the Army, to get Truman's approval. With very little discussion, Truman approved MacArthur's recommendation on June 30, 1950. Political pressure from Capital Hill, where support for the use of military force against Communist aggression was high, almost certainly played a part on this decision (see "Pressure on the Home Front," p. 30).

Truman thus committed ground troops to the conflict in Korea without formal consultation with either the JCS or Congress. Truman's actions violated Article I, Section 8 of the U.S. Constitution, which reserves to Congress the power to raise and support the armed forces as well as the sole power to declare war (see "The United States Constitution, Article 1, Section 8," p. 191).

Once Truman gave the green light, Collins issued this communiqué to MacArthur in Tokyo:

> Everyone here delighted with your prompt action in personally securing first hand view of situation. Congratulations and best wishes. We all have full confidence in you and your command.

Just a few days earlier, at a press conference, President Truman had tried to downplay U.S. intervention in Korea. He defended the commitment to supply air and naval support to the ROK and emphatically declared, "We are *not* at war." A reporter, trying to come up with a workable definition of U.S. involvement in Korea, asked the president, "Would it be possible to call this a police action under the United Nations?"

The president replied, "Yes that is exactly what it amounts to, a police action taken to help the UN repel a bunch of bandits." Truman did not realize at that time what "police action" would ultimately come to mean.

Chapter 4
U.S. FORCES MOVE IN

———

If the best minds in the world had set out to find us the worst
possible location in the world to fight this damnable war,
politically and militarily, the unanimous choice would have
been Korea.

—Dean Acheson

As U.S. commander of forces in the Far East, General Douglas MacArthur
had been directed to use "any and all" ground forces at his command.
Unfortunately, the ground forces closest to the Korean peninsula were
those that had been occupying Japan under MacArthur's command in Tokyo.
By most accounts, the duty of the occupying army in Japan was light, leaving
the soldiers unprepared for the fierce fighting that was to come. U.S. General
Matthew Ridgway, in *The Korean War*, wrote of "the idleness and luxury of
peacetime Japan, where [soldiers] lived on delicacies, whiled time away with
girl friends, and even found servants to shine their shoes."

In addition to the lack of combat readiness, the troops lacked adequate
equipment. The United States had slashed military spending after World War
II, concentrating instead on economic priorities at home and abroad. As a
result, the size of America's standing armed forces shrunk from 12 million
soldiers at the end of World War II to 1.5 million men and women by December 1948, the end of Truman's first term as president.

Truman was not oblivious to this state of affairs. As early as October
1945, he noted in a cabinet meeting that U.S. demobilization of its armed
forces was occurring so quickly that it would be better described as a disinte-

gration of the armed forces. But military spending continued to shrink, driven by Congressional opposition to new military spending, Republican desires to scale back U.S. involvement in international affairs, and Truman's own fiscal conservatism. By 1947 the nation's military budget had been cut to $10.3 billion, from a wartime high of almost $91 billion.

Many in the military believed that post-World War II demobilization and budget cuts had left the U.S. military disgracefully unprepared for war. As Chairman of the Joint Chiefs of Staff General Omar Bradley later wrote, the Army was in a "shockingly deplorable state" and "could not fight its way out of a paper bag."

Preparing to Engage the Enemy

Nevertheless, MacArthur and his staff began to put together a plan for an immediate confrontation with the NKPA. MacArthur had at his disposal several divisions of the Eighth Army stationed in Japan. The commander of the Eighth Army was General Walton H. Walker (nicknamed "Johnnie" after the scotch whiskey Johnnie Walker). He had served under the famous General George Patton in World War II.

Under Walker's command was Major General William F. Dean, commander of the Eighth Army's 24th Infantry division. Of the four Eighth Army division commanders, only Dean had actually led men in combat and knew Korea well. He had served a year in Korea during the U.S. occupation after World War II. Afterward, while serving in Japan, he became known to the Japanese as "the Walking General," as he preferred to walk rather than ride in staff cars whenever it was practical.

MacArthur and his staff put together a hasty plan to initiate immediate action against the rapidly advancing NKPA; there was much concern that delaying the deployment of U.S. ground forces would result in the Korean peninsula being completely taken over by the Communists. Also, as historian Russell Gugeler wrote in *Combat Actions in Korea*, "High ranking officers and riflemen alike shared the belief that a few American soldiers would restore order within a few weeks."

It fell upon Walker and Dean to put together the initial U.S. force that would confront the NKPA. Dean was to move his division as quickly as possible to Korea and move north to halt the NKPA advance to the south. It was

U.S. Military Units

The following lists the units in the U.S. armed forces, in order of size:

Squad—The smallest infantry unit, with 10 to 12 soldiers, usually commanded by a sergeant.

Platoon—Two or more **squads**, usually commanded by a lieutenant.

Company—Two or more **platoons**. Considered the basic army unit, usually composed of about 100 soldiers commanded by a major or a captain.

Battalion—Two or more **companies**, consisting of 30 or more officers and as many as 1,000 soldiers, usually commanded by a lieutenant colonel.

Regiment—Two or more **battalions**, usually commanded by a colonel.

Division—Two or more **regiments**. A major tactical unit, with 15,000 to 20,000 soldiers and officers, usually commanded by a major general.

Corps—Two or three **divisions**, consisting of 30,000 to 60,000 soldiers and officers, and usually commanded by a lieutenant general.

Army—Two or more **corps**. The largest unit, consisting of 120,000 to 200,000 soldiers, usually commanded by a general.

decided that a single "combat team" would be airlifted from Japan to Pusan, the southernmost city in Korea. The remaining troops and equipment would arrive by sea.

On July 1, 1950, the U.S. airlifted a group of 540 men—whose average age was 20—to Korea; they were to be remembered as "Task Force Smith" after their commander, Colonel Charles B. "Brad" Smith.

Task Force Smith

The hurried nature of the deployment of the first troops was further complicated by weather. The summer rainy season had hit both Japan and Korea, and heavy cloud cover and soggy landing field conditions at Pusan

U.S. Army Ranks

Enlisted Rank	Officer Rank
Private	Second Lieutenant
Private First Class	First Lieutenant
Specialist	Captain
Corporal	Major
Sergeant	Lieutenant Colonel
Staff Sergeant	Colonel
Sergeant First Class	Brigadier General (one star)
Master Sergeant	Major General (two star)
First Sergeant	Lieutenant General (three star)
Sergeant Major	General (four star)
Command Sergeant Major	General of the Army (five star)
Sergeant Major of the Army	

compromised Task Force Smith before it even landed in Korea. Only an hour away from Japan by air, the airlift was turned back to Japan once on the morning of July 1 because of poor visibility. Later attempts to land at Pusan were successful, and six planeloads of men arrived. The next day, even though the weather had cleared, the Air Force forbade the landing of any heavy aircraft until the landing strip could be reinforced. This meant that some of the heavier firepower and other equipment Colonel Smith needed had to be left behind in Japan.

Despite a relatively small fighting force and the absence of key military equipment, confidence remained high. Soldiers boasted to one another about the military skill of the U.S. Army, according to Russell A. Gugeler in *Combat Actions in Korea.* "As soon as those North Koreans see an American uniform over here," soldiers were heard to say, "they'll run like hell." (For more from Gugeler's account, see "Troop Recollections from the Early Days of the War," p. 202.) Colonel Smith was supremely confident as well. "No thought of retreat or disaster entered our minds," he later wrote.

From Pusan, Task Force Smith traveled by train to the city of Taejon and then marched on foot to Osan. Early on the morning of July 5 they dug them-

Troops with Task Force Smith at Taejon.

selves into an elevated position along the highway to meet the advancing NKPA. It was a cold, wet, miserable day.

At about 7:00 a.m., Colonel Smith looked through his binoculars and spotted a column of 33 Soviet T-34 tanks moving south along the highway. Because of the heavy cloud cover, Smith could not expect any support from the U.S. aircraft. His small force would be facing whatever was coming down the road without fire from the air. Smith passed on his orders to his men and waited for the tanks to get closer.

When the tanks came within range, Smith's men opened fire with recoilless rifle shells, bazooka shells, and high explosives from the biggest gun they had—one 105-millimeter howitzer, which was a short cannon. None of the first rounds fired were armor-piercing, so they had no effect on the heavily-armored tanks. Smith's troops did have some armor-piercing ammunition—but only six rounds, or shells.

Unfazed by the first rounds fired by Task Force Smith, the NKPA tanks kept rolling south. Smith gave the order to his bazooka team to wait until the tanks were within 700 yards, upon which they fired the six armor-piercing rounds in their possession. They scored direct hits, and the two leading tanks were stopped and burst into flames. The third tank stopped, fired at the lone howitzer, and took out Task Force Smith's artillery with a single round.

Two other tanks were disabled as the column passed and Smith's bazookas were able to fire on the T-34s from behind. But this only slightly affected the NKPA's armored advance. Their only weapons against the tanks now expended, Colonel Smith and his men watched in frustration as the remaining tanks rumbled southward to their destination.

At about 11:00 a.m., Smith spotted more movement coming down the Seoul-Pusan highway. Three tanks led a column of trucks. Smith assumed that it was a supply convoy, but the column actually was carrying two NKPA regiments, about 4,000 to 5,000 men. About half-an-hour later, when the column drew within range, Smith's men opened fire with everything they had: rifles, bazookas, mortars, and machine guns. Several trucks were hit and burst into flames, and the column came to an abrupt stop. Smith's men were shocked to see thousands of men rapidly deploying from the trucks, attacking them both head-on and advancing to their flanks—soon they were almost completely surrounded by the well-disciplined NKPA.

Within just a few hours of the first sighting of the enemy, about 100 of Smith's men were dead. By mid-afternoon, it was clear that Task Force Smith was in a hopeless situation. Smith gave the order to withdraw, a difficult maneuver in broad daylight under heavy enemy fire. The order created what would come to be commonly known in the Korean War as a "bug out." The men plunged into mucky, stinking rice paddies in a desperate attempt to flee the enemy. Many of the soldiers panicked, throwing away rifles, guns, ammo, helmets, and other items that might slow their escape. In their desperation, they left behind their dead and about 30 wounded men, many of whom were killed or captured by the NKPA.

The United States Army's first encounter with the enemy was a shocking, demoralizing event, with over 150 men killed, wounded, captured, or

U.S. soldiers, here seen loading a howitzer against oncoming North Korean troops, were stunned by their failure in the opening weeks of the war.

missing. It took five days for Smith's straggling survivors to regroup, retreating south to Ansong. They ultimately united with about 3,000 more men from the 24th Division, which had landed at Pusan on July 5 and been transported by rail to Pyongtaek.

The News Spreads

The news of what happened to Task Force Smith spread quickly through General Dean's men, planting seeds of doubt about the effectiveness of the Eighth Army's tactics and weaponry—and spreading fear about the true fighting capability of the NKPA.

For the next week, elements of the 24th Division encountered the enemy in a repeating pattern. Small units set up defensive positions and fired on the NKPA, which responded with frontal assaults and attacks on the sides, or flanks, of the U.S. units. These assaults produced more panicked and disorganized U.S. withdrawals, with soldiers leaving behind weapons that the NKPA would ultimately use against them. War correspondent Marguerite Higgins, the only female journalist to cover the conflict in Korea, was with the 24th Division in those early days (see A Woman in Combat, p. 54). In her book *War in Korea: The Report of a Woman Combat Correspondent*, Higgins wrote: "In the coming days I saw young Americans turn and bolt in battle, or throw down their arms, cursing their government for what they thought was embroilment in a hopeless cause…. It was routine to hear comments like 'Just give me a jeep and I know what direction to go in. This mama's boy ain't cut out to be no hero.'"

During these miserable days, the plight of the American soldiers was made even more acute by the poor quality of the weapons and other equipment they received. "We had World War II M-1 rifles whose barrels were so pitted and scarred that the bullets would twist all around when they came out," recalled one infantryman in *Remembered Prisoners of a Forgotten War*, by Lewis H. Carlson. "Everything was so loose that those rifles were always falling apart. As I recall, we did have three new sniper rifles, and those were the only new rifles we had. We also had 2.36 [inch] grenade launchers, which were like pea-shooters against the T-34 tanks we ran into." The oppressive heat and the shockingly poor performance of the ROK troops they encountered merely added to the disillusionment that swept through the ranks.

Generals Walker and Dean met to assess the situation on July 7 and 8 in Taejon, which was still well south of the fierce fighting that was steadily moving southward. Dean then shot off a personal letter to General MacArthur in which he declared his conviction that "the North Korean Army, the North Korean soldier, and his status of training and the quality of his equipment have been underestimated."

The American forces had been fighting the NKPA for just one week. During that time, the North Koreans had advanced 50 miles to the south, and U.S. forces had suffered nearly 3,000 casualties—dead, wounded, missing, or captured soldiers. In addition, valuable weapons, ammunition, and personal gear had been abandoned in the panicked retreats of American soldiers. "What had started out as something of a game had turned into a military nightmare for the American troops," wrote David Halberstam in *The Fifties*. "Here they were, tens of thousands of miles away from home in this godforsaken country, seemingly abandoned by their own country in a war no one was even willing to call a war."

At about the same time, the United States and the UN combined military efforts. On July 7, the United Nations asked the United States to oversee UN military efforts in Korea, and the U.S. agreed. The following day, President Truman named General MacArthur to command UN forces in Korea.

Disaster and Disarray at Taejon

Now that the leaders of the Eighth Army realized that the NKPA was not about to turn and run from American forces, they decided to make a stand at the city of Taejon, which had a natural barrier to the north, the Kum River. The superiority of the NKPA and the apparent lack of strength and resolve of the Eighth Army also forced General MacArthur to sent urgent requests to the Pentagon in Washington for more troops and equipment from the United States, as virtually all his fighting forces in Japan had already been committed to Korea. The grim situation also required MacArthur to postpone a planned invasion by sea at the port of Inchon, behind NKPA positions. Instead, those forces were deployed at Pusan, to back up the steadily retreating U.S. forces to the north.

"What had started out as something of a game had turned into a military nightmare for the American troops."

Part of General Dean's forces dug in on the southern side of the Kum River to await the advancing NKPA. On the morning of July 14, and again on July 16, the NKPA crossed the shallow river in barges, swimming, and on foot in a relentless attack. Dean's men fell back into Taejon in confusion and desperation. Of the 1,000 men deployed to defend the Kum River line, more than half were soon missing, presumed dead, or captured.

The NKPA was not only advancing across the Kum River to the north, but also to the east. Dean attempted to head off this maneuver by sending troops towards the town of Okchon. This diversion of troops made Dean's ability to hold Taejon even more doubtful, but on July 18 Walker implored him to try to hold the city for two more days to allow time for newly arrived reinforcements to deploy. Dean, who many observed to be so exhausted that he couldn't think straight, assured Walker that he could hold the city.

General William Dean was captured by North Korean forces outside of Taejon.

By July 20, NKPA T-34 tanks and infantry were roaming the streets of Taejon, and U.S. forces were engaged in street-to-street fighting. During these clashes, General Dean's behavior as an officer took a strange turn. While most officers commanding a large force would maintain a position at a field command post in order to assess situations and order troop movements, Dean took command of a small bazooka unit and went "hunting" for tanks. In one encounter, the bazooka gunner fired on a tank several times. Each shot missed, however, and soon the gunner had exhausted his ammunition. A frustrated Dean emptied his .45 caliber pistol on the massive machine. Later, the small team "stalked" a T-34, taking a firing position on the second floor of a building. The gunner fired three rounds at the tank and it burst into flames. Reportedly, Dean cried, "I got me a tank!"

Shortly thereafter, Dean returned to his headquarters; the city of Taejon was in flames and dead bodies littered the streets. Dean issued orders for troops to retreat, but in fact, most of the surviving soldiers had already fled the city. Dean and a few other officers climbed aboard jeeps to flee the burning city, but the NKPA had established roadblocks on the routes leaving the city. Dean abandoned his jeep and ran on foot into the hills. He hid from NKPA forces for 36 days, slogging through rice paddies and stumbling through forests and hills. Eventually South Korean civilians turned him over to the NKPA. He became the highest-ranking POW in the Korean War, his imprisonment lasting three years.

Dean was awarded the Medal of Honor by President Truman for heroism in his actions at Taejon, but Dean later expressed great ambivalence about the award. Writing in *General Dean's Story*, he stated that, "There were heroes in Korea, but I was not one of them.... I was a general captured because he took a wrong road. I lost officers and fine men. I'm not proud of that record, and I'm under no delusions that my weeks of command constituted any masterly campaign." He went on to add that he was "humbly grateful" for the Medal of

Honor. "But I came close to shame when I think about the men who did better jobs—some who died doing them—and did not get recognition. I wouldn't have awarded myself a wooden star for what I did as a commander."

In two days of trying to hold Taejon, 4,000 American soldiers were deployed; of those, 1,150 were dead, wounded, or missing. In two weeks of American fighting in Korea, only 8,660 of the 16,000 Eighth Army troops could be accounted for. In the meantime, the NKPA had advanced a total of 75 miles since their first encounter with the UN "police action."

Retreat to the Pusan Perimeter

After Dean's disappearance, General Walker named General John Church as commander of the badly battered 24th Division. Historians have described the 58-year-old Church as "frail and sickly" and a poor choice to be the commander of a demoralized infantry. The ROK forces, meanwhile, had been placed under General MacArthur's command along with other UN forces, which were beginning to arrive from Great Britain, Turkey, Canada, Australia, and other nations. All of these troops disembarked in Pusan, along with a deployment of U.S. Marines.

Considering how outmanned and outgunned the U.S. forces had been, General Johnnie Walker wanted to consolidate all the UN forces into one location and establish a new defensive perimeter. He proposed to MacArthur his plan to withdraw farther south and to defend a line behind the Naktong River in order to protect the ROK government in Taegu. MacArthur did not give him a definitive answer directly, but instead made a public statement that there would "be no Dunkirk in Korea." This was a reference to a port in France that had been the site of a mass evacuation of Allied troops during World War II. Despite the horrible casualties inflicted on the Eighth Army, MacArthur told reporters that "The enemy has lost his great chance for victory in the last three weeks.... I have never been more confident in victory—in ultimate victory—in my life than I am now."

After MacArthur shot down his idea for a withdrawal behind a more sustainable perimeter behind the Naktong River, Johnnie Walker delivered a speech to his division commanders and their staffs on July 29:

> We are fighting a battle against time. There will be no more retreating, withdrawal, or readjustment of the lines or any

other term you choose. There is no line behind us to which we can retreat. Every unit must counterattack to keep the enemy in a state of confusion and off balance. There will be no Dunkirk. A retreat to Pusan would be one of the greatest butcheries in history. We must fight until the end. Capture by these people is worse than death itself. We will fight as a team. If some of us must die, we will die fighting together. Any man who gives ground may be personally responsible for the death of thousands of his comrades. I want you to put this out to all men in the division. I want everybody to understand that we are going to hold this line. We are going to win.

This speech, known as Walker's "Stand or Die" speech, was not well received among the officers and soldiers, who knew who they were up against and how little strength they really had. They also knew that Walker's words "no line behind us to which we can retreat" were meaningless because the Naktong River flowing behind them was a defensible line. His reference to keeping the enemy in "a state of confusion and off balance" must have been especially ironic to men who had known nothing *but* that state since they first encountered the enemy.

Over the next few days, despite MacArthur's confidence and Walker's proclamation, the Eighth Army was forced to withdraw to positions behind the Naktong River. This meant that the total area of South Korea under UN control was a small rectangle of territory—about 100 miles long and 50 miles wide—in the southeast corner of the peninsula. The outer boundary of this territory came to be known as the Pusan Perimeter.

Chapter 5
THE INCHON INVASION

━━◍━━

We shall land at Inchon and I shall crush them.

—General Douglas MacArthur

By August 1, 1950, scarcely a month had passed since UN forces led by the United States first encountered the NKPA. UN forces had been pushed back to a tiny holdout at the southern tip of the Korean peninsula. The United States Eighth Army had suffered more than 6,000 casualties, including 1,884 killed, 2,695 wounded, 523 missing, and 901 taken prisoner. The casualties incurred by the South Korean military (ROK) were a staggering 70,000. At the time, U.S. military leaders estimated North Korean (NKPA) casualties at between 31,000 and 37,000 soldiers. Much later, it was learned that by August 1, the NKPA had lost nearly 58,000 troops.

By August 1, when the Pusan Perimeter was established, some estimates suggest that the NKPA forces numbered 70,000. UN forces, consisting of about 45,000 ROK soldiers and 30,000 American troops, slightly outnumbered the enemy when the perimeter line was drawn. However, long-awaited reinforcements from both the Army and the Marines arrived on August 4, bringing the total UN forces to 92,000. In addition, much-needed equipment and updated weaponry arrived every day, including bazookas capable of piercing the heavily armored T-34 tanks. The most significant addition to the UN force was the arrival of several tank battalions manning new Sherman tanks. This gave the Eighth Army an armored force it had lacked in the first operations.

While heavy fighting continued along the new lines behind the Naktong River, the establishment of the Pusan Perimeter permitted American military

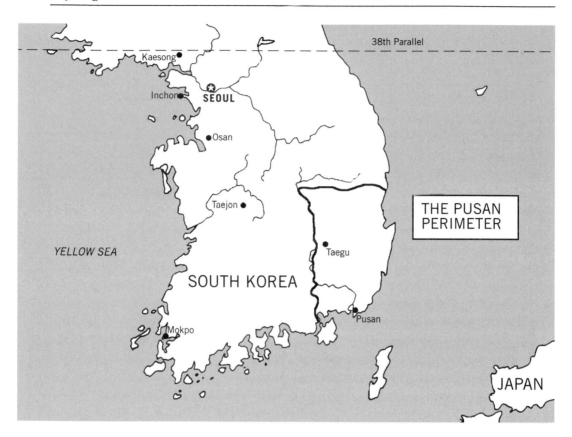

The Pusan Perimeter

leaders to reassess their strategy and adjust their assumptions about the enemy. Responding to the alarming rate at which U.S. forces had been beaten back, the Joint Chiefs of Staff (JCS) sent top staff to Tokyo to meet with MacArthur and to conduct a brief tour of the UN position to assess the situation. Among that group was General Matthew B. Ridgway, whose candid observations ultimately led to significant changes in the way the United States fought the NKPA (see Ridgway biography, p. 159).

Ridgway noted with dismay that the commander of the Eighth Army, General Johnnie Walker, could not even name top commanders in the ROK. He saw this as a clear indication that U.S. and ROK forces were not coordinating their efforts. He spoke critically of the Eighth Army, decrying "a lack of knowledge of infantry fundamentals ... a lack of leadership in combat echelons" and "the absence of an aggressive fighting spirit." Ridgway's report to the JCS pulled no punches:

General Matthew Ridgway talking with an American soldier in Korea.

> [The quality of the U.S.] soldier now engaged in Korea is not up to World War II standards. [U.S. troops] are easily stampeded. When attacked they do not respond with the fundamental infantry reaction to fire and movement, but instead call for artillery and air support and then withdraw if this does not suffice to interrupt the attack. Our troops do not counterattack an enemy penetration. Our forces do not maintain outpost protection nor flank protection.... Our troops do not dig in and make no pretense at camouflaging their positions. They do not seek cover and concealment while moving by day.... They are visible to the enemy by terrestrial [ground] observation.... Tactical air support is not satisfactory.

Privately, Ridgway believed Walker should be relieved of his command. But he refrained from saying so. He knew that if he made such comments, it might appear that they were motivated by a desire to serve in Walker's place. Regarding General Douglas MacArthur, Ridgway expressed nothing but admiration. Years later, in fact, he described MacArthur as "confident, optimistic, proud, eloquent, and utterly without fear."

Before the group of top JCS staffers left the Far East to return to Washington, they met with MacArthur at his command headquarters in Tokyo on August 8. At this meeting, MacArthur spent two and a half hours telling the group in great detail and with great passion how he would win the war in Korea. He truly believed that time was of the essence and that the United States needed to initiate a decisive move before the winter months set in.

With this in mind, MacArthur called for a daring amphibious assault on the South Korean port of Inchon, now located behind NKPA frontlines. To invade at Inchon, MacArthur would need additional forces beyond those

A Woman in Combat

Marguerite Higgins was an exceptional person: at a time when few women were in male-dominated fields like journalism, she had the distinction of being the only female correspondent in combat during the Korean War. She was a veteran reporter, having accompanied U.S. forces during the liberation of Nazi death camps at the end of World War II. She became the Far East Bureau Chief for the *New York Herald Tribune* in May 1950 in Tokyo, Japan.

Just a month into her new job, war broke out in Korea. She was there, with the troops, within two days. Being a war correspondent is a tough job for anyone—15 journalists were killed during the course of the Korean War—but it was even tougher for a woman. Higgins had to endure not only harsh conditions, but also sexist attitudes and behavior from enlisted men, officers, and her male counterparts. Several months into the conflict, General Johnnie Walker ordered her home; MacArthur overruled this order and Higgins stayed, but that didn't make her job any easier. She related much of her experience in *War in Korea: The Report of a Woman Combat Correspondent*, published in 1951. She accompanied the U.S. Marines that landed at Inchon, and her story of that event is excerpted here:

> I was to go in the fifth wave to hit at Red Beach.... It was an ear-shattering experience. We had to thread our way past the cruisers and carriers that were booming away at the beach, giving it a final, deadly pounding. The quake and roar of the rocket ships was almost unendurable.

already committed to Korea. Prior to the August 8 meeting, however, Ridgway, the JCS, and its top staffers were united in their conviction that MacArthur should not be given those forces.

MacArthur, though, made an impassioned and persuasive case for the Inchon plan at the meeting. "He won us all over to his views," Ridgway later wrote. "I know that after this brilliant exposition, and after I had studied the plans for ... the Inchon landing, my own doubts were dissolved. On the return flight, [we] agreed that we were prepared to support MacArthur's request

> After 20 minutes we rounded Wolmi Island—it looked as if a giant forest fire had just swept over it. Beyond was Red Beach. As we strained to see it more clearly, a rocket hit a round oil tower and big, ugly smoke rings billowed up. The dockside buildings were brilliant with flames. Through the flames it looked as though the whole city was burning.

Higgins approached the Inchon waterfront in a landing craft that came under heavy machine gun fire from the North Koreans, and she and the Marines crouched low as the boat lunged onto the beach next to a sea wall. The lieutenant in charge ordered the troops out of the landing craft, shoving them as they exited. Soon Higgins found herself crawling on the beach with 50 or 60 Marines, inching their way toward the sea wall. When one Marine next to Higgins ventured over the sea wall,

> He jumped back so hurriedly that he stamped one foot hard on to my bottom. This fortunately had considerable padding, but it did hurt, and I'm afraid I said somewhat snappishly, "Hey, it isn't as frantic as all that." He removed his foot hastily and apologized in a tone that indicated his amazement that he had been walking on a woman. I think he was the only marine who recognized me as a woman— my helmet and overcoat were good camouflage.

Higgins relates her story with a sense of humor, underplaying the bravery required to be a war correspondent on the front lines. She voluntarily put herself in a dangerous situation to report the events of the war to people back in the United States. In doing so, she also furthered the cause of women breaking into a traditionally male-dominated profession.

when we got home." By August 18, Truman had agreed to commit another division (about 15,000 troops) to MacArthur and his planned offensive.

Turning the Tide: Naktong Bulge, Taegu, and "Bowling Alley"

Throughout the month of August 1950, the NKPA continued to hammer UN forces along the Pusan Perimeter. North Korean premier Kim Il Sung had tried to rally his troops to "take Pusan by Liberation Day," August 15, the anniversary of Korean independence from Japan in 1945. Reinforcements of fresh UN forces armed with heavy artillery, tanks, and improved air support thwarted this ambitious goal, however. Soon, North Korea shifted its mission to trying to take the city of Taegu by Liberation Day. Taegu was where Syngman Rhee, president of the ROK, had set up his government after fleeing Seoul.

The tide was about to turn, however, in favor of the UN forces. Buoyed by reinforcements and a clearer understanding of NKPA tactics, American and South Korean troops registered a series of important, hard-fought victories in the defense of the Pusan Perimeter.

The first of these triumphs took place at the "Naktong Bulge," a curving stretch of the Naktong River about seven miles north of where it meets the Nam River. On August 5, the North Koreans launched an attack against the American forces by crossing the Naktong at night (the NKPA often staged assaults at night because it limited the effectiveness of American aircraft and artillery). They had built underwater bridges made up of sandbags, barrels, logs, and rocks. These bridges, rising from the riverbed itself, enabled the NKPA to bring heavy equipment and hundreds of men across with little difficulty. In fighting that lasted several days, the NKPA was able to penetrate almost eight miles into the Pusan perimeter. But newly arrived troops from the U.S. Marines were called in. Utilizing a combination of air power (both bombing and machine gun strafing) and coordinated ground attacks with U.S. troops, UN forces drove the NKPA back across the Naktong.

Still, Kim Il Sung and the NKPA were determined to try to take Taegu. By August 15, the NKPA had worn down ROK defenses and pushed as far as Tabu, about 15 miles from Taegu. Determined to stop the advance, General Johnnie Walker sent a tough Army outfit known as The Wolfhounds (officially the 27th regiment) to pitch in with ROK forces to stop the NKPA.

Deploying in a two-mile pass between two small mountain ranges, the Wolfhounds and the ROK staged a blistering defense against the NKPA. The Wolfhounds were fully prepared for any approach by the road, with land mines and heavy artillery in place. Each night, a column of NKPA tanks would appear, only to have the forward tanks blasted by UN fire. The North Korean column would then withdraw, only to repeat their movements the following day. This seven-night battle came to be known as "The Bowling Alley," both for the noise, which sounded like pins being knocked down in a bowling alley, and the persistent, repetitive approach of the NKPA tanks. In his memoir *From Pusan to Panmunjom*, ROK commander General Paik Sun Yup remarked, "At the time, I found it difficult to understand the Americans' humor when they referred to a grisly battlefield with such a lighthearted term." Indeed, the NKPA suffered as many as 4,000 casualties before they finally abandoned this effort.

Taegu had been saved, a triumph that provided a badly needed psychological lift to UN forces. The NKPA, meanwhile, had been badly battered in its attempt to break through the Pusan Perimeter. It suffered about 10,000 casualties by month's end, and its line of supply had been stretched more than 200 miles by the offensive, making it exceptionally vulnerable to enemy attack.

If MacArthur's plan to invade North Korean-held territory was ever going to work, the time was now.

The Risks at Inchon

The plan to invade Inchon was risky but carried potentially enormous benefits if it was successfully executed. The amphibious landing would take NKPA forces, which were weak everywhere except at the Pusan Perimeter, by surprise. If UN forces took the city, they could then easily cut supply lines from North Korea and trap NKPA troops operating in the south. A landing at Inchon would also enable UN forces to re-take Seoul, the South Korean capital. Part of the plan, too, was for Walker's Eighth Army to bust out of the Pusan Perimeter so that NKPA forces would be trapped between "giant pincers," according to MacArthur.

Many analysts continued to voice doubts about the plan's chances of success, however. For example, some military leaders doubted whether Walker's forces had enough manpower and hardware to successfully push out of Pusan. They pointed out that some of the forces defending the Perimeter were to be pulled out and shipped to Inchon for the invasion, reducing the number of troops that would be available to Walker. Further, an advance of 180 miles to the north was a lot to ask of men who were already exhausted from weeks of brutal fighting.

Doubts were also raised about the terrain that awaited any invading force at Inchon. "We drew up a list of every natural and geographic handicap—and Inchon had 'em all," remarked one naval officer. One difficulty was the narrow opening to the harbor, which would make it easier for the NKPA

General Douglas MacArthur, shown here (center, seated) surveying the assault on Inchon from the deck of the USS *McKinley*, convinced numerous doubters that his invasion plan would succeed.

to defend with artillery and mines. Perhaps more daunting was the nature of the tides at Inchon. Because Inchon was a relatively shallow harbor, the tides were very long, with the seawater receding completely for hours, turning the landing area to vast mud flats. Any approach by large vessels would have to be done at the tides' highest points, which occurred twice a day, 12 hours apart. This would limit MacArthur's ability to launch a surprise attack.

In addition, strategists had to take into account the presence of a small island, called Wolmi, that guarded the entrance to the harbor. The island contained a garrison of heavily armed North Korean troops that would have to be defeated before the mainland assault could begin. Any assault on Wolmi, however, would alert North Korean forces on the mainland to the presence of enemy troops.

Another obstacle confronting military strategists was the series of seawalls and piers that dominated the Pusan waterfront. Instead of landing on a large beach, the assault troops would be forced to scale the seawalls with ladders, which could expose them to withering fire from North Korean troops. And even if U.S. and South Korean forces succeeded in entering the city, they faced the possibility of being drawn into an urban warfare scenario—one in which NKPA forces forced them to take the city one bloody street at a time.

Finally, the weather loomed as a potential threat—the proposed amphibious attack was scheduled for typhoon season, and a storm could make both the sea and land operation next to impossible.

Given these factors, many military leaders remained skeptical of MacArthur's Inchon plan. He responded by insisting that the element of surprise would be so great that victory would be assured. At an August 23 meeting in Tokyo of top military leaders—including Secretary of Defense Joe Collins—MacArthur continued to press for the Inchon invasion. "Are you content to let our troops stay in that bloody perimeter [Pusan] like beef cattle in the slaughterhouse?" he snapped. "Who will take the responsibility for such a tragedy? Certainly I will not." Even though MacArthur acknowledged the risks and the difficulties of a landing at Inchon, he argued that "We must act now or we will die.... We shall land at Inchon and I will crush them."

MacArthur's arguments carried the day, and preparations for the Inchon invasion accelerated. Forces tapped for the invasion included a combination of U.S. Army, U.S. Marine, and South Korean units, collectively called "X Corps," led by MacArthur's chief of staff, Ned Almond.

The Inchon Invasion

In the days leading up to the planned date of the invasion, UN aircraft repeatedly bombed North Korean military positions in the Inchon region. Then, on the morning of September 13, 1950, 260 ships steamed toward Inchon in heavy seas with MacArthur at the helm. As feared, a typhoon struck the region, but fortunately it swung to the northeast, making seasickness the worst threat to the fighting forces aboard ship.

U.S. Marines in amphibious assault craft move toward Inchon.

On September 14, the first destroyers to reach Inchon's harbor discovered underwater mines. They quickly disarmed them, clearing the way for the landing force. The ships continued forward, drawing within shelling range of the NKPA fortifications on Wolmi Island at the mouth of the harbor. NKPA forces attacked, but withering fire from UN ships and aircraft soon silenced the North Korean artillery. The next morning, at high tide, U.S. Marines landed on Wolmi and were able to secure the island with relatively little resistance; no Marines were killed and only 17 were wounded.

On the afternoon of September 15, at about 5:00 p.m., the full invasion force rolled into Inchon Harbor at high tide. As MacArthur had expected, the North Koreans were completely unprepared for such an invasion. Even though the assault on Wolmi Island had alerted the mainland of trouble, the North Koreans had been unable to add to the 2,000 NKPA troops occupying Inchon at the time. As a result, the 13,000 U.S. Marines who poured ashore encountered surprisingly little resistance. Only 21 Marines were killed in the liberation of the city, the loss of which constituted a devastating strategic and psychological blow to North Korea.

The attack had unfolded just as MacArthur had planned. In only two days of fighting, UN forces secured Inchon—both the harbor and the city—and captured Kimpo Airfield, just a few miles outside Inchon. The invasion cost UN forces little: there were only 174 casualties, including 21 deaths. More men and equipment followed the initial invasion force, bringing the total of UN troops to more than 50,000. With this assault, X Corps had established a new front well behind the enemy lines at the Pusan Perimeter.

A small South Korean child crying in the street as UN forces seize Inchon.

Breakout of the Pusan Perimeter

To the south, another offensive was looming. One day after the Inchon landing, on September 16, General Johnnie Walker launched his offensive against North Korean troops stationed along the Pusan Perimeter. Walker's Eighth Army troops were weary from weeks of continual fighting with the North Koreans, but morale was high with the news of the success of X Corps at Inchon. The offensive at the Pusan Perimeter was not without difficulties, though. One of the most formidable tasks was taking high ground commanded by the NKPA, and the first three days of the offensive did not go well. But the situation changed on September 19, when the two NKPA divisions that had been attacking the perimeter suddenly withdrew. It has never been determined what prompted the withdrawal, but historians speculate it was to move forces north to defend Seoul, which NKPA forces had captured early in the summer, from UN forces on the move from Inchon.

The Eighth Army, however, was challenged by an enormous engineering problem when they reached the Naktong River. Handicapped by what histori-

UN forces settle in after taking Inchon.

an Clay Blair termed "a scandalous shortage of bridging equipment and bridge builders," crossing the river turned into a logistical nightmare. The Eighth Army's progress slowed to a crawl, much to Walker's frustration. When he heard a rumor at headquarters that MacArthur had said Walker wasn't up to the task of leading the Eighth Army out of the Pusan Perimeter, he shot a communiqué to Tokyo: "I don't want you to think I'm dragging my heels, but I have a river across my whole front and the two bridges I have don't make much."

Furthermore, much of the artillery, ammunition, and manpower that had once been at Walker's disposal had been redeployed to Inchon. However, by making do with what it had and by exploiting the resources the NKPA had left behind (like the underwater bridge they had built to cross the Naktong a month earlier), the Eighth Army was able to eventually jump the river and grind northward, even as the North Korean fighters—perhaps as many as 40,000 men—withdrew to defend Seoul and to regroup farther north.

With the X Corps at Inchon and the Eighth Army driving north from Pusan, MacArthur's plan to trap NKPA forces between "giant pincers" seemed to be working.

Chapter 6
THE LIBERATION OF SEOUL

—◦◦◦◦◦—

I regard all of Korea open for our military operations.

—Gen. Douglas MacArthur

The victorious X Corps under General Ned Almond continued to drive into the interior. Having secured the city of Inchon and the Kimpo Airfield, X Corps pushed toward the Han River and Seoul, the capital city of South Korea. Following the Inchon invasion, MacArthur hoped for a rapid advance and takeover of the fallen city. Retaking the capital would be a tremendous morale boost for the troops, plus it would restore the city's role as the center for South Korean communications, industry, and transportation, since north-south roads and railway lines ran through Seoul.

By September 18, 1950, UN forces had reached the Han River, but North Korean forces had brought in 20,000 troops—some of them withdrawn from the Pusan Perimeter—to defend Seoul. From September 22-25, UN and NKPA troops fought bitterly to the west of Seoul. On September 25 the North Koreans finally withdrew. Seizing a public relations opportunity, General Almond pronounced that Seoul had been liberated exactly "three months to the day" since South Korea had been invaded on June 25.

This wasn't true, however. Fierce street-to-street fighting continued for three more days, inflicting heavy casualties on both sides and even worse havoc on the capital city. The UN ground forces were supported by heavy artillery fire and air support from Kimpo Airfield and offshore aircraft carriers. Thousands of civilians were caught in the crossfire, their homes and workplaces destroyed, and many innocent lives were lost. A British journalist, Reginald Thompson, described the scene of the liberation of Seoul (quoted in Robert D. Heinl's *Victory at High Tide*):

> It is an appalling inferno of din and destruction with the tearing noise of dive bombers blasting right ahead, and the livid flashes of the tang guns, the harsh, fierce crackle of blazing wooden buildings, telegraphs and high-tension poles collapsing in utter chaos of wires. Great palls of smoke lie over us as massive buildings collapse in showers of sparks, puffing masses of smoke and rubble upon us in terrific heat.... Few people can have suffered so terrible a liberation.

Another war correspondent, Rutherford Poats, who wrote for the United Press, was with the U.S. Marines as they advanced through the city. In his book, *Decision in Korea*, he recalled the scene:

> Telephone and power lines festooned the streets or hung from shattered poles that resembled grotesque Christmas trees. Bluish smoke curled from the corner of a clapboard shack— the only building even partially spared destruction along the left side of the street. A young woman poked among a pile of roof tiles and charred timbers for her possessions, or perhaps for her child. A lump of flesh and bones in a mustard-colored Communist uniform sprawled across the curb up ahead, and the white-robed body of an old man lay on a rice-straw mat nearer the street corner.

Though South Korea's capital city lay in ruins, UN forces had indeed recaptured it. On September 29, General MacArthur flew South Korean President Syngman Rhee into Kimpo Airfield for an elaborate, emotional ceremony. With tears in his eyes, Rhee proclaimed to MacArthur, "You are the savior of our race." It was a gratifying day indeed for MacArthur, who in a separate ceremony awarded Generals Ned Almond of X Corps and Johnnie Walker of Eighth Army the Distinguished Service Cross for their bravery in the operations. (Walker's forces had met up with Almond's two days earlier, having made a three-day dash from the Pusan Perimeter to Seoul.)

When MacArthur returned to his headquarters in Tokyo later that day, there were messages from President Truman, General Dwight David Eisen-

UN troops fight their way through the streets of Seoul.

hower, former British Prime Minister Winston Churchill, and the Joint Chiefs of Staff (JCS). President Truman wrote: "No operation in military history can match either the delaying operation where you traded space for time in which to build up your forces, or the brilliant maneuver which has now resulted in the liberation of Seoul." The communiqué from the JCS was glowing: "We remain completely confident that the great task entrusted to you by the Untied Nations will be carried to a success."

Yet, historians puzzle over the apparent lack of planning on the part of MacArthur, the JCS, and the UN Security Council about how they should proceed once Seoul had been reclaimed. Historians observe that the NKPA was basically allowed to escape the Pusan Perimeter, Inchon, and Seoul. The roads leading to North Korea were left open and retreating forces were not pursued by ground or air. The "giant pincers" envisioned by MacArthur—with the Eighth Army from the south at Pusan and X Corps from the north at Inchon—had failed to trap the North Koreans in their withdrawal north. While MacArthur received many accolades for his success at Inchon, the plan, as a whole, did not achieve its objective of crushing the invading NKPA.

A Dramatic Shift in Policy

By this point the U.S.-led UN force had freed most of the territory North Korea had taken from June to September 1950. But the NKPA was still a formidable foe, and its status as a threat to South Korea had not substantially diminished. With this in mind, the military leadership of the UN and ROK forces began planning their next steps. But these plans were abruptly altered by a dramatic policy shift at the highest levels in Washington.

The United States had first entered the war with a limited objective: to drive the NKPA quickly back across the 38th parallel to accomplish a policy of "containment." However, there was growing sentiment in the Truman administration—and among the American public—to deal with the "Korean problem" once and for all. There was every reason to believe that the North Korean government would strike again, once the NKPA had recovered from its recent losses. The only way to deter future attacks would be to leave a strong occupying UN military presence in South Korea, which would not be a popular decision in the United States. Also, South Korean president Syngman Rhee had no intention of stopping his forces at the 38th parallel; he was determined to wreak revenge on the Communists to the north and to unify Korea by force.

Even before the landing at Inchon, the Truman administration and the UN Security Council were paving the way for a UN invasion of North Korea. Together with 70 other nations, the United States recommended a resolution that would result in action that would "ensure conditions of stability throughout Korea."

The final language included in the resolution when it was finally issued on October 7, 1950, however, introduced an idea that was not included in the earlier UN resolutions approving the use of military force in defending South

Korea. The new resolution of October 7 said that "the essential objective of the resolutions of the General Assembly referred to above [the resolutions of June 25 and June 27] was the establishment of a unified, independent and democratic Government of Korea." Yet the resolutions of June 25 and June 27 did not include any such language; they only called for UN member nations to support South Korea in its defense against North Korean aggression. The new United Nations goal of establishing a unified Korea—and defeat rather than contain Communism—thus marked a dramatic shift in its stated purpose for being on the Korean peninsula.

Policy aside, the UN resolution of October 7 was almost immaterial to UN forces. The JCS had already given a directive to MacArthur 10 days earlier, authorizing him to conduct military operations north of the 38th parallel. In fact, The JCS directive gave MacArthur the authority to conduct military operations as far north as the Yalu River—the border between North Korea and China.

The Chinese Issue a Warning

The October 7 UN Resolution also was meaningless to South Korea, as President Syngman Rhee had ordered ROK forces to cross the 38th parallel into North Korea a week earlier. Rhee desperately wanted to unify the entire Korean peninsula under his rule, by force if necessary. Confident of UN backing, Rhee's orders reflected his determination to seize the opportunity provided by North Korea's retreat from South Korea.

Meanwhile, from Tokyo, MacArthur sent a surrender ultimatum, approved by Washington, to Pyongyang, North Korea's capital. North Korean premier Kim Il Sung was strangely silent. Instead, the Chinese issued an ominous response warning that they would not "tolerate seeing their neighbors being savagely invaded by imperialists."

MacArthur dismissed the threat. Instead, he repeatedly assured the Truman administration that China would not intervene. He believed that if the Chinese had any intention of joining the fight, they would have done so immediately after the Inchon invasion. But MacArthur's conviction—shared by many other U.S. analysts—soon proved to be based on faulty assumptions.

Indeed, leaders in the United States—including foreign policy, military, and intelligence leaders—were almost unanimous in their belief that the Sovi-

The U.S. Chiefs of Staff for the Truman administration at the outbreak of the Korean War. Standing from left are Air General Hoyt Vanderberg; Army Chief of Staff General Joseph L. Collins, and Admiral Forrest Sherman of the U.S. Navy. Seated from left are Secretary of Defense Louis Johnson and General Omar N. Bradley, Chairman of the Joint Chiefs of Staff.

et Union was the real threat when it came to intervention in Korea and possible escalation to "total war." They regarded China as a much less likely source of trouble. Historical documents indicate, however, that the American leadership badly misjudged China's position. Soviet documents reveal that as early as May 1950, Chinese Prime Minister Mao Zedong had agreed to join with the Soviet Union and support the North Korean invasion of South Korea.

Chinese leaders reaffirmed their determination to support North Korea in October 1950, when they agreed to extend military aid to the NKPA in return for Soviet promises of military weaponry and air cover. "Their main argument [for entering the war] was that if all of Korea was occupied by the Americans, it would create a mortal danger to the Chinese revolution," noted Colonel Harry G. Summers in "The Korean War: A Fresh Perspective."

For both the Soviets and the Chinese, the U.S. decisions to get involved in Korea and, more specifically, to pursue the North Koreans beyond the 38th parallel posed a significant threat to the growth of Communism in Asia. These two superpowers, allied in their ideology, saw the U.S. invasion of North Korea as tangible evidence of "capitalist imperialism" and a potentially serious threat to their governments.

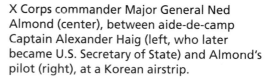

X Corps commander Major General Ned Almond (center), between aide-de-camp Captain Alexander Haig (left, who later became U.S. Secretary of State) and Almond's pilot (right), at a Korean airstrip.

Preparing for Invasion

Confident that the Chinese military would stay on the sidelines, MacArthur set in motion his plans to pursue the North Korean army all the way to the Yalu River. In fact, he boldly predicted that the conflict would be over by Thanksgiving and that U.S. troops would be home by Christmas of 1950.

MacArthur's plan was to move the bulk of X Corps troops who had landed at Inchon (on the western side of the peninsula) to the port city of Wonsan (on the eastern side of the peninsula, about 110 miles north of the 38th parallel). Wonsan would then serve as a staging site and supply center for troops moving northward through North Korea. X Corps would then take Pyongyang, the capital, as efficiently as UN forces had taken Seoul. Meanwhile, the Eighth Army troops who had come by road and rail from Pusan would establish a line running east and west and drive any remaining NKPA troops north.

To move from Inchon to Wonsan, X Corps would have to cross to the other side of the peninsula. As military planners tried to decide how best to move the troops and the massive amount of equipment required, disagree-

General Douglas MacArthur receives a medal from President Harry S. Truman during their October 14, 1950, meeting on Wake Island.

ments flared. One option was to move the troops by land, but detractors of this scheme predicted that troops and equipment would get bogged down crossing the difficult terrain. "Half of our heavy equipment—bulldozers, big guns, and heavy trucks—would have been left in ditches by the side of the road," argued X Corps Commander Ned Almond. But Admiral C. Turner Joy, commander of U.S. Naval Forces, argued that X Corps "could have marched overland to Wonsan in a much shorter time and with much less effort than it would take to get the Corps around to Wonsan by sea." Ultimately, MacArthur decided that X Corps would move by sea—requiring a long, slow 800-mile boat ride all the way around the peninsula.

As X Corps began its journey, divisions of the ROK army, who crossed by land, reached Wonsan on October 10. They encountered almost no resistance to their arrival. While X Corps was still at sea, the ROK secured the airfield and took the city, negating the need for another dramatic amphibious landing, like at Inchon. Thousands of mines were discovered in the shallow Wonsan Harbor. U.S. Navy minesweepers arrived on October 10 to begin clearing the harbor. Part of X Corps landed at Iwon, north of Wonsan; the rest of the troops arrived on shore after the harbor was cleared.

Truman and MacArthur at Wake Island

On October 15, 1950, President Harry S. Truman and General Douglas MacArthur, World War II hero and Supreme Commander of UN Forces in East Asia, met for the first and only time. Their meeting at Wake Island, a small island in the South Pacific, was motivated in part by politics. Truman's advisers suggested the president needed to show his support of MacArthur, particularly after his successes at Inchon and Seoul. Another reason for the meeting was to discuss the threat issued by the Chinese earlier that month. Many analysts have called the Wake Island meeting "historic," but in his book *The Forgotten War*, historian Clay Blair disagrees:

> Then, and later, journalists and some historians would inflate the "historic" importance of the Wake Island meeting. However, nothing "historic" occurred, other than the first meeting of Truman and MacArthur. The hurried and brief "discussions" and "exchanges of views" during the short official session were almost farcical, merely oral reviews of positions previously spelled out in far greater detail in cables [telegrams] or letters.

Their meeting lasted only an hour and a half. MacArthur assured Truman that victory was at hand, that the Chinese would not intervene—and if they did, that massive U.S. air superiority would drive them back across the Yalu. Though reliable intelligence suggested that as many as 300,000 Chinese ground troops were lined up along the Chinese/Korean border, MacArthur showed little concern. On the official record of the day's meeting, MacArthur said of Chinese ground forces that, at most, only "50,000 or 60,000 could be gotten across the Yalu. They have no air force. Now that we have bases for our Air Force in Korea, if the Chinese tried to get down to Pyongyang, there would be the greatest slaughter."

Retreat of the NKPA

By the middle of October, the North Koreans were in full retreat. Utilizing shattering air raids and fierce ground assaults, troops from both the Eighth Army and the ROK captured Pyongyang, the capital city of North Korea. Premier Kim Il Sung and his government fled to the city of Sinuiju on the Yalu River, bordering China.

MacArthur took the opportunity of this victory to fly to Pyongyang on October 20 to address the troops and the press. A provisional government for the city was established, comprised of non-Communist citizens. American strategists generally agreed that the NKPA would likely continue sporadic guerilla attacks in the region, which meant that an occupying UN force would need to remain in a unified Korea for some time. Still, many believed that the worst of the war was over.

MacArthur, meanwhile, continued his push northward. His stated goals were to fully demolish any remaining resistance and to prevent the NKPA from rising up again, should the UN withdraw the majority of its forces. On October 20, MacArthur issued orders to the Eighth Army (west of the Taebaek mountain range) and X Corps (east of the range) to push north and "to use any and all ground forces … as necessary to secure all of North Korea." The two armies promptly obeyed, even though they were unable to communicate with each other. As they headed north into North Korea, they were divided by a 75-mile expanse of virtually impassable mountains, leaving each force isolated and vulnerable to attack.

MacArthur's orders were given without the full consent of the Joint Chiefs of Staff (JCS) and the Truman administration. The directive that MacArthur had received on September 27 had plainly given him the authority to invade North Korea, but to place only ROK troops on the front line at the Yalu River. The purpose of this directive was to avoid any direct confrontation between U.S. and Chinese forces. Washington feared that such a confrontation might result in a prolonged and bloody ground war and might even precipitate the use of nuclear weapons between the two superpowers— or "total war." MacArthur's orders to his forces, to push all the way to both the Chinese and Soviet borders, was a radical departure from the intentions of both Washington and the UN Security Council.

This decision would prove to be the greatest mistake of MacArthur's career, and one of the gravest errors in judgment in U.S. military history.

Chapter 7

ENTER THE CHINESE

<figure>⊶⊷</figure>

To the ROKs and Americans, the oncoming waves of massed manpower were astonishing, terrifying, and to those Americans who believed the war was over, utterly demoralizing.

—Historian Clay Blair

In early October, the first reports of South Korean (ROK) encounters with Chinese forces began to surface. While U.S. military leaders initially dismissed the Chinese fighters as a handful of "volunteers" who had crossed the Yalu River, it soon became obvious that the Chinese had not only built up their forces behind the border, but were well-positioned inside Korea. It is estimated that between October 13 and October 20, more than 180,000 troops crossed from China into Korea. Their movements and presence were largely undetected by UN intelligence and air reconnaissance; they crossed the Yalu River at night, and the first troops to arrive wore North Korean uniforms or camouflaged their distinctive Chinese uniforms.

A New Kind of Enemy

This new force in the conflict brought an entirely different type of warrior into the picture. Fresh from victory against the Nationalists in the Chinese Civil War, the Chinese Communist Forces (CCF) were highly trained and highly motivated. Of all the armies involved in the Korean War, the Chinese were probably the worst equipped. Yet in some ways they were also the most formidable fighting force.

The Chinese troops were masters at guerrilla warfare. They used small groups to ambush and harass larger forces, often attacking under cover of darkness. By focusing on nighttime movements and assaults, they effectively neutralized the UN's big airpower advantage. As the war progressed they became notorious for short, intensive attacks that inflicted many casualties. But they were adept at withdrawing quickly, which minimized their own losses. They lacked sophisticated radio and telephone communication, but made effective use of bugles and whistles to signal commands and movements. They had very little artillery, and only a modest supply of mortars (smaller, muzzle-loading cannons). Rifles, pistols, and hand grenades were their main weapons. When their supply of ammunition ran out, they resorted to hand to-hand combat, using rifle butts, bayonets, and their own hands.

The typical Chinese soldier wore a mustard-colored, two-piece quilted cotton oversuit, with summer clothing underneath. Since the Chinese had virtually no air support, no trucks, no Jeeps, and no tanks, the common foot soldier had to carry everything he would need to fight and live for weeks at a time. They wore no steel helmets like other armies, and few had boots; most only had fur-lined caps and poorly constructed shoes. There were no supply trucks carrying food and water. Soldiers carried about five days worth of cooked rice and beans; by carrying pre-cooked food, they avoided setting up camps with kitchens and their telltale fires.

UN Forces Meet the CCF

In late October, the CCF began the first of several major Chinese offensives against UN forces. The CCF attacked ROK units at Unsan and Ojong, not far from the western end of the border with China. More than 2,700 South Koreans were lost in these attacks. Clearly, the Chinese had entered Korea to fight.

Reports from ROK commanders to UN headquarters that the Chinese were attacking them went mostly unheeded. American military leaders remained convinced that the attackers were North Koreans, not Chinese. In *From Pusan to Panmunjom*, ROK General Paik Sun Yup recalled his frustration:

> The Americans continued to fool themselves because the Chinese had yet to challenge a U.S. Army division directly, and because to the American eye, the Koreans and Chinese looked and sounded very much alike. To us, of course the differences were vast.

Within a few days, however, the United States was forced to confront the grim reality that they were now engaged in mortal combat with the largest Communist ground force ever assembled.

On November 1, elements of the Eighth Army arrived in Unsan to reinforce the ROK units that had been so badly damaged by skirmishes with the CCF. The Eighth Army soldiers arrived there with the misinformation that no more than 2,000 Chinese foot soldiers were in North Korea as "volunteers." There was still a persistent belief among UN leaders that the war was essentially over and that they were simply mopping up the last of the defeated NKPA. That afternoon, however, under cover of smoke from forest fires set by the Chinese, about 20,000 CCF troops marched on the town.

U.S. Marines with captured Chinese troops.

At dusk, the Chinese attacked American and South Korean positions from three sides. With their bugles, horns, whistles, and drums, they frightened the bewildered U.S. forces. Firing at the sounds in the night, the UN defenders gave away their positions, making themselves targets for machine gun fire and mortar and grenade attacks. As the fighting went on through the night, the Eighth Army units began to run out of ammo and retreated in disarray, leaving behind trucks, tanks, and artillery. The next day, knowing that some forces were still trapped and under attack, a rescue force was sent in. Their brave efforts availed nothing, and they suffered 350 casualties. The fighting went on for several days at Unsan. The Chinese lost about 500 men. Of the Eighth Army regiment that fought there, around 600 of its 800 men were killed or captured.

General Johnnie Walker, when apprised of the situation in Unsan, ordered a general withdrawal to a position about 50 miles to the south. Meanwhile, though, the Chinese mysteriously disappeared into the mountains. The massive force that had completely overwhelmed the ROK and UN forces for three solid days was suddenly nowhere to be found.

Shortly after the initial encounter between the CCF and the United States Army, the CCF published a pamphlet for its soldiers. The pamphlet acknowledged U.S. air-to-ground attack capabilities as "exceptional." But it called the infantry "weak" and added that "Their men are afraid to die, and will neither press home a bold attack nor defend to the death.... Their habit is to become active only during the daylight hours." The Chinese assessment of the will of the U.S. Army in Korea to date was largely true, and the sudden and mysterious withdrawal of the CCF was a welcome event.

On the other side of the peninsula, General Ned Almond's X Corps was proceeding up the eastern side of the Taebaek mountain range in pursuit of the remnants of the beaten NKPA. As the X Corps moved forward, the ROK reported that it had captured 16 CCF soldiers who told their captors that thousands of Chinese were in the region. Yet Almond didn't change his orders. He directed X Corps to continue toward the Yalu River, hoping for victory by Thanksgiving.

MacArthur Bombs the Yalu

Between November 7 and 24, 1950, the Korean War entered a quiet lull that puzzled UN commanders. Had UN military experts read the writings of Chinese Communist Premier Mao Zedong, they would have been familiar with his strategy for combat. He had written that the best way to defeat a powerful enemy was to conduct short, harassing missions, then withdraw to re-supply and refresh the troops. Since the Chinese army was entirely dependent on ground forces, this was a necessary strategy. The disappearance of the troops that attacked so forcefully at Unsan misled UN headquarters into making the assumption that earlier estimates that nearly 200,000 Chinese troops had infiltrated the region were incorrect.

MacArthur did finally acknowledge the threat of growing Chinese involvement, however, by ordering aerial bombing of bridges along the Yalu River. The Joint Chiefs of Staff (JCS) ordered him to cease this action immediately, as it was contrary to the directive they had earlier given him forbidding U.S. attacks on the Chinese border. MacArthur shot back an impassioned communiqué, saying the only way to stop Chinese forces from entering Korea was to destroy the bridges on the Yalu. He added his usual flair for the dramatic: "Every hour this is postponed will be paid for dearly in American and other United Nations blood."

The General's dire warnings marked a "stunning reversal on MacArthur's part," wrote David Halberstam in *The Fifties*. "Until then he had been saying

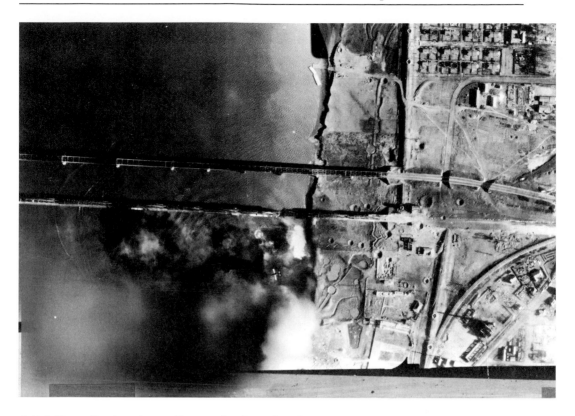

A U.S. Navy dive bomber pulls out of a dive after dropping a 2,000-pound bomb on the Korean side of a bridge spanning the Yalu River, on the Chinese-Korean border.

with great disdain that the Chinese would not come in; now he seemed to be promising a slaughter of his own men. What he had said would never happen was happening."

When MacArthur further reported that Chinese fighters were attacking UN aircraft, the JCS gave MacArthur permission to continue with his operations. He subsequently bombed the Yalu from November 8 until December 5. They urged him not to cross over into Chinese territory, however, in order to avoid provoking China's Communist leadership.

Preparing for an Offensive

As the bombing continued, MacArthur began drawing up plans for an advance north, a "final offensive" to secure the entire Korean peninsula. To the east, X Corps moved quickly north, as NKPA forces offered little resistance. The orders for X Corps were to proceed north along the Taebaek Range, then cross to the west in the area of the Chosin Reservoir. The Eighth Army would proceed north from its perimeter at Sinanju at the Chongchin River, north of Pyongyang, the captured North Korean capital.

There were conflicts, though, between Eighth Army General Johnnie Walker and X Corps General Ned Almond, the leaders of these two forces. Some military leaders at the time (and many military historians since) thought that the two should be united under one command. If that were to happen, it would mean Walker would be in command, as he was Almond's superior. Almond, however, had been MacArthur's chief of staff in Tokyo for years, and he had made it clear that he would not serve under Walker. So, separated not only by the formidable Taebaek Range but also by internal politics, U.S. forces were divided in their advance to the north.

Walker, whose men had already made contact with the Chinese, advocated a slow, steady advance, while Almond wanted to move as quickly as possible to the Yalu and attain MacArthur's objective of destroying NKPA and Chinese opposition before winter set in. But Almond had not yet encountered the Chinese, and none of the UN forces were fully prepared for an enemy they could not defeat with weapons and tactics—the weather (see "A Third Enemy: Winter," p. 84).

Eighth Army: "Home by Christmas"

Winter fell on Korea almost overnight. By Thanksgiving, snow had fallen and temperatures had dropped to 15° Fahrenheit. Few UN soldiers had standard winter gear, including winter boots, wool caps, gloves, and overcoats. Weapons and equipment, from rifles to radios to cannons to vehicles, refused to function in the bitter cold.

Nevertheless, on November 24, 1950, one day after UN troops ate a specially prepared Thanksgiving turkey dinner, the "Home by Christmas" offensive officially began. The offensive included the Eighth Army, the ROK First Division, and British and Turkish troops, numbering 118,000 men. The offensive began with heavy artillery support, and the Eighth Army advanced with little resistance for the first 36 hours.

On the evening of November 25, the Eighth Army was confident in its progress. A cold, clear moonlit night found most men preoccupied with stay-

The onset of the Korean winter badly hindered UN operations. Here two ground crew members attempt to carry out maintenance duties on a U.S. Air Force light bomber (a B-26 Night Intruder) in a heavy snow storm.

ing warm. Some were lucky enough to set up camp in abandoned Korean houses, but most were in the open. Few had troubled to dig foxholes in the frozen ground, and many had unwisely built campfires.

And then the second Chinese offensive began. At about 8:00 p.m., the quest for comfort was replaced by fear and confusion as swarms of Chinese soldiers attacked in massive force. Pouring over the hills in a burst of blowing bugles, shaking rattles, and chants, they fired flares to light the battleground, shot burp guns (lightweight machine guns), and hurled grenades at the unsuspecting American soldiers. In *The Forgotten War*, Clay Blair quoted infantryman James Marks, who remembered the scene:

All up and down the river valley, all hell had broken loose. Tracers and explosions left and right. Flares would explode, giving too much light, then flutter down and extinguish themselves in frozen corn stubble. The Chinese blew bugles and whistles and shouted American profanity. I thought their bugles were playing "Silent Night, Holy Night." Between shots and explosions, I could hear the wounded crying for help.... Men sprinted in every direction. I grabbed our medic (who was killed later that night): "What'n hell's going on?" "Get out of here. We're overrun."

The next day, General Johnnie Walker informed General MacArthur in Tokyo that Chinese Communist Forces were "attacking in strength," but that it was too early to tell if it were a major offensive. But by November 28, he requested—and received from MacArthur—the authority to withdraw the Eighth Army. The withdrawal took place along a single road. One six-mile stretch of the road wound between high ridges and mountains, where NKPA and Chinese were positioned to fire upon the rattled troops. Anytime a vehicle became stuck or disabled, the retreat slowed, and enemy snipers were free to pick off the hapless retreating UN forces; this became known as "The Gauntlet." One division involved in the retreat lost 3,000 men that morning.

X Corps Dashes into Disaster

Meanwhile, General Ned Almond, commander of X Corps, had been under pressure from MacArthur to press north quickly so that the late November UN offensive would be as unified as possible. The X Corps thus plunged headlong into massive resistance in an attempt to make an impressive and gallant surge to the Yalu River. (For an account of the experiences of one group of soldiers from X Corps, see "Defeat at Chosin Reservoir," p. 210.)

By November 27, X Corps had crossed over the Taebaek Range and was thinly dispersed close to the Chosin Reservoir. The CCF, however, had massed forces in the gap between X Corps to the east and the Eighth Army to the west, and was poised to attack X Corps along its western flanks. The attack came, as elsewhere, after dark, with the characteristic sounds of Chinese assault: bugles, horns, whistles, screams, mortars, grenades, and burp guns.

This first encounter with the Chinese elicited the same reaction from X Corps that the ROK and the Eighth Army had felt: fear and confusion. X

Corps was spread out between three towns, Yudam, Hagaru, and Koto, and the CCF was able to set up roadblocks between the villages, isolating some of the units. By midnight on November 28, three battalions of X Corps were completely surrounded by CCF troops. Incredibly, earlier that morning, Ned Almond had flown into Hagaru, where he had spoken these incongruous words intended as encouragement: "The enemy who is delaying you for the moment is nothing more than remnants of a Chinese division fleeing north.... We're still attacking and we're going all the way to the Yalu. Don't let a bunch of Chinese laundrymen stop you."

Almond may have been trying to deny the overwhelming force the CCF had mustered in Korea. But it was clear from a communiqué MacArthur issued that same day that the UN command was finally beginning to understand the massive and overwhelming size of the Chinese presence on the Korean Peninsula:

> It is quite evident that our present strength of force is not suffi-
> cient to meet this undeclared war by the Chinese with the
> inherent advantages which accrue thereby to them.... This
> command has done everything possible within its capabilities
> but is now faced with conditions beyond its control and
> strength.... My strategic plan for the immediate future is to
> pass from the offensive to the defensive with such local adjust-
> ments as may be required by a constantly fluid situation.

The legendary general was conceding that the Chinese were too much for the UN forces to handle. In what was certainly a low point in his career, MacArthur reluctantly ordered the most massive withdrawal—or retreat—in U.S. military history.

Withdrawal from the Chosin Reservoir

By November 30, it was decided that X Corps must retreat from the Chosin Reservoir area. The first designated stop in the withdrawal was Hagaru, where the wounded would be airlifted back to safety. Then, able-bodied troops and equipment would proceed south to the port of Hungnam, where they would be evacuated by ship. But that evening, as troops were preparing for the withdrawal in below-zero weather, the CCF attacked again. Fighting through the night, with the aid of artillery and close air support, X

A Third Enemy: Winter

November 1950 brought to UN troops the shock of a formidable new foe in the Korean conflict: the relentless Chinese ground forces. But another enemy entered the equation with a pervasiveness and severity that rivaled the tenacity of the Chinese: winter.

A U.S. soldier uses his poncho for protection from winter winds.

The high altitude of North Korea and Arctic air moving down from the north conspired to expose both UN and Communist forces to temperatures below zero Fahrenheit for weeks at a time. Cold brought many complications to the battlefield. Equipment malfunctioned, vehicles failed to start, and guns misfired or failed to work at all. The already dangerous combat conditions were further complicated by poor visibility from blinding snowstorms, and the stress of the cold brought an additional weariness and loss of battlefield awareness. The otherwise simple tasks of loading and firing weapons became arduous with frostbitten hands.

Digging foxholes into the frozen ground was nearly impossible and moving through deep snow slowed individual troops, making them more vulnerable to enemy fire. Vehicles not built for snowy conditions became

Corps managed to inflict some 600 casualties on the Chinese, with a loss of more than 100 of their own men.

Thus began a "fighting retreat" south, as the American soldiers fought their way through Chinese troops that had infiltrated along the roads to Hagaru, setting up roadblocks along the way. By December 3, X Corps broke through to Hagaru, where a massive airlift of the wounded began; in four days, more than 4,500 wounded soldiers were evacuated.

hopelessly mired in snow, ice, and muck, slowing any mechanized movements.

These obstacles underscored the lack of foresight with which U.S. forces had been sent to Korea. A majority of U.S. troops were poorly clothed, many of them without gloves, winter boots, wool socks, or even proper winter headgear. They lacked tents, sleeping bags, overcoats, and camp stoves to warm the troops at night. Frostbite was common, and it was not uncommon for a soldier's skin to be removed along with a sock that had frozen to his foot.

The canned "C-rations" that soldiers were issued were solid blocks of ice, and eating food that had not been thawed caused miserable digestive problems. Treating the wounded was also problematic, as even the blood for transfusions was frozen and unusable. The effect of bitter cold on the wounded already suffering shock meant more battlefield deaths, and surgeons with frozen hands could not perform the lifesaving tasks they would be able to perform under normal conditions.

Irv Langell, a U.S. infantryman who suffered during that first winter as both a soldier and as a prisoner of war, recalled the experience in Lewis Carlson's book *Remembered Prisoners of a Forgotten War*:

> I look back and ask myself, "How in hell did we survive?" The winter of 1950 in Korea was one of the coldest in history. What did we have? Very little clothing. How did we live? We huddled and cuddled. We scraped by and when somebody died, his clothes were fair game. That's the way it was. Those were the facts of life.

On December 6, X Corps was on the move again. The Chinese had not attacked Hagaru during the evacuation of the wounded, but instead had moved further south. CCF assault teams were deployed ahead of the main body of the withdrawing troops to secure the hills before the main column came through. As a result, X Corps encountered resistance virtually all the way to Hungnam.

In Hungnam's harbor, a huge fleet of U.S. Navy ships awaited not only the fleeing UN forces, but thousands of Korean refugees. Beginning on

The entrance of the Chinese stopped the UN advance in its tracks and forced a quick retreat.

December 11, over the course of two weeks, nearly 205,000 people were evacuated from Hungnam by ship, the number divided fairly evenly between UN soldiers and refugees. When the last of the fighters and civilians were safely aboard ship, naval gun ships decimated the city so that none of its resources would be available to the advancing Chinese and NKPA.

Meanwhile, the evacuated soldiers on board pondered the heavy toll of X Corps' hasty advance into Chinese-held territory, and its even hastier retreat. All told, one in four of the soldiers of X Corps had been killed, wounded, or gone missing in action.

Chapter 8
CHANGES IN COMMAND

⤙⤚

On New Year's morning, I drove out north of Seoul and into a dismaying spectacle. ROK soldiers by truckloads were streaming south, without orders, without arms, without leaders, in full retreat.... They had just one aim—to get as far away from the Chinese as possible. They had thrown away their rifles and pistols and had abandoned all artillery, mortars, machine-guns, every crew-served weapon.

—General Matthew B. Ridgway

By December 1950, the exhausted American forces stationed in Korea were looking back on earlier promises that they would be "home by Christmas" with sadness and anger. By December 15, UN forces had retreated south of the 38th parallel, and whatever "real estate" had been gained the previous fall was now lost. Six months into the Korean conflict, the United States-led UN had traversed the length of the Korean peninsula, advancing twice and retreating twice. Momentous changes were soon to come, however, in positions of high command; one as the result of an accident, and one as the result of an administrative decision.

Ridgway Takes the Helm of Eighth Army

General Johnnie Walker, who was considered an able, though uncharismatic, leader of the Eighth Army, was known for speeding around the countryside in an open jeep. He had even outfitted his official jeep with a steel bar in the front passenger seat so he could stand and observe as his driver sped

General Walton H. Walker lost his life in Korea in a jeep accident.

past installations. On December 23, a Korean truck suddenly pulled into the path of Walker's fast-moving jeep while it was climbing up an icy incline. The truck struck the jeep at nearly full speed. All the inhabitants of the jeep were thrown from the vehicle, and Walker was pronounced dead on arrival at a nearby military surgical hospital. He had just celebrated his 61st birthday.

General MacArthur was informed of Walker's death within minutes, and he immediately phoned Army Chief of Staff Joe Collins in Washington. MacArthur and Collins had already agreed that, should anything happen to Walker, Lieutenant General Matthew B. Ridgway would be his replacement as commander of the Eighth Army. Ridgway had been serving as deputy to the Army chief of staff (a member of the Joint Chiefs of Staff) in Washington. Ridgway briefly met with MacArthur in Tokyo, then headed for the Korean Peninsula. By December 26, Ridgway was in Korea at the front, inspecting his troops.

General Ridgway immediately put himself in the midst of the troops— and the danger—so he could get a first-hand view of the situation. Driving to the front in a jeep, he stopped frequently to interview men of all ranks, from officers to enlisted men, in order to understand their mindset. What he found disturbed him greatly, as he remembered in his memoir, *The Korean War*: "After meeting all ranks of officers and men, it was my impression that they were deficient in vigor, bravery, and fighting spirit." He also observed that most men lacked proper winter clothing, and he immediately ordered that winter gear be sent to Korea. From that point on, he began to carry extra pairs of gloves to hand out to any barehanded soldier he met.

On his second day in Korea, Ridgway took to the air in the Eighth Army command plane, which he had christened *Hi Penny!* for his wife. Writing in his memoir, he recalled his first survey of the terrain in which his army was fighting:

General Matthew Ridgway (rear left)—seen here at a Korean command post with Major General Doyle Hickey (rear right) and General Douglas MacArthur (front left)—dramatically improved the fighting capacity and morale of the Eighth Army within a matter of weeks.

[It] was of little comfort to a soldier commanding a mechanized army. The granite peaks rose to 6,000 feet, the ridges were knife-edged, the slopes steep, and the narrow valleys twisted and turned like snakes. The roads were trails, and the lower hills were covered with scrub oaks and stunted pines, fine cover for a soldier who knew how to conceal himself. It was guerilla country, an ideal battleground for the walking Chinese riflemen, but a miserable place for our road-bound troops who moved on wheels.

The first days and weeks of Ridgway's command were critical, and he assessed the need for a different approach in leadership, strategy, and tactics.

One of the most important things he did was to "clean house," not by firing those in high command, but by systematically rotating tired or disillusioned older officers with younger officers eager to prove themselves at the front.

Perhaps most importantly, the special status that X Corps had enjoyed, operating independently of the Eighth Army, was brought to an abrupt halt. Ridgway unified the entire United States fighting force, with General Ned Almond reporting to him. As Clay Blair later reported in *The Forgotten War*, one officer present during Ridgway's restructuring of the command said, "My opinion is that Ridgway told [Almond] how things were going to go in Eighth Army from now on. Almond got the point, and that's how it went. There wasn't any question as to who was the army commander."

The New Year's Offensive

Ridgway and his staff correctly anticipated a third Chinese offensive would take place around New Year's Eve, 1950. UN forces, including elements of both America's Eighth Army and the South Korean army, were positioned near the 38th parallel, and on December 31, 1950, the CCF crossed the 38th parallel and invaded South Korea. As the CCF attacked in force once again, all UN forces retreated to positions below the 37th parallel. This was a contingency that Ridgway had planned for, though, with the rearward positions well-fortified so that a line could be held.

Following the CCF attack and the UN retreat, Ridgway met with South Korean President Syngman Rhee on January 2, 1951. Ridgway denounced the performance of ROK troops, reporting that they exhibited a deplorable unwillingness to stand and fight. In fact, they had repeatedly abandoned their positions in the face of Chinese attack, leaving behind costly weaponry and equipment that the United States had supplied. "We aren't going to get anywhere with your army until you get some leadership" he told Rhee. He further told Rhee that he would not give the South Koreans any more equipment until they "got rid of their incompetents."

This prompted Rhee to visit ROK troops at the front, along with Ridgway, and to launch his own "housecleaning" of officers. For the first time since the war began, a United States armed forces commander was taking an active role in working closely with the ROK army leadership.

By January 3, it was clear that Seoul, the capital of South Korea, would have to be surrendered for a second time to the Communists, and Ridgway ordered a

Korean siblings amid the machinery of war, which took a greater toll on civilian populations with each passing month.

general withdrawal. In addition to clearing Seoul of UN forces and ROK government officials, hundreds of thousands of refugees also fled the Communists. Many of the bridges across the Han River had been destroyed in previous fighting, which meant that military equipment, military personnel, government officials and their families, and civilians all had to cross at the same point.

Ridgway himself was on the scene. He ordered that no civilians were to cross the bridge until all official and military personnel and equipment had crossed. In his memoir, Ridgway recounts the scene poignantly:

> The scene is one that shall always live in my mind: men, women, and children, patriarchs with storybook beards, grand-

Soldiers with the 24th Infantry Regiment board trucks that will take them to the firing line in Korea.

mothers carried on their sons' backs like children, stolidly waiting their turn in the dusk and the near-zero cold, without a destination except some spot far away from the Chinese, with nothing left to them beyond what they could carry, a terrible procession of the meek and disinherited bound only to escape the terrors of Communism and to cling to the freedom so briefly known.

Ridgway's final preparation for his own departure from Seoul was to go to his own "bleak room" and pack his belongings. He left one item behind, a pair of pajama bottoms with the seat split, tacked to the wall beneath a sign that read: "TO THE COMMANDING GENERAL CCF: WITH THE COMPLIMENTS OF THE COMMANDING GENERAL EIGHTH ARMY."

Ridgway and the remnants of the command post at Seoul finally departed on January 4. He was determined not to surrender any further ground to the Chinese or CCF and to switch from a defensive to an offensive position as soon as possible. To bolster the spirits of the troops, Ridgway issued a heartfelt communiqué to every individual assigned or attached to Eighth Army, explaining his perspective on U.S. involvement in the war (see "Why Are We Here? What Are We Fighting For?" p. 94).

UN Progress

After the New Year's offensive, the Chinese withdrew once again to replenish food, ammunition, and other supplies. Ridgway ordered patrols forward of the line he'd established at the 37th parallel, in order to ascertain the whereabouts of the enemy; these patrols encountered little resistance. The goal was to recapture the South Korean capital and regain the 38th parallel; Seoul was heavily guarded, but UN forces slowly began moving their line north toward the city.

Beginning on February 11 the Chinese initiated a counter-attack—its fourth major offensive—at Chipyong, southeast of Seoul. Hit hard, UN forces requested permission from Ridgway to withdraw; he refused. For the first time, orders from the top prevented the "bug out" that had been the standard operating procedure in virtually every major encounter with the enemy. With no order to withdraw, the UN forces fought hard and defeated the Chinese, who lost more than 5,000 men in the battle of Chipyong. By March 15, Communist forces withdrew from Seoul, and the South Korean capital, which was a ghost town by now, changed hands for the fourth time since the war began.

MacArthur Sacked; Ridgway Sent to Tokyo

Meanwhile, relations between General Douglas MacArthur and the Truman administration (including the Joint Chiefs of Staff) plummeted to a new low. Actually, the relationship had been strained from almost the beginning of the war. Though MacArthur had a shining moment in the invasion at Inchon, the JCS repeatedly had to restrain MacArthur's zeal for pushing the conflict beyond what the Truman administration envisioned. For example, MacArthur had given orders to advance north of the 38th parallel well in advance of his

"Why Are We Here? What Are We Fighting For?" (Letter to the Eighth Army from Lt. Gen. Matthew B. Ridgway)

The answer to the first question, "Why are we here?" is simple and conclusive. We are here because of the decisions of the properly constituted authorities of our respective governments. As the Commander in Chief, United Nations Command, General of the Army Douglas MacArthur has said: "This command intends to maintain a military position in Korea just as long as the Statesmen of the United Nations decide we should do so." The answer is simple because further comment is unnecessary. It is conclusive because the loyalty we give and expect precludes any slightest questioning of these orders.

The second question is of much greater significance, and every member of this command is entitled to a full and reasoned answer. Mine follows.

To me the issues are clear. It is not a question of this or that Korean town or village. Real estate is, here, incidental. It is not restricted to the issue of freedom for our South Korean Allies, whose fidelity and valor under the severest stresses of battle we recognize; though that freedom is a symbol of the wider issues, and included among them.

The real issues are whether the power of Western civilization, as God has permitted it to flower in our own beloved lands, shall defy and defeat

official instructions to do so. He also had ordered United States air strikes and troop movements right to the Chinese border, contrary to the National Security Council's directive on September 27, 1950, to use only ROK forces in that area. These actions were nothing less than insubordination, and many in the Truman administration became convinced that MacArthur saw himself as above civilian control.

Because of MacArthur's stature as a World War II hero and his success in the reconstruction of Japan, the JCS—and Truman—often felt they had to handle MacArthur with kid gloves. In his book *The Korean War*, Ridgway recalled an exchange that took place after a JCS meeting in early December 1950. The JCS meeting had just concluded a long debate about how to make MacArthur obey his directives:

Communism; whether the rule of men who shoot their prisoners, enslave their citizens, and deride the dignity of man, shall displace the rule of those to whom the individual and his individual rights are sacred; whether we are to survive with God's hand to guide and lead us, or to perish in the dead existence of a Godless world.

If these be true, and to me they are, beyond any possibility of challenge, then this has long since ceased to be a fight for freedom for our Korean Allies alone and for their national survival. It has become, and it continues to be, a fight for our own freedom, for our own survival, in an honorable, independent national existence.

The sacrifices we have made, and those we shall yet support, are not offered vicariously for others, but in our own direct defense.

In the final analysis, the issue now joined right here in Korea is whether Communism or individual freedom shall prevail; whether the flight of fear-driven people we have witnessed here shall be checked, or shall at some future time, however distant, engulf our own loved ones in all its misery and despair.

These are the things for which we fight. Never have members of any military command had a greater challenge than we, or a finer opportunity to show ourselves and our people at their best—and thus to do honor to the profession of arms, and to those brave men who bred us.

The meeting broke up with no decision taken. The Secretaries of State and Defense left the room and the Joint Chiefs lingered to talk among themselves for a few moments. I approached Hoyt Vandenberg, whom I had known since he was a cadet and I an instructor at West Point. With Van, I had no need for double-talk.

"Why," I asked him, "don't the Joint Chiefs send orders to MacArthur and *tell* him what to do?"

Van shook his head.

"What good would that do? He wouldn't obey the orders. What *can* we do?"

At this, I exploded.

"You can relieve any commander who won't obey orders, can't you?" I exclaimed. The look on Van's face is one I shall never forget. His lips parted and he looked at me with an expression both puzzled and amazed. He walked away without ever saying a word and I never afterward had occasion to discuss this with him.

In March 1951 Chinese forces withdrew as the UN advanced to retake the original border between North and South Korea. By mid-March, when UN forces regained control of Seoul, the time seemed right for peace negotiations. On March 20, the Truman administration put together a plan for a cease-fire that would put an end to the killing while negotiations continued on key issues. While the plan was being drafted, the JCS issued a directive to MacArthur, telling him not to advance past the 38th parallel until after Truman had presented his cease-fire proposal to North Korea and China.

While the State Department was still drafting the cease-fire proposal, the overconfident MacArthur broadcast his own cease-fire proposal on March 24, essentially including an ultimatum to the Chinese: "The enemy therefore must now be painfully aware that a decision of the United Nations to depart from its tolerant effort to contain the war to the area of Korea through expansion of our military operations to his coastal areas and interior bases would doom red China to the risk of imminent military collapse."

This was not the language of diplomacy, nor did it reflect the spirit of the Truman administration's cease-fire proposal. In fact, it was a clear indication that MacArthur had stepped well outside the bounds of his authority, and in doing so, risked an escalation of Chinese involvement in the conflict. Without the approval of the UN Security Council, the President, Congress, or the JCS, MacArthur was essentially threatening total war—including the implied use of nuclear weapons—with China.

MacArthur's taunting communiqué, in fact, led many to conclude that he actually desired a war with China. "The Red Chinese had made a fool of the infallible 'military genius,'" wrote JCS Chairman Omar Bradley in *A General's Life*. "The only possible means left to MacArthur to regain his lost pride and military reputation was now to inflict an overwhelming defeat on those Red Chinese generals who had made a fool of him. In order to do this he was perfectly willing to propel us into all-out war with Red China, and possibly with the Soviet Union, igniting World War III and a nuclear holocaust."

Whatever his motivation, MacArthur's bombshell broadcast completely undermined the Truman administration's proposed cease-fire. Other instances of insubordination followed quickly, and the president officially removed him from command on April 12, 1951. That same day, the president made a radio address to the American people outlining his reasons for the change in command and explaining U.S. policy in the Far East. Mac-Arthur was replaced by General Matthew Ridgway as Supreme Commander of United Nations forces in the Far East; General James A. Van Fleet succeeded Ridgway as commander of the Eighth Army (see "President Truman's Radio Report to the American People on Korea and on U.S. Policy in the Far East," p. 222).

Still a hero in the eyes of many, Mac-Arthur returned to the United States, where

Lieutenant General Matthew Ridgway succeeded MacArthur as Commander in Chief of UN forces in Korea.

he was greeted with ticker tape parades and other public appearances, including an address before a joint session of Congress. During this time, he was frequently mentioned as a possible Republican candidate for president. Meanwhile, Truman's decision to dismiss MacArthur wounded his presidency. But historian Bevin Alexander strongly defended Truman's decision. In *Korea: The First War We Lost*, he wrote, "Whether MacArthur had been right or wrong made little difference; by taking it upon himself to make policy unilaterally, he was operating outside the American political system."

Chapter 9

TWO YEARS OF BLOODY STALEMATE

In carrying out the instructions of my government, I gained the unenviable distinction of being the first United States Army commander in history to sign an armistice without victory.

—General Mark W. Clark

The spring of 1951 brought to an end the cycle of UN advances and retreats—referred to by some soldiers as the "yo-yo war." The CCF mounted two more major offensives, attacking both the Eighth Army and X Corps on April 22 and May 16. By this point, though, CCF forces had proved they weren't invincible, and the UN forces had proved they were up to the task.

Both the CCF and UN forces had dug into defensive positions just north of the 38th parallel, the original dividing line before North Korea invaded the South. The international community was beginning to call for stabilization and peace, and the only outspoken proponent of Korea's unification by force was South Korean President Syngman Rhee. General Matthew Ridgway, the UN Commander of forces in Korea, was put into the difficult position of maintaining both offensive and defensive positions along the new "border," while supporting the idea of a cease-fire and negotiations.

Talks Proposed

The Truman administration had been planning on proposing a cease-fire as early as March 1951, but MacArthur's belligerent message to the Chinese had ruined that plan. Then, when the administration was prepared to try again, they faced the puzzle of deciding who to approach. The official "enemy" was North Korea, which had invaded South Korea. But the Soviet Union had supported their efforts early on with military advisers and equipment, and the Chinese had arguably committed more men than the NKPA. Initiating negotiations was further complicated by the fact that neither the United Nations nor the United States officially recognized Communist China as a nation; therefore there were none of the diplomatic channels that would normally exist between countries.

In June, however, former U.S. diplomat George Kennan had a meeting with the Soviet Union's ambassador to the United Nations, Jacob Malik (the same ambassador who had boycotted the UN a few weeks before the Korean conflict began). On June 23, Malik broadcast a message on UN radio, stating that the Soviet Union supported a cease-fire and peace negotiations between the warring nations. On June 30, the Joint Chiefs of Staff ordered Ridgway to broadcast a message to the Communist leaders that if they were interested in discussing a cease-fire, then representatives from the UN would be sent to meet with them. The JCS message suggested that the negotiators meet on a Danish hospital ship in Wonsan Harbor. On July 2, China and North Korea sent a joint response: "We are authorized to tell you that we agree to suspend military activities and to hold peace negotiations, and that our delegates will meet with yours." The Communists did not agree with the proposed meeting place, however, and suggested Kaesong, a town on the 38th parallel.

After receiving this message, the JCS sent a directive to Ridgway, stating that military operations were to continue until diplomatic agreement had been reached on a cease-fire or armistice. They also wanted that stance communicated to the Communists prior to the beginning of any talks. On July 3, Ridgway sent a message to North Korean Premier Kim Il Sung agreeing to meet in Kaesong beginning July 10. "Since agreement on Armistice terms has to precede cessation of hostilities," he added, "delay in initiating the meeting and in reaching agreement will prolong the fighting and increase the losses."

It was now a little more than a year since North Korea had invaded South Korea on June 25, 1950. In that year, according to official U.S. Army statisticians, the conflict had resulted in nearly two million battle casualties, broken down in this way:

CCF	600,000	(dead, wounded, and captured)
NKPA	600,000	(dead, wounded, and captured)

ROK civilians	469,000	(170,000 dead; 299,000 wounded and captured)
ROK Army	212,554	(21,625 dead; 190,929 wounded and captured)
U.S.	78,800	(21,300 dead; 57,500 wounded and captured)
Total	1,960,354	casualties

Though the UN and Communists had agreed to a meeting place and time, the talks progressed slowly. They dragged out over the next two years, against a backdrop of bloody stalemate at the front, continued hardship for Korean civilians on both sides, and unrelenting captivity for thousands of prisoners of war.

Troubled Talks

The peace talks at Kaesong began on schedule on July 10, with representatives from the UN, South Korea, North Korea, and China. But they got off to a rocky start. Ridgway, of course, had originally proposed that the talks take place on what was arguably neutral "ground," a hospital ship at anchor in Wonsan Harbor. Kaesong, however, was behind enemy lines, and the Chinese and NKPA military presence was nothing less than overbearing. The UN members were subject to screening and searches by armed NKPA and CCF soldiers, and no Western press was allowed near the site of the negotiations. Communist reporters, however, were allowed free access to the talks.

On July 12, when a contingent of journalists from UN member countries was denied access again, the lead UN negotiator, Navy Admiral Turner Joy, walked out with his team. On the radio, Ridgway denounced the Communist manipulation of the site of the peace talks. On July 15, the Communists backed down and agreed to allow Western reporters access to the talks.

The early sessions were also marred by petty arguments and issues, such as whose chair was taller and whose flag was displayed more prominently. The first 10 sessions alone were devoted to identifying what items were to be on the agenda. The two sides finally agreed that the key points in the negotiations would be:

1. A decision on the location of the military demarcation line, or border, and the demilitarized zone, a buffer between the two hostile forces.

2. A cease-fire and armistice arrangement, and an organization to over-see it.

3. A plan for exchanging prisoners of war.

4. An agreement on established governments for North and South Korea.

The first item was a major sticking point, with neither side willing to budge. The Communists wanted the demarcation line to be the 38th parallel, as it was before the North Korean invasion. The UN delegation insisted that the current line, several miles north of the 38th parallel, should be the new demarcation line. Both sides were immovable, and at one point the two negotiating teams sat in stony silence for a period of more than four hours.

In late August, the Communists accused the UN of bombing the neutral zone around Kaesong with chemical weapons and called off negotiations. The United States denied the claim and the Communists never provided any evidence to support their claim. In September, the Communists again claimed that the United States had bombed Kaesong, and once again, the United States denied it. After an investigation, however, it was discovered that a U.S. bomber had indeed mistakenly bombed a target. General Ridgway apologized to the Communists, but they formally rejected his apology. The talks remained suspended for a full two months, while deadly fighting continued on the front.

Close Combat: Punchbowl, Bloody Ridge, and Heartbreak Ridge

Despite the hopes for peace that had sprung forth when peace talks began, there was no relaxation in hostilities between the forces massed at the front. Both UN and Communist forces were dug in, and desperate battles were fought over increasingly meaningless bits of land. The type of warfare had shifted from the large movements of the first year of the war to a stalemate reminiscent of the trench warfare of World War I. Both sides paid dearly in human lives, with no decisive victories for either side.

Ridgway and his UN forces intended to keep military pressure on the Communists during the negotiations, and their determination to do so intensified when peace talks stalled. Rather than engaging in large-scale offensives, however, Ridgway and Eighth Army Commander General Van Fleet planned a series of "limited objective" offensives. Several of these took place in and around a vast, geologic formation that U.S. soldier called the "Punchbowl," particularly during August-October 1951. In his memoir, Ridgway described the area:

U.S. B-26 light bombers batter the harbor at Wonsan, North Korea.

[An] area the enemy held dear was an ancient volcanic crater we named the Punchbowl, about 25 miles north of Inje and the same distance from the east coast.... Its rim was nearly knife sharp all around the edges, rising abruptly several hundred feet above the crater floor, and thickly wooded on every side. The enemy was solidly entrenched on the rim here and well armed with mortars and artillery. Much blood was to be spilled in the coming months to win control of this area.

In an effort to solidify the UN defensive line, an ROK offensive was launched to take the northern ridge of the Punchbowl. Heavy artillery nearly wiped out all the vegetation where the enemy was entrenched, but it failed to destroy the underground bunkers built by the Communists. From these heavily fortified positions, NKPA and Chinese forces were able to repel ROK attacks. In early September, the Eighth Army joined in the attack, and three weeks of fierce fighting ensued. Finally, the NKPA and CCF withdrew from "Bloody Ridge," but not until casualties reached 15,000 on the communist side. The Eighth Army, meanwhile, suffered 2,700 casualties in the clash.

Meanwhile, beginning in mid-September, a similar battle raged at another Punchbowl location, dubbed "Heartbreak Ridge." In fighting that lasted 30 days, tremendous casualties were suffered on both sides; Communist casualties at Heartbreak Ridge were estimated at 25,000, with UN casualties numbering around 4,000.

These and similar operations all along the front during the summer and fall of 1951 offered no significant strategic benefit to either side, but the clashes resulted in as many as 60,000 UN casualties and nearly 235,000 Communist casualties.

Peace Talks Resume

On October 25, 1951, Communist and UN delegates reconvened, this time at Panmunjom, on the west coast of the Korean peninsula, near the 38th parallel. The negotiations picked up where they had left off, still attempting to agree on an initial demarcation line from which to establish a cease-fire. The Communists proposed that the existing battle lines be established as the demarcation line, but Ridgway opposed this. He felt that the Communists should also concede Kaesong, which he felt had significant strategic and symbolic significance. By this time Ridgway was a firm advocate of playing "hard ball" with the Communists, and he expressed suspicions that their proposals cloaked some hidden treachery.

By November 12, it looked like the delegates were just a few weeks away from an agreement. But Ridgway continued to press the JCS and the Truman administration for further concessions from the Communists. In one letter to the JCS, Ridgway declared: "I have strong inner convictions that more steel and less silk, more forthright American insistence on the unchallengeable logic of our position, will yield the objectives for which we honorably contend. Conversely I feel that the course you are directing will lead step by step to sacrifice of our basic principles and repudiation of the cause for which so many gallant men have laid down their lives. We stand at a crucial point. We have much to gain by standing firm. We have everything to lose through concession. With all my conscience, I urge we stand firm."

Back in Washington, the U.S. military leadership questioned Ridgway's conclusions. Omar Bradley, President Truman's chief military adviser, commented that "I don't know why we're arguing about Kaesong. It doesn't mean anything to us." Ridgway remained intransigent, though, and some members of the Truman administration expressed concern that his rhetoric was starting to sound eerily like MacArthur's.

In late November, the negotiators at Panmunjom finally reached agreement on a crucial issue. They decided that the existing battle line, which was slightly north of the 38th parallel, would

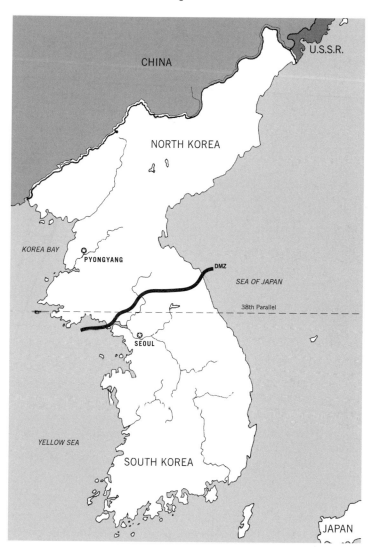

The demilitarized zone as ratified by negotiators in November 1951.

be the final dividing line between North and South Korea. The agreement on the military line of demarcation was officially ratified by both sides on November 27, 1951. This agreement brought into existence a demilitarized zone, or DMZ, that extended two kilometers on either side of the boundary. The agreement was contingent on a truce being reached within 30 days, but it served to limit the fighting somewhat, since neither side was enthusiastic about risking lives for land that it might later have to give up.

In the end, the two sides failed to reach an agreement within the 30-day time period, primarily because the issue of repatriation of prisoners of war remained unresolved. As a result, blood continued be to shed along the 38th parallel for another two years, although not at the fever pitch of the war's opening months.

Debate over POWs

With the demarcation line settled, the negotiators then turned to the next two items on the agenda, provisions for the armistice and the exchange of prisoners of war. The UN—with Ridgway the most vocal leader—was insistent that North Korea not be allowed to continue to build up its military to create another imbalance that would leave South Korea vulnerable to a second invasion. Both Ridgway and Truman initially objected to even the rehabilitation of roads and railways for North Korea, which could be used to strengthen military capabilities. They relented, however, in the face of the argument that the devastated country needed to rebuild its infrastructure for the general benefit of civilians. One provision that remained as a condition of the armistice, however, was that North Korea would be prohibited from building airstrips that could accommodate jet aircraft.

A more significant problem was agreeing to terms for the exchange of prisoners of war (POWs). The combatants were guided by the Geneva Conventions, which are a series of agreements among nations that cover the rules of war, including humane guidelines for the conduct of soldiers and the treatment of civilians, wounded combatants, and prisoners of war. Under the Geneva Conventions, an all-for-all prisoner exchange would have been a simple matter. However, the issue of Chinese involvement in the conflict and the desire on both sides for ideological victory slowed the peace talks to a crawl.

For humanitarian reasons, the UN side wanted "voluntary repatriation," so that prisoners would not be forced to return to Communist countries

In December 1952 President-elect Dwight D. Eisenhower fulfilled a campaign promise to assess the situation in Korea personally.

against their will. The UN wanted to give Chinese prisoners the choice of returning to Communist China if they desired, or joining Chinese nationalists on the island of Formosa (now called Taiwan). Many nationalists had lived on Formosa since Chiang Kai-shek fled there when the Communists came to power in the late 1940s. The UN negotiators recognized that if a large number of Chinese refused to return to Red China, it would constitute a moral victory for the UN and a blow to the Communists.

Another issue was the large number of South Korean natives who had been pressed into service by the invading NKPA. Many of these Koreans were not POWs in the truest sense. Most of these men were neither Communists nor North Koreans, and it was believed that forcing them back into the hands of the enemy would mean torture and murder for most of them, and possibly slavery for others.

The UN negotiators presented the idea of "voluntary repatriation" in early January 1952. The Communists were outraged, so the UN downplayed its estimates of how many of their detainees would choose not to return to China or North Korea. The two sides agreed to a poll of prisoners in April 1952; when the returns came in, the Communists were incredulous. Of 132,000 military POWs held by the UN, only 70,000 said they would agree to return to Communist control. Armed with this information, the Chinese and North Korean negotiators walked out on the peace talks, claiming UN treachery.

More Changes in Command

President Harry Truman decided to forego seeking re-election in 1952, prompted in part by the growing unpopularity of the war among U.S. citizens. The war had cost more than 100,000 casualties, and Truman's handling of the whole affair, including his sacking of MacArthur, had cost him political support. In the fall of 1952, the Republican party nominated as their presidential candidate World War II hero General Dwight D. Eisenhower, who had been Supreme Commander of Allied Forces in Europe during World War II. The Democrats, Truman's party, nominated Adlai Stevenson.

Eisenhower's candidacy required him to give up his post as Supreme Commander of NATO forces (the North Atlantic Treaty Organization) in Europe, which is considered one of the top posts in the military. His successor in this prestigious position was General Matthew Ridgway, who took the post on May 12, 1952. General Mark Clark, who had been a commander of U.S. forces in Italy during World War II, was designated as Ridgway's replacement.

Eisenhower handily beat Stevenson in the November election, partly on the strength of his stated commitment to bring the Korean conflict to an end. Voters believed in this tough commander who had led the famous D-Day invasion at Normandy toward the end of World War II. Eisenhower immediately made good on a campaign promise to personally assess the situation in

A group of U.S. POWs being interviewed by the press at Freedom Village, Korea, after their release.

Korea. Even before he took the oath of office and occupied the Oval Office, he went to Korea to appraise the situation.

Eisenhower visited Eighth Army commander General James Van Fleet in early December. Van Fleet presented Eisenhower with an elaborate and aggressive plan for all-out war against the Communists, including the use of nuclear weapons. Eisenhower rejected these proposals, favoring a negotiated end to the conflict and the removal of U.S. forces as soon as possible.

Another significant change in command took place halfway around the world with the death of Soviet Premier Joseph Stalin on March 5, 1953. His replacement, Georgy Malenkov, soon broadcast a speech calling for peace in Asia. The sudden absence of Stalin, who had consistently called for Communist world domination, signaled a softening in the North Korean and Chinese negotiating positions.

POW Exchanges and Armistice

Almost immediately after Stalin's death, the Chinese and North Koreans publicly expressed willingness to allow the exchange of sick and wounded POWs. This resulted in what came to be known as "Little Switch," which began on April 20, 1953. The UN returned more than 5,100 North Korean and 1,000 Chinese POWs, and about 500 civilian detainees. The Communists released about 700 prisoners, mostly South Koreans but also about 150 Americans, as well as soldiers from Great Britain, Turkey, and other UN countries.

Official talks resumed on April 26, in the midst of Little Switch, and discussions centered on establishing a commission of neutral nations to oversee the exchange of remaining POWs. Again, the talks stalled, as the two sides could not agree on who might be truly neutral. South Korean President Syngman Rhee almost completely derailed the peace process by continuing to make inflammatory statements about uniting Korea by force. He also announced that South Korea would not support any of the conditions of the armistice. He stated that if the United Nations would not support his mission to reunite Korea, then South Korea would go it alone. President Eisenhower sent a team of diplomats to reason with Rhee, and Rhee agreed to issue an apology to the Communists.

Finally, on July 27, 1953, Communist and UN delegates, including General Mark Clark, signed the armistice that brought an end to a little over three years of fighting. While North Koreans celebrated the end of the war as a victory, the event passed quietly in South Korea and in the United States; for the UN forces this was more an end to a meaningless stalemate than a victory.

The remainder of the POWs on both sides were exchanged in late 1953, primarily between August 5 and September 6, in an operation known as "Big Switch." The Communists returned 12,773 prisoners, including approximately 7,800 South Koreans, 3,600 Americans, 1,000 British, and a few hundred soldiers from other UN countries. The UN released 75,823 North Korean and Chinese prisoners of war to the Communists in the demilitarized zone. Another 22,600 POWs who did not wish to return to Communist

On July 27, 1953, an armistice ending the war in Korea was finally signed, after two years of negotiation.

China or North Korea were released to the Neutral Nations Repatriation Commission (NNRC), a group that included representatives from several neutral nations led by India. In addition, 359 UN soldiers held by the Communists as prisoners of war decided to remain with the Communists, including 335 Koreans, 23 Americans, and 1 Briton.

The repatriation proceedings during both Little Switch and Big Switch were marked by controversy. After Little Switch, returning Communist troops that had been held by UN forces charged that they had been beaten, starved, and psychologically abused. After Big Switch, heated debate about voluntary repatriation included charges that Communist captors had tortured and tried to brainwash UN prisoners of war.

111

The last two years of negotiating and fighting did nothing to change the demarcation line that had been established when the peace talks began. U.S. forces suffered an estimated 62,000 casualties during this bloody stalemate, with 12,300 killed.

The Human Cost

In the wake of the armistice, historians tried to tally the total number of casualties among both fighting forces and civilians during the war. The exact figures, however, are unknown. The best estimates from the U.S. Department of Defense are as follows:

Nearly one million UN casualties, including

- More than 850,000 ROK casualties
- More than 17,000 non-American UN casualties
- More than 157,500 American casualties, including nearly 37,000 battlefield deaths

Almost one and a half million Communist casualties, including

- More than 520,000 North Korean casualties
- More than 900,000 Chinese casualties
- Nearly three million Korean civilian casualties

In addition, hundreds of towns and villages were destroyed, creating large homeless populations in both North and South Korea. Finally, much of the peninsula's infrastructure—power plants, highways, bridges, harbors, business districts—had been pulverized.

Chapter 10

ATROCITIES OF
THE KOREAN WAR

—◄▩◄▩◄▩►—

There were few who dared write the truth of things as they
saw them.

—Reginald Thompson, British war correspondent

In every war, there are incidents of violence committed against innocent
people. In the Korean War, where atrocities were committed by all parties
in the conflict, historical controversy has raged ever since regarding the
degree of responsibility for each side. All agree, however, that the level of
atrocities suffered by civilians and prisoners of war (POWs) was particularly
shocking. These non-combatants should have been protected by the laws of
war, which had been drafted by the international community in response to
the many atrocities perpetrated in World War II and other wars (see "The
Geneva Conventions," p. 124).

Much of the information about these atrocities was not published during
the war, nor was it part of official government records on either side. Instead,
many of the stories have surfaced in the form of post-war recollections of the
victims.

Execution and Imprisonment of "Communist Sympathizers"

Almost immediately after the North Koreans invaded South Korea, people in South Korea became suspicious of anyone who might have any sympathy for the Communists. Many believed that North Korea had positioned
Communist infiltrators at various levels of government. The result of this

A South Korean civilian, arrested by the ROK for allegedly being sympathetic to the Communists, crouches on the ground.

mass paranoia was the imprisonment and summary execution of thousands of people without any due process or substantial proof of their alleged conspiracy against the government of South Korea.

Less than a month after the North Korean invasion, South Koreans were attacking their neighbors with alarming dispatch. In *The Bridge at No Gun Ri*,

South Korean women grieve after discovering the bodies of family members who were arrested as political prisoners and then executed by the North Korean military.

the authors Charles J. Hanley, Sang-Hun Choe, and Martha Mendoza relate the experience of one war correspondent:

> In early July 1950, O.H.P. King, an Associated Press correspondent, reported that the national police chief in Suwon said police firing squads summarily executed 60 alleged "Communists" or "Communist sympathizers" in the two days after MacArthur's much-publicized visit to the town. King, in touch at that time with the U.S. Army advisory team, wrote later that he was "shocked that American officers were unconcerned and not interested in helping me ascertain the answers to the many questions the executions raised."

Many journalists either experienced such violence first hand or interviewed witnesses to and survivors of the violence. In *Korea: The Unknown War*, historians Jon Halliday and Bruce Cumings collected the accounts of these journalists—including representatives from both foreign and American press. One British correspondent, James Cameron of London's *Picture Post*, wrote about the treatment of South Korean political prisoners held in what he called concentration camps in Pusan in August 1950:

> This terrible mob of men—convicted of nothing, un-tried, South Koreans in South Korea, suspected of being "unreliable." There were hundreds of them; they were skeletal, puppets of string, faces translucent gray, manacled to each other with chains, cringing in the classic Oriental attitude of subjection, the squatting fetal position, in piles of garbage.... Around this medievally gruesome marketplace were gathered a few knots of American soldiers photographing the scene with casual industry.

Cameron was deeply disturbed by the situation and took his concern to UN officials, who did nothing. Though Cameron diligently recorded the plight of the prisoners at Pusan with photographs and detailed reporting, the *Picture Post* chose not to publish the story.

Many journalists and historians have tried to provide context for the behavior of the South Koreans. They note that the North Korean occupation of much of South Korea included extensive brutality. As Spencer C. Tucker wrote in *Encyclopedia of the Korean War*, "The widespread cruelty of the Communist occupation during the opening months of the conflict set the moral tone for the rest of the war. It also led South Koreans who were lukewarm or opposed to the government of Syngman Rhee to rally to it as far preferable to that of the Communists."

During the months of June to September 1950 alone, for example, North Korean forces killed over 20,000 South Korean civilians. The Communists also rounded up and murdered members of the South Korean government and police. In numerous instances, North Korean captors executed their prisoners with a single bullet to the back of the head and left their bodies in roadside ditches with their hands tied behind their backs with wire. After the North Korean retreat from Taejon, 5,000 bodies were discovered there, the worst of many reports of instances in which U.S. forces discovered trenches filled with hundreds of dead South Korean men, women, and children. U.S. forces also found many dead bodies of American prisoners of war who had been executed.

These Korean civilians were killed when they became caught in the line of fire during a guerrilla assault.

The Guerrilla Threat

One of the difficulties facing American and other United Nations troops was the very real threat of guerrilla warfare. There were indeed incidents of enemy attacks by people—men and women—who appeared to be civilians. In order to blend in with groups of civilians, North Korean soldiers sometimes covered their uniforms with the traditional white garb of Korean peasants, with their weapons hidden in sacks on their backs. Further, there was no easy way to identify by appearance alone whether a Korean was from the South or the North. Fear and confusion gripped the newly arrived U.S. troops, especially as stories of attacks—both real and imagined—sped among the ranks. In *Korea: The Unknown War*, authors Jon Halliday and Bruce Cumings point out several cases of American complicity in attacks against civilians. They also, however, emphasize the difficulty faced by American troops in identifying the enemy:

> Americans first felt the combination of frontal assault and guerrilla warfare in the battle for Taejon. Local peasants, including women and children, would come running along the hillsides near the battle lines as if they were refugees. At a given signal, the "refugees" snatched rifles, machine-guns, and hand grenades from their bundles and brought down withering fire on the troops below. The [American] retreat from Taejon ran into well-organized roadblocks and ambushes, often placed by local residents. Americans thought anyone in "white pajamas" (thus they described the Korean native dress) might potentially be an enemy. From this point onwards, American forces began burning villages suspected of harboring guerril-

las, and in some cases they were burned merely to deny hiding places to the guerrillas.

In the very early stages of the war, more than 380,000 refugees streamed south from North Korea, and the possibility that North Korean guerrillas were hiding among them was a very real concern. This insidious threat of an enemy who was not distinguishable by uniform, racial distinction, or even gender may have been a root cause of one alleged atrocity, the incident at the bridge of No Gun Ri.

No Gun Ri and the Associated Press Report

In July 1950, a series of events occurred near the village of No Gun Ri involving South Korean villagers and U.S. troops. These events constitute one of the most controversial episodes of the Korean War, yet the facts remain unclear to this day, and different participants offer very different recollections and interpretations of the events.

The episode at No Gun Ri was not publicized at the time of the war. It first became widely known in 1997, when a group of South Korean survivors petitioned the United States for an apology and reparations. Their petition, which was rejected, prompted an investigation by journalists from the news organization the Associated Press (AP). The AP initiated an investigation that included reviewing hundreds of documents and conducting interviews with more than 100 veterans. The AP also interviewed survivors and reconstructed events that led up to the alleged massacre. Their initial report was issued on September 29, 1999. For its reporting on the incident, the Associated Press was awarded a Pulitzer Prize for investigative journalism. Three of the AP journalists—Charles J. Hanley, Sang-Hun Choe, and Martha Mendoza—later published a book, *The Bridge at No Gun Ri: A Hidden Nightmare from the Korean War*. The following description of the events at No Gun Ri summarizes their coverage of the incident.

On July 23, 1950, American soldiers ordered the evacuation of two small villages in the North Chungchong Province in South Korea. They told villagers that they had to leave because of the impending advance of the NKPA, and they assured them that they would be escorted to safety in the American stronghold in Pusan. However, on July 25, the American troops abandoned the South Korean refugees in the village of Ha Ga Ri. The following day, the refugees resumed the journey south on their own.

The refugees arrived at the village of No Gun Ri on July 26 and were met by American soldiers (later identified as a company from the 2nd Battalion of the 7th Division of the First Cavalry Division). The Americans had arrived in Korea only three days earlier and had been informed by their commanders of the risks of guerrilla infiltrators among refugees. They stopped the refugees on a railroad bridge and searched them for weapons; none were found.

Suddenly, the American soldiers scattered as U.S. planes flew in from over the nearby mountains. The planes began shooting the civilians trapped on the bridge, spraying men, women, children, and their livestock with machine gun and rocket fire. Survivors estimated that at least 100 people were killed in the attack from U.S. warplanes, as described in this excerpt from *The Bridge at No Gun Ri*:

> From every direction, in every direction, people were running, panicked, helpless, not knowing what was happening, children with hands over their ears, adults dragging children by their arms. Some scratched into the ground trying to hide. Others lay bloody and silent, dismembered, strewn about. Still others lay sprawled crying pitifully for help. Cows screamed. The limbs of people and animals rained down. As he lay on the ground, teenager Chung Koo-shik felt something hot land on his back. It was the head of a baby… .
>
> Soldiers converged on the scene, villagers recalled, checking bodies with a nudge of their boots, gathering people on the tracks, on the adjacent hillside, in the small field between the tracks and road, and herding them toward the trestle. Parents carried children. People supported wounded relatives who could walk. Sobbing, or in silent shock, they slowly shuffled toward the cavernous tunnels under the bridge… .
>
> Inside it was bedlam. Frantic villagers cried out children's names. Boys and girls screamed for their mothers and fathers. Family groups crawled to the safest spots, away from the road, shoving and pushing for space on the jam-packed sandy floor. Choon-ja's grandmother finally glanced out toward the road and saw a man's body with a straw mat on its back. "There's my husband!" she wailed, but she dared not go to him.

According to the AP reporters' account, those who were able—about 400 refugees—ran down into the concrete culverts beneath the bridge. For the next three days, American troops fired on the Korean refugees from both sides of the culverts. The defenseless refugees were forced to pile the bodies of their family members and neighbors at the mouths of the culverts to protect themselves from gunfire. In the sweltering July heat, many wounded civilians died of thirst. As one survivor of No Gun Ri recalled, "The American soldiers played with our lives like boys playing with flies." On July 29, the Americans suddenly disappeared, probably due to encroaching NKPA troops.

Additional investigations revealed that no official record exists of the activities of that particular Army company for those three days. Subsequent inquiries have uncovered communications authorizing Air Force strafing of refugees and communiqués from Army commanders to nearby troops that authorized the shooting of civilians who tried to cross frontlines. For example, one order from First Cavalry headquarters stated, "No refugees to cross the front line. Fire [on] everyone trying to cross lines. Use discretion in [the] case of women and children."

Follow-Up Investigations

When the AP story first appeared in September 1999, the initial response was shock and horror that U.S. troops had been involved in such an appalling incident. The revelations by AP immediately generated a storm of governmental and journalistic activity as other journalists and military investigators rushed to cover the story. U.S. military investigators started an in-depth investigation that would take a year-and-a-half to complete. At the same time, newspapers and magazines picked up the story and began their own investigations. During the ensuing months, many journalists conducted significant research and analysis, and the AP, *U.S. News & World Report*, the *New York Times*, and the *Washington Post* all provided extensive coverage.

Edward Daily, one of the veterans who had been an important source for the AP story, soon became the public face for the incident. He was interviewed by many journalists and appeared on national TV news programs. Daily traveled to Korea to meet with survivors of No Gun Ri; he traveled with Tom Brokaw to the No Gun Ri site for an NBC news program. Daily shared memories of the event that were poignant, vivid, and brutal.

But veteran military journalist Joseph L. Galloway then published an article in *U.S. News & World Report* that challenged many aspects of the AP account. Galloway said that Edward Daily had essentially lied. Daily was a veteran of the Korean War, but he had lied about his service records, his medals, his status as a prisoner of war, and his involvement at No Gun Ri. In fact, he had been nowhere near the village at that time. *U.S. News* challenged other elements of the AP story, including the veracity of several other veterans who had contributed eyewitness accounts. A succession of challenges to the AP story followed. AP agreed that Daily had apparently lied, but argued that there was enough other evidence and other witnesses to support the story. According to some observers, however, challenges to the veracity of Daily and other witnesses undermined the authority and credibility of the AP story.

"The American soliders played with our lives like boys playing with flies."

In the ensuing coverage, several key issues emerged as subjects of dispute: whether the witnesses in the AP story were credible; whether U.S. troops and U.S. aircraft had been ordered to fire on Korean civilians; whether the estimates of the number of civilian deaths were accurate; whether there had been returning fire from the Koreans under the bridge; and whether disguised North Korean guerrillas had infiltrated the group and were hiding among the villagers.

On January 11, 2001, the United States Department of the Army Inspector General released its report on the incident at No Gun Ri. The Review Team had examined over one million documents, analyzed the results of forensics examinations, studied press coverage, interviewed about 200 American witnesses, and analyzed oral statements of about 75 Korean witnesses. In its final 300-page report, it found that American troops had been unprepared for combat, with inadequate experience and equipment; that troops had been unprepared to deal with the numerous uncontrolled refugees fleeing the North Koreans; that troops had good reason to be afraid that North Korean soldiers had infiltrated refugee groups; that troops may have conducted inadvertent air strikes on Korean civilians; and that troops did not receive oral or written orders to shoot and kill Korean civilians. The summary of the report also included the following:

> It is clear, based upon all available evidence, that an unknown number of Korean civilians were killed or injured by the effects of small-arms fire, artillery and mortar fire, and strafing

that preceded or coincided with the NKPA's advance and the withdrawal of U.S. forces in the vicinity of No Gun Ri.... The firing was a result of hostile fire seen or received from civilian positions or fire directed over their heads or near them to control their movement. The deaths and injuries ... wherever they occurred, were an unfortunate tragedy inherent in war and not a deliberate killing.... Neither the documentary evidence nor the U.S. veterans' statements reviewed by the U.S. Review Team support a hypothesis of deliberate killing of Korean civilians. What befell civilians in the vicinity of No Gun Ri in late July 1950 was a tragic and deeply regrettable accompaniment to a war forced upon unprepared U.S. and ROK forces.

U.S. President Bill Clinton issued a statement acknowledging that a tragedy did in fact occur, expressing deep regret "that Korean civilians lost their lives at No Gun Ri," and offering condolences to those who lost loved ones in the tragedy. His statement did not include an apology to the victims and their survivors. Secretary of Defense William Cohen offered these remarks:

> The passage of 50 years has reduced the possibility that all of the facts can be known about the tragic incident that took place in the vicinity of No Gun Ri in South Korea. We have determined, however, that U.S. soldiers killed or injured an unconfirmed number of Korean refugees in the last week of July 1950 during a withdrawal under pressure in the vicinity of No Gun Ri.... While recollection of these events is painful, neither Americans nor Koreans should bury their history. Innocent Korean civilians died as a result of the war forced upon our two countries, and we should never forget them, as we should never forget the brave soldiers who fought to defend freedom.

Cohen also announced that the United States would erect a memorial in the vicinity of No Gun Ri to commemorate the innocent Korean civilians who lost their lives in the war.

Many people took issue with the findings in the U.S. government report. South Korean survivors of No Gun Ri pressed for reparations from the U.S. government, and many journalists and historians disputed different aspects of the report. Meanwhile, controversy continued to rage about the findings by the initial AP reporters, although many observers felt they were somewhat vindicated by the findings in the U.S. government report. As Michael Dobbs wrote in the *Washington Post,*

> The first lesson from the No Gun Ri controversy is that eyewitness accounts, particularly 50 years after the event, can be misleading. People have selective memories, even when they are making every effort to be truthful.... A second lesson from this controversy is that written records also can be unreliable.... A third lesson from No Gun Ri is that history is an imperfect science, journalism even more so. History is constantly being rewritten as new evidence emerges. We should distrust anyone who claims to have come up with the "definitive" version, or interpretation, of history.

Indeed, there are currently many different interpretations of what happened at No Gun Ri—from the South Korean survivors, the U.S. Army, the AP, and other reporters and historians. In the years since No Gun Ri, many of the events still seem ambiguous and contradictory, and the full story may never be conclusively known.

The Tiger Death March

Another notorious incident of war crimes against both POWs and civilians was the "Tiger Death March," which occurred over a nine-day period beginning on October 31, 1950. About 850 North Korean-held prisoners— including 80 civilians—left Manpo in North Korea, marching nearly 100 miles north along the Yalu River to Chunggang. In addition to U.S. soldiers, the prisoners included such noncombatants as missionaries, nuns, priests, diplomats, and business people from Europe and the United States. Many of the prisoners had been captured weeks or months earlier and were already weakened by fatigue, hunger, thirst, illness, and injuries. Many had been captured during the summer and were inadequately dressed for the extreme winter weather conditions they now faced.

The commander of the march was "The Tiger," the prisoners' nickname for the ruthless man who ordered the prisoners to march onward despite their

---

The Geneva Conventions

It's not uncommon to hear people say "the Geneva Convention," but in fact, the term is "Geneva Conventions," referring to a series of resolutions and protocols agreed to by an international body regarding the rules of war. The first Geneva Convention was established in 1864, prompted by Red Cross founder Henri Dunant's concern for the treatment of wounded combatants. Since then, there have been three additional "conventions" and two protocols, which together outline humane guidelines for the conduct of soldiers and the treatment of civilians, wounded combatants, and prisoners of war (POWs). The conventions also address the conduct and treatment of medical personnel and journalists. The International Red Cross continues to monitor adherence to the conventions among warring countries, and the conventions are subject to updates as weaponry and tactics and strategies change.

The atrocities that were perpetrated during the Korean War centered primarily on the treatment of civilians and prisoners of war. Some basic guidelines of the Geneva Conventions are as follows:

For Civilians:

- Civilians are not to be subject to attack, whether directly or as the result of indiscriminate attacks in areas where both military personnel or targets and civilians are present.

---

wounds, hunger, weakness, and age; no one ever learned his real name. A Salvation Army missionary who translated the Tiger's orders told of the commander's heartlessness from the very first day. The Tiger told the translator to communicate to the prisoners that they would be marching 16 miles the first day. When the translator protested that there were wounded, elderly, and sick people among them, the Tiger snarled, "Let them march till they die!"

In the following nine days, the Tiger kept a grueling schedule, apparently so that UN forces would not overtake them and liberate the prisoners. The prisoners were freezing cold, their wounds and illnesses were untreated, and they were starving and thirsty and weary to the point of exhaustion. They spent their nights huddled together, either in the open air or in unheated

- Private property must not be destroyed unless it is justifiable as a military necessity.

- Civilians must not be tortured, raped, or enslaved.

- Civilians must not be used as hostages.

- Civilians must not be subject to outrages upon personal dignity.

- Civilians must not be subject to collective punishment and reprisals.

For POWs:

- POWs must be treated humanely.

- POWs must not be subject to torture or medical experiments of any kind.

- POWs must be immediately removed from combat zones and may not be used as "human shields."

- POWs must be protected against intimidation, violence, insults, and public humiliation.

- POWs must be questioned in their native language and are not required to give information beyond their names, ranks, birth dates, and serial numbers.

buildings. Soldiers along the way abused them, kicking them and hitting them with their rifle butts if they began to straggle. The prisoners showed tremendous courage, compassion, and kindness, trying to help those who were slower and weaker. One morning, the Tiger called together the American Army officers to tell them of his plan to kill anyone who lagged behind. He made his point by executing one officer, Lieutenant Cordus Thornton, whose men had made slow progress the day before. In Lewis H. Carlson's book *Remembered Prisoners of a Forgotten War*, civilian prisoner Larry Zellers described that day:

> The Tiger moved smartly to face the victim and ordered him to turn around. Pausing for a moment, the Tiger pushed up the

back of Thornton's cap and put his pistol against the back of Thornton's head. I noticed right in front of me a little Turkish girl who was probably 15 or 16. She was sobbing softly to herself. Some people were averting their eyes. I kept looking, at least I had my face turned in that direction, but when I knew the gun was going to fire, I shut my eyes for a brief two or three seconds until it was over.... The Tiger called for [the interpreter] to come to his side and translate for him. "You have just witnessed the execution of a bad man. This move will help us to work together better in peace and harmony."

The emaciated prisoners were forced to move at a grueling pace, marching through snowstorms and over mountains. Many, too weak to go on, simply stopped and waited by the side of the road. Prisoners who collapsed in this manner were shot and rolled into the ditch. The number of deaths during the march and those that resulted later due to injury, malnutrition, exposure, and illness from the march were appalling. Twelve months after the march began, only 300 of the original 850 prisoners remained alive.

American Prisoners of War Captured by North Korea and China

POWs on either side of a conflict are supposed to be offered protection under the Geneva Conventions. But the North Korean Army ignored those guidelines, particularly in the very first days of the war. There are numerous accounts of American prisoners of war found left behind in ditches by their captors, their hands bound with wire and bullets in their heads.

The Geneva Conventions were created to offer protection to POWs against violence, abuse, torture, and maltreatment of any kind. Many Americans reported extremely harsh conditions under the North Koreans, including lack of food and healthy drinking water, lack of medical attention, torture, and murder. In Lewis H. Carlson's book *Remembered Prisoners of a Forgotten War*, infantryman Irv Langell, who was captured early in the fighting, described a typical example of psychological torture:

We came to a small village and were told to sit on a split-log bench. A soldier soon came by, looked at us, and drew out a .45 pistol and put it to [fellow prisoner] Roger's head. In broken English, he asked, "You believe in God?" We both shook

North Korean and Chinese prisoners at a UN POW camp at Pusan.

our heads yes. He pulled the trigger, but it just clicked, and he walked off laughing.

Many UN POWs died in the first weeks and months of the war under the NKPA. Exact numbers are not known, but of the more than 8,000 soldiers unaccounted for, experts believe at least half of these died in POW camps.

Conditions for POWs improved somewhat when the Chinese entered the war and set up permanent camps near the Chinese border. The Chinese treated the prisoners better than the North Koreans did for political reasons. The Chinese "reeducated" some prisoners, though, through schemes of indoctrination that lauded the virtues of Communism and characterized Western capitalism as evil and corrupt.

After the war, there were many accusations that American prisoners of war had been "brainwashed" by their North Korean and Chinese captors. During "Big Switch," prisoners on both sides were given the choice of whether to remain with their captors; 23 American soldiers chose to remain with the Chinese. This caused problems for many remaining American POWs. Some were greeted with distrust and suspicion by fellow Americans who wondered if they had been brainwashed into acting as Communist spies. A few prisoners, of course, did collaborate with the enemy. A few more prisoners strictly followed military protocol by completely refusing to comply with their jailors. Most prisoners, though, simply tried to survive under intolerable conditions. (see "One U.S. Soldier's POW Experience," p. 229.)

Chapter 11

THE LEGACY OF THE KOREAN WAR

By calling the Korean conflict a "forgotten war," we both name it, and we remember it—a paradox. What is it that we are remembering to forget?

—Historian Bruce Cumings

The Korean War has been called "the forgotten war," "the unknown war," "the wrong war," and "the first war the United States ever lost." Many Korean War veterans felt that the purpose of the war was not clear and that the American public did not support them and did not show them the respect given to veterans of earlier wars—much like Vietnam veterans would feel several years later. "America tolerated the Korean War while it was on but could not wait to forget it once it was over," confirmed historian David Halberstam in *The Fifties*.

By the time the armistice was signed and the fighting stopped on July 27, 1953, the toll of the Korean conflict had become truly staggering. More than four million men, women, and children had been killed or wounded during the war. Hundreds of thousands of people were displaced and homeless. North and South Korea were no closer to reunification, and the dividing line between the two countries had been re-drawn almost exactly as it had been prior to June 25, 1950.

Despite the lack of a decisive victory for either side, the Korean War was a pivotal event in world history: it was the first actual armed struggle in the Cold War between Communism and democracy. As the Truman Presidential Library points out in its online exhibit (www.trumanlibrary.org), "The Korean peninsula is the only place in the world where the interest and the security concerns of the United States, China, Japan, and Russia directly intersect." In the years since the armistice was signed, the two Koreas have become, in a sense, laboratories for two opposing ideologies. Meanwhile, they maintain an uneasy and fragile truce.

The Effect on the Koreas

Unquestionably, North and South Korea were most deeply affected by the war. In addition to the human cost, much of the countryside and cities were laid to waste by armed combat. Homes were destroyed, and families were split. At the close of the war, the two nations' infrastructures and economies lay in ruins.

After the war, North Korea remained under the control of the ruthless dictator Kim Il Sung, who suppressed all dissent. His rule continued for 40 years, making him one of the longest-ruling leaders of the 20th century and the only leader to stay in power throughout all of the Cold War. After Kim Il Sung's death in 1994, he was succeeded by his son, Kim Jong Il, who rules the country with a mighty military force. North Korea has remained staunchly Communist since the war's end, even in the face of the dissolution of the Soviet Union and the growing influence of Western-style capitalism and culture in China.

In many ways, North Korea has reverted to the peninsula's earlier status as "the hermit kingdom." Foreign intervention of any kind is rebuffed, and North Korea remains very much a closed country. This isolationism prevents North Korea from reaping the benefits of foreign aid programs, financial investment, and other fruits of capitalism. Poverty and famine continually challenge its economy. Many observers say this is due to the disproportionate size of the nation's armed forces. Since the war, North Korea has greatly expanded its armed forces, which now include over one million members. In fact, North Korea's armed forces include almost double the number of troops as South Korea, even though the country's overall population is about half that of South Korea. It has also displayed ambitions of becoming a nuclear power, a prospect that greatly alarms South Korea, the United States, and many other nations.

In recent years, North Korea has established itself as a "non-aligned nation" which, for example, belligerently refuses to participate in internation-

A Korean War soldier's bullet-pierced helmet lies next to his body.

al moves to disarm nuclear warheads. U.S. leaders often refer to North Korea as a "rogue nation," and many analysts believe that if the United States were to withdraw its military presence from South Korea, the North would once again invade the South.

South Korea, by contrast, has enjoyed a flourishing economy as well as political growing pains in the last half-century. Immediately after the war, Syngman Rhee developed agreements with the United States to ensure South Korea's security in the future and to establish long-term economic aid. This aid allowed South Korea to rebuild its economy after the war, and today its gross national product is estimated to be almost one trillion dollars, making it the world's 11th largest economy. South Korea's per capita income is estimated at about $20,000 per person, roughly 20 times that of North Korea.

But politically, South Korea has had problems. Rhee's presidency turned corrupt and violent, and he was forced to resign in 1960. Civil unrest, assassinations, and military coups d'etat have rocked the country several times since then, and a new constitution was drafted in 1987. Though South Korea's economic growth is impressive, its advances in freedom and democracy continue to fall short of U.S. standards.

A key issue of the war, reunification, remains unresolved. In recent years, both North and South Korea have made small but significant overtures toward conciliatory moves—though North Korea's unpredictable leadership has also issued threatening statements periodically. After almost 60 years, the peninsula is still divided, and a demilitarized zone (DMZ) continues to separate the two countries. Today, reunification seems very unlikely.

The Effect on the United States

The Korean War also had a tremendous effect on the United States, particularly on foreign policy and military strategy. Since the war's end, many historians have tried to evaluate U.S. conduct in the war. Some commentators have criticized the Truman administration for not consulting Congress before going to war. Others have criticized the U.S. government for not adequately preparing forces to face a well-armed North Korean army. Still others have taken issue with the decision to cross the 38th parallel and pursue the fight to the Yalu River, which was not a clearly stated goal of the first UN resolution.

Other observers contend that despite the tremendous cost, which was certainly greater than the Truman administration calculated, the Communists were ultimately turned back from their invasion of South Korea. According to this perspective, the Truman Doctrine of containment was validated. In the end, as Allan R. Millett noted in *The Journal of Military History*, "Just which Korean War one reads about depends on what lessons the author intends to communicate, for the history of the war reeks with almost as much didacticism as blood."

Prior to the Korean conflict, the United States had always scaled back its military establishment immediately after the conclusion of a war. Even after World War II, U.S. military expenditures were drastically cut back, which crippled U.S. efforts in Korea at the beginning of the war. But after Korea, the U.S. maintained the armed services at full strength. And the U.S. Congress, which authorizes all military funding, showed an increasing willingness to invest a greater proportion of government revenue in the military, even in peacetime.

The Korean War also marked a change in the way U.S. leaders viewed America's role in the world. The U.S. came to view itself as the world's peacekeeper. After this war, the U.S. reversed a gradual slide toward isolationism and created mutual defense treaties with nations around the globe. One key mutual defense pact was NATO (North Atlantic Treaty Organization), a defense pact with Western European nations intended to assure Western Europe's safety from the Soviet Union. The Korean War was the decisive moment, according to many historians, that the U.S. emerged as a world power prepared to take military action to protect its interests around the world.

"The history of the war reeks with almost as much didacticism as blood."

U.S. military strategy required some readjustment after Korea. Fighting in Korea had been different than in previous wars, because of its limited objectives. In earlier wars, the U.S. had always fought for a total victory. But that approach was impossible because of the threat posed by the Soviet Union and the possible use of nuclear weapons. Military planning in Korea therefore had to avoid drawing the Soviet Union into the war. Viewed as a pawn between the superpowers, Korea was not considered worth the risk of a nuclear war. After the war, though, the United States was seen as a powerful military establishment willing to use force to stop the threat of Communism.

Within the United States, the aftermath of the war brought feelings of frustration. It was hard for people to believe that the powerful United States, with the help of UN forces, had been unable to defeat a tiny country like North Korea. One apparent lesson of the war was that it was difficult to win a ground war in Asia against a committed enemy. Yet that lesson would seem remote just a few years later, when the United States became involved in Vietnam. Thus the Korean War earned the name "the forgotten war" as the American people put the conflict behind them and moved on with their lives.

The Effect on the International Community

The war's effect on the Soviet Union was ambiguous. Some say that the Soviets were happy to see U.S. forces fighting in Korea rather than in Europe. It has also been speculated that the Soviets were pleased that the war destroyed any prospect of the United States and China establishing diplomatic ties. Others, though, argue that the war had a chilling effect on Soviet expanionist ambitions. According to this view, the U.S. response in Korea acted as a deterrent to the Soviets.

Many say the war had a positive impact for China. Before the war, China was viewed with pity by many Westerners, who considered it impoverished and backward. But instead of pity, China elicited respect and fear in the war's aftermath. Chinese Communist forces had advanced beyond the border and decimated U.S. forces in Korea, a stunning development that greatly enhanced China's international prestige. Thus the Korean War created a dramatic shift in the global balance of power, as a new Communist superpower was born. Later, China's actions in Korea emerged as a key consideration for U.S. military strategists and policymakers in their assessments of the Vietnam conflict.

Shortly after the war, the events in Korea—the first violent campaign of the Cold War—were seen as a polarizing force in the international community. Certainly there had been other acts of aggression from the Communist world, including the Soviet Union's subjugation of Eastern Europe, the Berlin blockade, and the explosion of the first Soviet nuclear bomb. But the events in Korea earned particular revulsion because a Communist aggressor had invaded part of the "free world." At this tense moment in the Cold War, many worried where they would strike next.

Yet people's worst fears were not realized. Less than 40 years later, the Cold War came to an end. The Berlin Wall, which had separated East and West Berlin and stood as a symbol of Communist repression, was torn down in 1989. Two years later, in 1991, Communism collapsed in the Soviet Union. Today only a few countries in the world remain under the rule of Communist governments—including Cuba, China, Vietnam, and North Korea.

Continued U.S. Occupation

More than 50 years after the armistice was signed, the UN and the United States still have a large contingent of troops stationed in South Korea. The U.S. Army routinely keeps 37,000 soldiers along the DMZ at the 38th parallel. U.S. troops have remained there since the close of the war, because South Korea felt threatened by North Korea's continued alliance with China and the Soviet Union after the armistice was signed in July 1953.

U.S. Marines pay their respects to comrades who fell on the Korean War battlefield.

Just a few months after the armistice was signed, military commentator S.L.A. Marshall wrote about the continuation of the U.S. presence in South Korea in *Atlantic Monthly* magazine. He acknowledged that the United States could not extricate itself until South Korea's military strength reached the point that it could resist any future aggression from the North. Like many others, though, Marshall was under the impression that the U.S. military presence in Korea was temporary. "Korea is a strategically profitless area for the United States, of no use as a defensive base, a springboard to nowhere, a sinkhole for our military power. We don't belong there."

Today, the continued presence of U.S. troops in South Korea is seen by many analysts as powerful evidence that once the United States commits its military power overseas, events often take on an unpredictable life of their own. These events can often make it extremely difficult for the United States to extricate itself from the region, especially in instances when its leadership commits troops and other military resources without a realistic and flexible "exit strategy." As historian Bruce Cumings explained in his book *North Korea: Another Country*:

> The 50th anniversary of the presumed end of [the] war came and went in July 2003, but the war is still not over and appears unlikely to be resolved anytime soon. We remain technically at war with North Korea.... The longevity and insolubility of the Korean conflict makes it the best example in the world of how easy it is to get into a war and how hard it is to get out.

BIOGRAPHIES

Dwight D. Eisenhower (1890–1969)
President of the United States at the end of the Korean War

Dwight David Eisenhower was born on October 14, 1890, in Denison, Texas. He was the third of seven sons born to David Eisenhower and Ida (Stover) Eisenhower. The family moved to Abilene, Kansas, in 1892. Eisenhower's father worked as a shopkeeper and his mother as a homemaker; the family was poor, but held high expectations of moral integrity and educational excellence for their sons.

Eisenhower (nicknamed "Ike") graduated from Abilene High School in 1909 and worked in a local creamery until 1911, when he won an appointment to the United States Military Academy at West Point. He graduated in 1915, and began his military career with the U.S. Army as an infantryman in Texas. While stationed in Texas, Eisenhower met and married Mamie Geneva Doud in 1916. They had two sons, Doud Dwight (who died of scarlet fever at age three) and Jon Seldon Doud.

During World War I Eisenhower served as a training officer and administrator at military bases in Texas, Georgia, and Maryland. He was promoted to major in 1920, a rank he held for the next 16 years. His first overseas assignment was in the Panama Canal Zone in 1922, where he served until 1924. In 1925 he attended the Command and General Staff School at Fort Leavenworth, Kansas, then served as a battalion commander at Fort Benning, Georgia, until 1927. He graduated from the Army War College in 1928.

Eisenhower briefly served under famed World War I hero General John Pershing with the American Battle Monuments Commission, and then joined the staff of General George V. Mosely, Assistant Secretary of War. He served as Mosely's executive officer from 1929 to 1933. Eisenhower then became chief military aide to General Douglas MacArthur, who was Army Chief of Staff at the time. He accompanied MacArthur to the Philippines and served there from 1935 to 1939, gaining a promotion to lieutenant colonel in 1936.

Military Fame During World War II

After the outbreak of World War II, Eisenhower returned to the United States from the Philippines and held a series of high-level administrative positions in Washington, D.C. Army Chief of Staff General George C. Marshall quickly took note of his administrative and organizational skills. In June 1942 he designated Eisenhower as commanding general for the European Theater of the war in June 1942, despite the fact that he had never seen combat nor commanded men under fire. Eisenhower promptly went to London, England, where he engineered the Allied invasion and occupation of North Africa.

Eisenhower's greatest military triumph during World War II, however, was probably his planning and execution of "Operation Overlord." Better known as "D-Day," this successful Allied amphibious invasion of Normandy, France on June 6, 1942, was a pivotal victory for the United States and its allies. In recognition of the successful D-Day operation, Eisenhower was promoted to General of the Army in December 1942.

In 1944 Eisenhower became Supreme Commander of Allied forces. He held this position, which gave him command over more than 4 million men and women, until Germany surrendered in the spring of 1945. During this period, President Franklin D. Roosevelt relied on Eisenhower's skill not only as a military commander but also as a diplomat. Indeed, Eisenhower worked in close concert with other Allied leaders, including British Prime Minister Winston Churchill, French President Charles DeGaulle, and Soviet Premier Joseph Stalin, during the last months of the war. After the German surrender, Eisenhower was made Military Governor of the U.S. Occupation Zone in Europe. He served in this role until November 1945, when he was named Army Chief of Staff on the Joint Chiefs of Staff (JCS), the primary military advisory group to the president of the United States.

Eisenhower served in Washington, D.C., as Army Chief of Staff until 1948, when he retired from the Army. He then accepted the presidency of Columbia University in New York City, a position he held until the summer of 1952. In January 1951, however, he took a leave from Columbia to help nurture the newly created North Atlantic Treaty Organization (NATO). He was named Supreme Commander of NATO troops in Europe and oversaw the organization of NATO headquarters in Paris. In 1952, however, he resigned and launched his long-expected campaign to become the next president of the United States.

America's 34th President

Both the Democratic Party, which needed a candidate after President Harry S. Truman had declined to seek a second term, and the Republican Party pursued Eisenhower as a candidate. Previously unaligned with either party, Eisenhower ultimately chose to run as a Republican; he purportedly said the Democrats had been in office for 20 years and it was a time for a change. Armed with the campaign slogan "I like Ike" and enormous personal popularity because of his World War II exploits, Eisenhower gained the Republican Party's nomination, then easily beat Democratic candidate Adlai Stevenson in the 1952 presidential election.

In December 1952 the president-elect fulfilled a campaign promise to visit Korea to get a firsthand perspective on the war. Eisenhower spent most of his three-day trip at the front, inspecting the frigid winter camps and talking with front-line commanders. By the time he returned to the United States, he was convinced that unifying Korea under a democratic government would be a horribly costly enterprise—and one that might well trigger an even wider war with Communist Asia. He decided that a negotiated settlement that would leave both South Korea and North Korea intact was the only practical solution. "My conclusion as I left Korea," he later wrote in *Mandate for Change*, "was that we could not stand forever on a static front and continue to accept casualties without any visible results."

Once he took the oath of office, Eisenhower aggressively pursued a peace settlement with the North Koreans and the Chinese. This decision was at odds with his campaign rhetoric, which had repeatedly criticized the Truman administration for its failure to stamp out Communism in North Korea. He sensed, however, that American weariness with the war had became so great that a diplomatic settlement would not significantly hurt him politically. On July 27, 1953, the Armistice Agreement was finally signed, bringing an end to the fighting. The following year, South Korean President Syngman Rhee tried to convince him to direct nuclear strikes against North Korea, but Eisenhower flatly refused to even consider the notion.

Eisenhower After Korea

President Eisenhower served two terms as the 34th U.S. president (1953–1961), earning the second term with a rematch victory over Stevenson in the

1956 elections. He thus became the first Republican president to serve two complete terms since General Ulysses S. Grant.

During his presidency Eisenhower presided over years of heady economic growth and prosperity across much of America. He also paved the way for the development of America's interstate highway system, sent in U.S. troops to enforce racial desegregation of schools in Little Rock, Arkansas, and signed into law the addition of Alaska and Hawaii as states of the Union.

In foreign affairs, historians describe Eisenhower's approach as moderate and restrained. But he did play a major role in guiding the United States' early involvement in Vietnam, which he saw as another nation at risk of a complete Communist takeover. After his departure, in the 1960s, Vietnam erupted into one of the most divisive and costly wars in American history. In his farewell address to the nation, Eisenhower made a remarkable speech in which he warned about the tremendous growth and influence of America's military-industrial complex—a colossus that he and his fellow Cold War warriors had helped to bring to reality.

After completing his second term, Eisenhower turned over the White House to Democrat John F. Kennedy, winner of the 1960 presidential election over Eisenhower's vice president, Richard Nixon. Eisenhower retired with his wife Mamie to their farm near Gettysburg, Pennsylvania. He died after a long illness on March 28, 1969, in Washington, D.C.

Sources

Ambrose, Stephen E. *Eisenhower*. 2 vols. New York: Simon and Schuster, 1983-1984.

Bongard, David L., and Ken Stringer. *Harper Encyclopedia of Military Biography*. New York: Harper Collins, 1992.

Broadwater, Jeff. *Eisenhower and the Anti-Communist Crusade*. Chapel Hill: University of North Carolina Press, 1992.

Divine, Robert A. *Eisenhower and the Cold War*. New York: Oxford University Press, 1981.

Eisenhower, Dwight D. *The White House Years*. 2 vols. Garden City, NY: Doubleday, 1963-1965.

Melanson, Richard A., and David Mayers. *Reevaluating Eisenhower: American Foreign Policy in the 1950s*. Urbana: University of Illinois Press, 1986.

Schneider, Carl, and Dorothy Schneider. *World War II: An Eyewitness History*. New York: Facts on File, 2003.

Kim Il Sung (1912–1994)
President of North Korea

Kim Il Sung was born Kim Sung-ju on April 15, 1912, during the height of Japanese domination of the Korean peninsula. (In the Korean language, the "family name" or surname comes first; so, "Kim" is the last name in this case.) Kim later adopted "Il Sung" in remembrance of an earlier anti-Japanese resistance fighter who had died in action. There are significant differences in the accounts of Kim's early life; there is the "official" version perpetrated by the Communist North Korean government and Kim himself, and there are other accounts by independent sources.

The state-sponsored versions of Kim's biography generally paint him as a life-long Communist who was destined from an early age to become a leader of his people. It is believed that Kim was born to a peasant couple, but the official version is that his father was a schoolmaster. One legend of Kim as a young man is that he rebelled against his Japanese-controlled schoolmasters by scratching out the Japanese language titles of books with a penknife and by exhorting his schoolmates to speak Korean in defiance of laws mandating exclusive use of the Japanese language.

In 1925 Kim's family fled Japanese oppression, settling in the Manchurian region of China. His formal education ended at the eighth grade level when he was expelled from school and jailed for "illegal political activities" against the Japanese, who were attempting to expand their rule into Manchuria during this time. It is believed that both of his parents died around the time he was jailed. Shortly after his release, Kim joined the underground Chinese Communist Youth League. He then began leading Chinese and Korean expatriate guerilla forces against Japanese military outposts in China.

Kim and his fellow guerrillas fled Manchuria in the face of increased Japanese occupation in 1940. He and his comrades retreated to a province in Siberia, where they may have received Soviet instruction in military tactics and Communist doctrine. Kim reportedly married a fellow Korean partisan during that time. But her name remains unknown, and scholars are uncertain whether the union ended with divorce or her death. It is known that his second wife, Kim Chong Suk, joined his band of rebels as a young woman. In 1942 she gave birth to his son and eventual successor, Kim Jong Il. She died in the late 1940s while giving birth to a stillborn child.

Leader of North Korea

In August 1945 Japan surrendered the territories they had occupied during World War II, including Korea. Kim Il Sung returned to North Korea, now occupied by the Soviet Union. By this time Kim had risen to the rank of major in the Soviet Red Army, and he was an important resource for the Soviet government on military and political issues in the region.

Shortly after his return, Kim was hand-picked by the Soviets to establish a provisional government in the north. Several months later, he founded the North Korean Provisional People's Committee. By the end of 1946 he had also organized the North Korean Workers Party, the sole political party in the north, and the Korean People's Army (KPA), which shortly became the North Korean People's Army (NKPA). In February 1947 the Soviet-sponsored provisional government was formally replaced by the North Korean People's Assembly, led by Kim.

When the United Nations sponsored elections in May 1948, the North Korean administrative government refused to participate. The North Koreans instead established their own sovereign state called the Democratic People's Republic of Korea, which claimed authority over the entire Korean peninsula. The Republic's general assembly elected Kim Il Sung premier in September 1948, beginning Kim's 46-year reign.

Obsessed with Reunification

Kim advocated reunification of the Korean peninsula by any means necessary. Many scholars believe that Kim's primary motivation for reunification was not ideological, but nationalistic. Dae-Sook Suh, author of *Kim Il Sung: The North Korean Leader* writes:

> The war has always been analyzed from the cold war viewpoint: the confrontation of superpowers, a complex accusation

of collusion among North Korea, the Soviet Union, and China, and the concept of aggression by persuasion....The objective of the war for Kim was quite different. It was neither the development of the concept of limited war, nor was it the expansion or containment of communism in Asia. The war for Kim was primarily the function of his own political ambition, and his effort to resolve the question of Korea's division.

For the first few years of his leadership, Kim's regime sponsored guerrilla forces in South Korea and subversive political action. When these activities failed to dislodge the UN-sponsored South Korean government of Syngman Rhee, the Soviets gave their blessing to an all-out military offensive. Kim's North Korean People's Army invaded South Korea in June 1950.

To Kim Il Sung, the Korean War was the "fatherland liberation war," and he believed—erroneously, as it turned out—that the offensive would trigger a popular uprising across the south against Syngman Rhee's government in Seoul. When this uprising failed to materialize, Kim was genuinely surprised. Most historians characterize the Korean War as being instigated by the Soviet Union, and the involvement of the Chinese after the UN moved north of the 38th parallel seems to suggest a greater Communist bloc agenda

Kim's original intent was to push south, capture Seoul, and reunify Korea militarily. He misjudged the American-led United Nations response, however. After enjoying early success, the NKPA suffered a series of crushing defeats, most notably at Inchon. When the U.S.-led UN forces crossed the 38th parallel and occupied Pyongyang in October 1950, Kim panicked and asked for immediate help from his Communist allies. From that point forward in the war, Kim was pushed aside, and the war was effectively managed by the Chinese military under commander Peng Dehuai. In fact, the Chinese remained in Korea long after the armistice was signed in July 1953, its troops finally leaving in 1958.

Pursues Policies of Isolationism and Militarism

After the armistice, Kim concentrated on building a strong industrial economy. He also developed his own style of Communism called *Chu'Che*, an odd blend of Marxist-Lenin Communism, isolationism, and his own personality cult. During this period, execution, imprisonment, or exile of opponents became commonplace, and they remained a hallmark of Kim's government for the remainder of his rule.

Kim's economic policies emphasized heavy industry and collective farming, and until the 1970s, North Korea's economy was more robust than that of South Korea. Kim's insistence on isolationism, however, eventually served to alienate him somewhat from the Soviet Union and China, despite their similar political ideologies. In addition, the government's single-minded pursuit of self-sufficiency and military might bred economic stagnation and environmental carnage throughout the country.

Kim's desire for unification and his hostility toward the United States remained central in his political machinations. North Korea was responsible for a number of assassinations of South Korean leaders, an attempt on the life of South Korean president Park Chun Hee in 1968, and the capture of the USS *Pueblo*, a U.S. intelligence-gathering vessel and its crew, in the same year; North Korea held the 82 crew members of the *Pueblo* for 11 months before releasing them. Throughout Kim's regime, relations with the United States ranged from strained to profoundly hostile. North Korea's development of nuclear energy and nuclear weaponry have been a sticking point in international relations with the West for decades.

In August 1984 Kim announced that his son would eventually succeed him as North Korea's leader. This announcement underscored the fact that Kim, though supposedly aligned with Communist ideals of a society for the people, had effectively constructed a monocracy. His absolute control over every aspect of North Korean society enabled him to revise history, crush his opponents, and ensure that power would remain in his own family after his death.

Over the years, Kim diverted significant sums of his country's treasury to monuments to himself and his reign. In 1972, a huge bronze statue of Kim was dedicated for his 60th birthday. To commemorate another of his birthdays, he erected an Arch of Triumph taller than the original Arc du Triomphe in Paris.

By the latter years of his rule, Kim was revered as almost a demi-god in his own country, having convinced the people through his self-deification campaigns that he was the "Supreme Ruler." According to one biographer, Kim attempted to defy death itself by employing more than 2,000 doctors, biologists, and pathologists for the sole purpose of extending the lives of himself and his son for as long as possible. In the end, Kim Il Sung died a very conventional death of a heart attack on July 7, 1994.

Sources

Bai, Bong. *Kim Il Sung: A Political Biography*. 3 vols. New York: Guardian, 1970.

Cotton, James, and Ian Neary, eds. *The Korean War in History*. Atlantic Highlands, NJ: Humanities Press, 1989.

Suh, Dae-Sook. *Kim Il Sung: The North Korean Leader*. New York: Columbia University Press, 1988.

Tucker, Spencer C. *Encyclopedia of the Korean War: A Political, Social, and Military History*. 3 vols. Santa Barbara, CA: ABC-CLIO, 2000.

Douglas MacArthur (1880–1964)
Supreme Commander of United Nations Forces in Korea

Douglas MacArthur was born on January 26, 1880, in Little Rock, Arkansas, to Arthur MacArthur Jr. and Mary Pinkney (Hardy) MacArthur. Douglas was the youngest of three boys, his older brothers being Arthur III and Malcolm. Arthur MacArthur Jr. was a career infantry officer who fought in the American Civil War. During MacArthur's younger years, his father was stationed at various posts in the western United States. MacArthur was later fond of saying, "I learned to ride and shoot before I learned to read and write," which may have been an exaggeration. He did, however grow up in a thoroughly military lifestyle, observing the discipline of life in various forts and bases. He also spent hours listening to his father's tales of heroics under General U.S. Grant in the Civil War and other soldiers' accounts of the later "Indian wars."

At the age of thirteen, MacArthur entered the new West Texas Military Academy. He was valedictorian of the academy's first graduating class. From there he moved on to West Point, the premier American school for aspiring Army officers. During his years at West Point he lived with his mother in a hotel on the academy's grounds. MacArthur excelled, graduating in 1903 with the highest grade point average of any West Point cadet in 25 years.

MacArthur's first commission was in the Philippines, as part of the U.S. Army's newly created "general staff." In 1904 he was promoted to first lieutenant and aide-de-camp to his father, now a general, and accompanied him to Japan for an eight-month tour. His father had an abiding interest in the Far East, and together they toured Japan's military bases and other Asian countries, including China and India.

In 1906, MacArthur was ordered to Washington, D.C., where he served as an aide to one of President Theodore Roosevelt's military advisors and also attended Engineers School. For the young officer, the proximity to the bold and boisterous Roosevelt, the famous proponent of "gunboat diplomacy," was intoxicating.

In 1913, as an Army captain, he was ordered on a commando mission to Veracruz, Mexico, where a rebellion threatened peace; it was MacArthur's first taste of battle. The mission was successful, and MacArthur reported that three different bullets pierced portions of his clothing during the fracas without injuring him.

It was around this time that the flamboyant MacArthur adopted some extravagances in his appearance. As a field officer, he could get away with some modifications to his uniform. He wore a battered campaign hat, his captain's bars sideways on his collar (instead of over his breast pocket), a brightly colored scarf around his neck and the trademark pipe between his teeth. In 1915, as the Army's first public relations officer, he promoted the use of the selective service to draft soldiers.

World Wars Vault MacArthur to Prominence

The United States entered World War I in 1917. MacArthur, now a colonel, served in France, where he led the 42nd Division. Under his leadership, his so-called "Rainbow Division" performed superbly, and MacArthur himself became known as a "soldier's soldier" with a knack for "[rallying] other men to the grim business of killing," wrote biographer Geoffrey Perret. By war's end, he had earned numerous combat decorations and a promotion to brigadier general.

MacArthur's stellar performance in World War I gained him an appointment as superintendent of West Point, where he is credited with introducing numerous changes that modernized the academy. In 1922, he married Louise Cromwell Brooks; they divorced in 1929. MacArthur, at this time, became increasingly concerned with the growth of Communism as a global political movement and its perceived infiltration of American institutions. "Pacifism, and its bedfellow, Communism, are all about us," he lectured.

In 1930 MacArthur was promoted to Army Chief of Staff. During the Depression, in 1932, he led an assault on World War I veterans who had encamped in the nation's capital, demanding bonus pay they had never received for combat duty. Most accounts have MacArthur leading the charge against the protestors on horseback, dispersing them with tear gas and bayonets. MacArthur later told the press that the Army's harsh hand with the protestors had saved the country from "incipient revolution."

Commissioned again to the Philippines in 1935, MacArthur was assigned the task of creating a defensive U.S. base in the Far East. He married Jean Marie Faircloth in 1937; they had one son together, Arthur. In 1941 he was named commander of all U.S. forces in the Far East.

After the Japanese attack on Pearl Harbor on December 7, 1941, MacArthur commanded U.S. forces in the Far East and the Pacific in World War II. MacArthur's World War II experience began ingloriously. Underestimating Japanese willingness to attack the Philippines, MacArthur was defeated when they did. Japanese air raids destroyed MacArthur's air power within hours of Pearl Harbor, striking bases before the planes were ordered to the air. He then lost the key Philippine island of Luzon to the Japanese invaders. President Franklin Roosevelt ordered MacArthur to withdraw to Bataan, then to Corregidor, and ultimately to Australia. Before MacArthur left Bataan, however, he uttered the famous line, "I shall return."

MacArthur kept his promise, making a triumphant return nearly three years later. Directing Pacific operations from Australia, MacArthur guided Allied forces through New Guinea, then liberated the islands of Southeast Asia from the Japanese. When he landed again in the Philippines in October 1944, wading ashore in the company of journalists, he spoke into a waiting microphone: "People of the Philippines: I have returned…. Rally to me." As commanding officer of operations in the Pacific theater, MacArthur accepted the unconditional surrender of the Japanese aboard the USS *Missouri* in Tokyo Bay on September 2, 1945.

After World War II, President Harry S. Truman appointed General MacArthur to head a peacetime mission of occupation and reconstruction in Japan. Over the next six years, MacArthur oversaw the development of a non-military society in Japan. Changes implemented under MacArthur's watch included the establishment of a democratic constitution, religious freedoms, civil liberties, the emancipation of women, the formation of labor unions, and land reforms. Across much of Japan, MacArthur came to be regarded as a benevolent, almost paternalistic, figure that helped rebuild the war-ravaged country into a thriving industrial nation.

MacArthur and Korea

As supreme commander of Allied Powers in the Far East, including Japan's former colonies in the region, MacArthur wielded authority over the

U.S. occupation of South Korea. But he made only one trip to Seoul in five years, for the 1948 ceremony inaugurating Syngman Rhee as the first president of the Republic of Korea. He placed most responsibility for South Korea's affairs in the hands of Lieutenant General John Hodge.

When North Korea invaded South Korea in June 1950, and the United Nations resolved to support the South, MacArthur was named supreme commander of UN forces in Korea. He commanded United States and other forces from his headquarters in Tokyo, Japan.

In the war's opening weeks, the North Korean People's Army (NKPA) battered the U.S.-led UN forces, which were poorly equipped and soft from years of inactivity. By late July 1950 the only South Korean soil under MacArthur's control was a 100-mile by 50-mile rectangle of land in the southeast corner of the peninsula. Since the major city in this territory was the port of Pusan, the outer line of UN defense of this land came to be known as the Pusan Perimeter.

A Decisive Triumph

Determined to change the war's momentum, MacArthur devised a daring plan to send an invasion force behind enemy lines at the port of Inchon. Many military advisors expressed strong initial opposition to the plan, but MacArthur ultimately prevailed and the Inchon invasion proceeded in September 1950. This amphibious operation proved spectacularly successful, and MacArthur received praise from Truman and the Joint Chiefs of Staff (JCS).

MacArthur pressed his advantage, retaking Seoul and pushing North Korean forces above the 38th parallel. He did this with the full approval of the United Nations and the Truman administration, which suddenly saw an opportunity to seize all of North Korea. But MacArthur's belief that China would stay out of the conflict if UN forces pursued North Korea's army above the 38th parallel proved to be a gross miscalculation. In a few short weeks, his boast that he would unify Korea under a democratic government in time to send U.S. troops home by Christmas was shattered by brutal winter weather and massive attacks by Chinese Communist forces pouring over the China-North Korea border.

In early November MacArthur finally acknowledged that a formidable Chinese military presence might exist in the Korea-China border region. He reacted by calling for intensive bombing of bridges on the Yalu River, the border between North Korea and China. He then essentially disobeyed JCS instructions when he ordered Eighth Army commander General Walton Walker to use "any and all ground forces …to secure all of North Korea." The JCS directive had permitted MacArthur to use only South Korean forces at the Chinese-North Korea border.

In the meantime, UN forces under MacArthur's command continued to surge through North Korea toward the Chinese border. "Complete victory seemed now in view, a golden apple that would handsomely symbolize the crowning effort of [MacArthur's] brilliant military career," wrote Matt Ridgway in *The Korean War*. "Once in reach of the prize, MacArthur would not allow himself to be delayed or admonished. Instead he plunged northward in pursuit of a vanishing enemy and changed his plans from week to week to accelerate his advance without regard for dark hints of possible disaster."

In late November 1950, the Chinese launched a devastating offensive against MacArthur's widely dispersed forces. The offensive was so effective that MacArthur was forced to call a hasty withdrawal of his forces all the way back to the 38th parallel. From this point forward, the general actively sought to expand the war, urging Washington to commit to a final military show-down with the Chinese.

Truman Dismisses MacArthur

MacArthur clashed with Truman and the JCS on multiple occasions around this time, especially after Washington abandoned the goal of Korean reunification. MacArthur finally exhausted Truman's patience for insubordination when he issued a statement to the Chinese and North Koreans that undermined a cease-fire proposal that Truman had in the works. This action alone prompted Truman to consider firing MacArthur. The deciding factor, though, was a letter MacArthur wrote in April 1951 to Joseph Martin, the Republican speaker of the House of Representatives. In the letter, MacArthur openly criticized the foreign policy of the Truman administration, saying, "If we lose this war to Communism in Asia, the fall of Europe is inevitable." He also urged widening the war to take on China. On April 5 Martin read the letter to Congress, deeply embarrassing the Truman administration. Afterward, Truman acknowledged in his dairy that "This looks like the last straw. Rank insubordination." Truman fired MacArthur on April 12, replacing him with Matthew Ridgway.

MacArthur's firing evoked public sympathy in Japan, where 250,000 citizens lined the route to the airport the day the venerable general and his wife departed. The controversy and outrage was even greater in the United States. "The firing was as divisive an act as anyone could remember—in terms of class, religion, culture, and geography," wrote David Halberstam in *The Fifties*. "It was not just that everyone had an opinion about what had happened, it was that everyone had to voice it. There were fights in bars between strangers and fights on commuter trains between men who knew each other and who had, up to that moment, been friends and had concealed their political differences.... It was to that nation, that outpouring of emotion, that MacArthur came home. At first it seemed like one vast parade that would never end."

Indeed, MacArthur and his wife were welcomed home by a massive ticker-tape parade in New York City. A few days later, he made a historic speech before a joint session of Congress that was broadcast to millions over the radio and the new medium of the day, television. During his address he quoted an old military ballad, "Old soldiers never die, they just fade away." MacArthur, who had concluded 52 years of military service to his country, said, "like that old soldier of that ballad, I now close my military career and just fade away—an old soldier who tried to do his duty as God gave him the light to see that duty. Goodbye."

For a time it appeared that MacArthur might make a serious bid for the Republican Party's 1952 presidential nomination, but public support for the idea gradually faded. The retired general and his wife settled in New York City, where MacArthur accepted a job as chairman of the board for the Sperry Rand Corporation in 1952. Plagued by illness in the last years of his life, MacArthur died at the age of 84 on April 5, 1964.

Sources

Blair, Clay. *MacArthur*. New York: Times Books, 1977.

Halberstam, David. *The Fifties*. New York: Villard, 1993.

MacArthur, Douglas. *Reminiscences*. New York: McGraw-Hill, 1964.

Manchester, William. *American Caesar: Douglas MacArthur, 1880-1964*. Boston: Little, Brown, 1978.

Perret, Geoffrey. *Old Soldiers Never Die: The Life of Douglas MacArthur*. New York: Random House, 1996.

Schaller, Michael. *Douglas MacArthur: Far Eastern General*. New York: Oxford University Press, 1989.

Syngman Rhee (1875–1965)
President of South Korea

Syngman Rhee was born Yi Sung-man on March 25, 1875, in P'yongsan, a town in Korea's Hwanghae Province. His Korean surname "Yi," which appears first per Korean custom, was later "Westernized" to "Rhee" and placed second, as with Western custom, by Rhee himself. Rhee's father was a *yangban*, an educated civil servant elevated in the Confucian society of the time to a position above the working and farming class. Despite his family's position in the traditional Korean aristocracy, however, Rhee grew up in very modest financial circumstances. As a very young boy, Rhee's mother educated him according to Chinese traditions and classicism, a reflection of China's influence on Korea at the time.

At the age of nine, Rhee had a transformational encounter with the West. He was struck by a case of smallpox that rendered him blind in both eyes. After trying traditional Oriental treatments of herbs and roots, his parents finally took him to an American Christian missionary, who was a doctor. The doctor administered medicine that restored the boy's sight. This experience has been cited as a factor in Rhee's later interest in Western culture and society.

As a teenager, Rhee began attending the Paichai School run by Methodist missionaries. He hid this activity from his parents, who were allegiant to the teachings of Buddhism and Confucionism. During this time, the seeds of Christian theology were planted in the young man's mind, along with ideas of independence from the oppression Korea had been subjected to over the years by China and Japan. While a student at Paichai, Rhee became involved in the nationalistic Independence Club and edited a newsletter advocating Korean independence from Japanese influence.

Political Activism Results in Imprisonment

In 1898 Japanese anger about the activities of the Independence Club prompted a violent crackdown. The organization was forcibly disbanded and its members arrested. Rhee was tortured and sentenced by the Japanese to life imprisonment. His missionary friends made frequent visits to him, and he converted to Christianity during his prison term. During his imprisonment, he also wrote a series of political essays that he was able to smuggle out of prison with the help of sympathetic friends. These essays, which urged Koreans to take responsibility for the future of the nation, were published anonymously in a variety of newsletters and newspapers. Some of these writings were later collected in a book called *The Spirit of Independence* (published in 1906), including this passage:

> To live in this nation is comparable to being a passenger on a ship in a cruel sea. How can you be so indifferent as not to be concerned with the affairs of your own nation, but to insist they are the business of high officials? …Do not wait for others to lead or to do what must be done, but arouse yourself.

In an effort to improve relations with the Korean people, Japan declared an amnesty for political prisoners in August 1904, and Rhee was released. Convinced that hope for Korean independence was tied to support from the West—the United States in particular—Rhee left for Washington, D.C., two months after his release. He departed with a student passport and the blessing of high-level Korean officials who were alarmed by Japan's growing sway over the peninsula's internal affairs.

Rhee arrived in the United States in December 1905. His first efforts to meet with President Theodore Roosevelt ended in failure, and several months went by. But in July 1905 Rhee and P. K. Yoon, a Korean Methodist minister who lived in Hawaii, finally met with the president. Roosevelt encouraged Rhee to work through traditional diplomatic channels, but later that year, Japanese and Korean officials signed an agreement making Korea a protectorate of Japan. The agreement gave Japan formal control over most facets of Korean life, and the Japanese formally annexed Korea five years later.

Disheartened by the turn of events in his native land, Rhee stayed in Washington, D.C, where he earned a bachelor's degree from George Washington University in 1907. He attended Harvard University and emerged with a master's degree in 1908. From there, he went to Princeton University, and in 1910 he became the first Korean national to be awarded a Ph.D. by an Ivy League school.

After graduating from Princeton, Rhee briefly returned to Korea, but in March 1912 he left again, marking the beginning of a 30-year period of exile. Operating first in Hawaii and then primarily from Shanghai, China, he emerged as one of the most prominent voices urging Korean independence from Japan. In 1919 Rhee was elected president of the Korean Provisional Government—a government-in-exile—on the strength of his nationalistic proclamations and years of activism. He and his fellow exiles bickered endlessly, however, and in 1925 Rhee was removed from the presidency by political opponents. Rhee never acknowledged the setback, however, and he continued to describe himself as the rightful president of Korea for the next two decades.

Emerges as International Figure

In 1933 Rhee traveled to Geneva, Switzerland, to petition the newly formed League of Nations to support Korean independence from Japan. His pleas did not bring any diplomatic results, but it did give him the opportunity to meet Francesca Donner, the daughter of a wealthy Austrian businessman. After their marriage in 1934, they had one son who died in childhood. They later adopted another son.

During World War II, Rhee became Korea's most visible political figure, despite his long absence from the peninsula. A tireless advocate of Korean independence—and unification, after Japan's surrender in 1945—Rhee gained valuable political connections in the West during these years. He gained particular favor with powerful American lawmakers because of his strong anti-Communist remarks. As a result, when Korea was surrendered along with other Japanese-occupied lands at the end of World War II, the United States decided to support his bid to lead the new government.

Over the next two years, Rhee's relations with U.S. officials were often turbulent. They regarded him as a savvy politician with a genuine loathing for Communism, but they also saw him as unscrupulous and overly obsessed with uniting the divided country under his rule. Ultimately, though, American diplomats continued to stand behind Rhee because they could find no other legitimate candidates with strong anti-Communist credentials.

First President of the Republic of Korea

By May 1948, when the United Nations sponsored elections in South Korea, Rhee was the clear frontrunner for the presidency. He won easily, assuming the reins of the newly established Republic of Korea (ROK). Rhee's government quickly received diplomatic recognition from the United States, but his relations with the Americans remained troubled. Well aware of Rhee's desire to unify the Korean peninsula by force if necessary, the United States purposely limited its investment in the South Korean military. By contrast, Rhee's counterpart to the north, North Korean President Kim Il Sung, received massive military assistance from his Soviet benefactors. Kim was also determined to unite the divided country—albeit under a Communist form of government—and in June 1950 he ordered a massive invasion of the South. The South Koreans and their American allies were totally unprepared for the onslaught, and they were nearly pushed off the peninsula entirely. After weeks of being routed, however, the tide slowly turned. In early 1951 the war settled into a bloody stalemate that dragged on for more than two years.

Throughout the war and the negotiations to bring an end to the conflict, Rhee proved to be an impediment to peace. He often threatened to "go it alone" if the United Nations pulled out, and he repeatedly sought to sabotage armistice talks in hopes that a continuation of the war would ultimately bring him the unified Korea he desired. Rhee did not subside until the United States promised a large contingent of occupying troops and millions of dollars in economic aid.

After the armistice was signed, Rhee was a reluctant participant in the democratic process. Unwilling to yield the presidency when his term expired in 1954, Rhee strong-armed a constitutional amendment removing its original two-term limitation to the presidency. During these years his administration became notorious for corruption, intimidation of political opponents, and inattention to domestic economic affairs. In 1960 Rhee was elected president for a fourth time. But protests against his government became so fierce and widespread that Rhee fled the country. It was later alleged by his opponents that he absconded with $20 million of the country's general fund.

Rhee retired to Hawaii, where he had many supporters among the state's Korean expatriate community. He lived in Hawaii with his wife and his adopted son until his death on July 19, 1965. His body was subsequently returned to South Korea, where it was buried in the national cemetery.

Sources

Allen, Richard C., *Korea's Syngman Rhee: An Unauthorized Portrait*. Rutland, VT: Charles E. Tuttle Company, 1960.

Cumings, Bruce. *Korea's Place in the Sun: A Modern History*. New York: W.W. Norton, 1997.

Oliver, Robert T. *Syngman Rhee: The Man Behind the Myth*. New York: Dodd, Mead, 1955.

Stueck, William W., Jr. *The Korean War: An International History*. Princeton, NJ: Princeton University Press, 1995.

Matthew B. Ridgway (1895–1993)
Commander of Eighth Army, Commander of UN Forces in Korea

Matthew Bunker Ridgway was born in Fort Monroe, Virginia, on March 3, 1895. His father, Thomas Ridgway, was a career army officer; his mother, Ruth Starbuck (Bunker) Ridgway was a homemaker who was an accomplished concert pianist. He had one younger sister, Ruth.

Raised on Army bases, Ridgway became acclimated to the rhythms of military life at an early age. He also spent a good deal of time with his father enjoying the outdoors, camping, and hunting. The Ridgway family moved frequently from post to post, and he attended elementary school in Washington state, Minnesota, and North Carolina. He graduated from English High School in Boston, Massachusetts, in 1912. He entered West Point in June 1913.

At West Point, Ridgway excelled in the language arts, scoring best in Spanish and English; he graduated 56th in a class of 139 cadets in 1917. As with many in his graduating class, he hoped that he would sail for France to join the Allies in World War I, but instead, he was stationed along the Mexican border. Toward the end of World War I, he was ordered to report to West Point as an instructor, which he felt was the "death knell" of his military career.

Ridgway's proficiency in Spanish, however, soon brought him assignments in Latin America, including Nicaragua and the Philippines. From 1932 to 1935, he served as technical advisor to the governor of the Philippines. He also continued his military education during the 1930s, attending the Infantry School, the Command and General Staff School, and the Army War College.

A Star Officer in World War II

By the time World War II broke out in 1939, Ridgway was in the War Department War Plan Division. He was promoted to brigadier general by his mentor, General George C. Marshall, and sent to Europe, where he excelled.

159

He first served as commander of the 82ⁿᵈ Airborne Division, leading paratroopers in invasions and campaigns in Italy. "He was a *great* combat commander," recalled one officer in Clay Blair's *Ridgway's Paratroopers*. "Lots of courage. He was right up front every minute. Hard as flint and full of intensity, almost grinding his teeth with intensity."

Ridgway parachuted with his troops during the pivotal June 6, 1944, "D-Day" invasion at Normandy, France. Later that year, he was assigned command of the 18ᵗʰ Airborne Corps in Belgium, France, and Germany. A strong leader with a perfectionist streak, his men joked that under his command, "There's a right way, a wrong way, and a Ridgway." He was promoted to lieutenant general in the waning weeks of the war, and in August 1949 he was named a chief aide to Army Chief of Staff Omar Bradley.

Ridgway considered himself be a spiritual man, and he often wrote and spoke about the influence of God in his life and the affairs of men. But he led a personal life that was not always consistent with his proclaimed morality. His reputation as both a cadet and an instructor at Wes Point was that of a womanizer; the other cadets called him "the Black Knight of the Hudson." Ridgway was married for the first time in 1917 to Julia Caroline Blount. They had two daughters together and divorced in 1930. Five days after the divorce from his first wife was final, he married Margaret Howard Wilson Dabney, a widow, and legally adopted her daughter. His second wife divorced him in 1947. By then, he had already met his third wife, Mary Princess "Penny" Long, who had recently divorced; they were married in 1947. Together, they had a son, Matthew.

Ridgway Goes to Korea

Ridgway was deeply involved in devising U.S. military strategy after North Korea staged its surprise invasion of South Korea in June 1950. But he did not have a command role in the conflict until December 23, 1950, when he was named to replace Lieutenant General Walton Walker, who had died in a jeep accident, as commander of the U.S. Eighth Army. Ridgway confronted a demoralized Army shaken by the entrance of the unrelenting Chinese infantry. But he moved decisively to improve morale by shuffling his officer corps and insisting on a higher level of care and regard for ordinary soldiers.

Ridgway also showcased his abilities as a military strategist, registering several important victories over Communist forces. The most impressive of these triumphs came in early 1951, when Eighth Army troops recaptured

Seoul and drove the Chinese north of the 38th parallel. "In the Italian and Normandy campaigns [of World War II], he was always out there where he could see the most and shifting his outposts nearer to the enemy," stated one enlisted man, as reported in George Mitchell's *Matthew B. Ridgway*. "In Korea it was the same—the Ridgway idea about how to fight may be summed up by his statement during one hot moment in the frontline, that 'the Communists can fire only so many shells, and I figure you may as well be moving forward as sitting here and catching them in our laps.'"

As the months passed, veteran U.S. military leaders openly marveled at the dramatic improvement in the performance of the Eighth Army. "It is not often in wartime that a single battlefield commander can make a decisive difference," wrote JCS Chairman Omar Bradley in *A General's Life*. "But in Korea, Ridgway would prove to be the exception. His brilliant, driving, uncompromising leadership would turn the tide of battle like no other general's in our military history."

When Truman sacked Douglas MacArthur in April 1951, Ridgway replaced him as commander of UN forces in Korea and the Far East. He also succeeded MacArthur as commander in chief of U.S. Armed forces in the Far East and supreme commander of Allied occupation forces in Japan. These myriad responsibilities forced Ridgway to relocate to Tokyo, where he continued to oversee military operations in Korea.

Commander of NATO

In May 1952 Dwight D. Eisenhower retired from the Army to pursue politics. Ridgway was quickly named to replace him as Supreme Commander of North Atlantic Treaty Organization (NATO) forces in Europe. He served in that post until October 1953, when he became Eisenhower's Army Chief of Staff. Ridgway retired from active duty in June 1955, partly due to his strong differences with the Eisenhower administration on military spending priorities. He believed that Eisenhower and his key aides were so determined to build a nuclear arsenal that they gave insufficient attention to conventional military forces. Ridgway left active military service with a host of military decorations, including the Distinguish Service Cross, the Distinguished Service Medal, the Legion of Merit, and the Silver Star.

Ridgway became director of Colt Industries in 1960. Over the next several years he emerged as an outspoken advocate for limiting U.S. involvement in Vietnam. In March 1968, President Lyndon Johnson invited Ridgway to participate on a panel advising the president on his Vietnam strategy. Ridgway and the panel—collectively known as the "Wise Men"—urged the United States to negotiate a settlement in Vietnam and bring its troops home.

In 1971, Ridgway's son Matt was killed at the age of 22 in an accident involving a train while he was working as a counselor at a camp in Minnesota. Expressions of sympathy from top leaders in the United States, including President Richard Nixon, were sent to the Ridgways.

Ridgway died of cardiac arrest in his home in Fox Chapel, Pennsylvania, on July 26, 1993, at the age of 98. Colin Powell, then Chairman of the Joint Chiefs of Staff, eulogized Ridgway at his graveside, saying, "No soldier ever performed his duty better than this man. No soldier ever upheld his honor better than this man. No soldier ever loved his country more than this man did. Every American soldier owes a debt to this great man."

Sources

Appleman, Roy. *Ridgway Duels for Korea*. College Station, TX: Texas A&M Press, 1990.

Blair, Clay. *Ridgway's Paratroopers*. New York: Doubleday, 1985.

Mitchell, George C. *Matthew B. Ridgway: Soldier, Statesman, Scholar, Citizen*. Mechanicsburg, PA: Stackpole Books, 2002.

Ridgway, Matthew B. *The Korean War*. Garden City, NY: Doubleday, 1967.

Soffer, Jonathan M. *General Matthew B. Ridgway: From Progressivism to Reaganism, 1895-1993*. Westport, CT: Praeger, 1998.

Tucker, Spencer C. *Encyclopedia of the Korean War: A Political, Social, and Military History*. 3 vols. Santa Barbara, CA: ABC-CLIO, 2000.

Harry S. Truman (1884–1972)
President of the United States, 1945–1953

Harry S. Truman was born in Lamar, Missouri, on May 8, 1884. His parents were John Anderson Truman and Martha Ellen (Young) Truman. He was the second son born to the couple, though his older brother died in childbirth. He had a younger brother, Vivian, and a younger sister, Mary Jane. The family moved about rural Missouri several times in Truman's childhood, finally settling in Independence on his grandmother's 600-acre farm, which his father worked.

Truman attended public schools in Independence, graduating from its high school in 1901. He worked for a time for a railroad construction contractor, then as a clerk in two Kansas City banks. In 1905 he joined the Missouri National Guard. A year later, he began to work with his father on his grandmother's farm in Independence. He attempted to gain entrance to the U.S. Military Academy at West Point, New York, and the U.S. Naval Academy in Annapolis, Maryland, but his application was rejected at both schools because of his poor eyesight.

Truman remained on the family farm until 1917, when the United States entered World War I. Truman was called to active service in August, and a few months later he was sent to France, where he commanded a battery in an artillery regiment. Truman later said that his combat experiences in Europe taught him that "a leader is a man who has the ability to get other people to do what they don't want to do, and like it."

When he returned from World War I in 1919, Truman married his childhood sweetheart, Bess Wallace, who he had known since the age of six. The couple had one child, Margaret. Also in 1919, he and a war buddy opened a haberdashery, selling clothes and accessories for men. The store failed due to the postwar recession, but instead of filing for bankruptcy, Truman paid off all the store's debts over a period of years.

Enters Politics at Local Level

In 1922, Truman was elected to his first public office, as an administrative judge in Jackson County, Missouri. His bid for a second term in 1924 failed, and he worked for a time at an automobile insurance company. He ran again as a Democrat for the presiding judgeship in Jackson County in 1926, which he won. His tenure was successful and he successfully defended his seat in the 1930 elections. He further burnished his reputation as a man of integrity and conservative economic principles during this time, and in 1934 Truman mounted a successful campaign to represent Missouri in the U.S. Senate.

As a Congressman, Truman carved out a niche as a fiscal conservative and opponent of large business interests. His successful 1940 campaign was due in part to support of African-American Democrats because of his outspoken stance on civil rights. In his second term in Congress, Truman became chairman of the Special Senate Committee to Investigate the Department of Defense. This committee, known as the "Truman Committee," was charged with ensuring that defense contractors delivered goods and services at fair prices, and it was credited with saving American taxpayers millions of dollars.

When President Franklin D. Roosevelt sought a running mate for his 1944 reelection campaign, the Democrats selected Truman, and the pair won. As Roosevelt's vice president, however, Truman was kept somewhat in the dark about the president's long, debilitating struggle with polio, and he was not involved in major foreign policy decisions during those turbulent World War II years. When Roosevelt died on April 25, 1945, Truman was sworn into office as the nation's 33rd president. Fully aware of the awesome responsibilities now on his shoulders, Truman reputedly told journalists covering his move to the Oval Office that "if you fellows know how to pray, pray for me now."

Truman in the Oval Office

After ascending to the presidency, Truman showed firm leadership in guiding the nation through the final months of World War II. His most difficult decision during this period was the one approving the use of atomic bombs on the Japanese cities of Hiroshima and Nagasaki. The bombings brought World War II to a quick close, as Japan agreed to an unconditional surrender, but Truman's use of the bomb remains the most debated action of his entire presidency.

Truman's postwar foreign policies emphasized the rebuilding of Europe and Japan and opposition to Communism. In fact, almost every action in Truman's foreign policy was associated with the perceived Communist threat—in Eastern Europe, Northern Africa, Southeast Asia, and the Middle East—and his conviction that Communism had to be contained came to be known as the Truman Doctrine. Other Cold War measures initiated by Truman included the establishment of the National Security Council, reorganization of the military by eliminating the Department of War and creating individual departments for each branch of service, and creation of the Central Intelligence Agency. He was also instrumental in the establishment of the United Nations.

Truman made significant domestic contributions as well, including executive orders desegregating the armed forces and forbidding racial discrimination in federal employment. He also established a Committee on Civil Rights and encouraged the Justice Department to work against segregation.

After serving the remainder of the late President Roosevelt's term, Truman narrowly defeated Republican Thomas E. Dewey in the 1948 election to secure another term. In June 1950 Truman's mettle in the face of what he saw as Communist expansionism received its sternest test yet when North Korean forces invaded South Korea. Upon hearing the news of the invasion from Secretary of State Dean Acheson, Truman reportedly said, "Dean, we've got to stop the sons of bitches, no matter what." Ten years later, when a television producer wanted to do an extended show on the decision to fight in Korea, Truman reportedly told him that would not be possible, since the decision was made in less than ten seconds. He did not consult Congress nor ask for a formal declaration of war in his decision to commit military support to South Korea. Truman quickly made use of the newly established United Nations, however, in gaining international support for military action. "If the Communists were permitted to force their way into the Republic of Korea [South Korea] without opposition from the free world, no small nation would have the courage to resist threats and aggression by stronger Communist neighbors," Truman later wrote in his memoirs.

Truman's "Police Action" in Korea

In the early stages of the Korean conflict, Truman characterized UN involvement as a "police action" against a "bunch of bandits." It shortly became clear, however, that the UN force, spearheaded by the United States, faced a formidable foe in the Soviet-backed North Koreans. Moreover, the war exposed serious shortcomings in the postwar U.S. military, most notably distressing shortages of battle-ready troops and inadequate investment in conventional armaments.

Truman tapped General Douglas MacArthur to lead the UN forces in Korea. Initially, the war went so badly for the U.S.-led UN forces that it seemed that they might be pushed off the peninsula and into the Sea of Japan. But the triumph at Inchon dramatically changed the complexion of the war. For a brief time, it even appeared that MacArthur might be able to unify all of the Korean peninsula under the banner of South Korean President Syngman Rhee. But MacArthur moved so aggressively into the Korea-China border region that China entered the war with a vengeance. This development stunned MacArthur and was a serious blow to the Truman administration, which had sensed that a major confrontation with China might be brewing. But as Secretary of State Acheson later admitted to Evan Thomas and Walter Issacson, authors of *The Wise Men*, "we sat around like paralyzed rabbits while MacArthur carried out this nightmare."

China's entrance into the conflict forced MacArthur to regroup around the 38th parallel and led Truman to abandon thoughts of unification. Instead, he worked to bring the conflict to a peaceful resolution, convinced that Korea was "not the place to fight a major war." This change of course deeply frustrated MacArthur, who wanted to take the war to a new level. He repeatedly undercut the Truman administration's diplomatic overtures, creating a thorny political issue for the president. MacArthur's continued belligerence finally forced Truman to sack the widely revered World War II hero in April 1951 and replace him with General Matthew Ridgway. Historians describe the removal of MacArthur as necessary. In fact, MacArthur's insubordination was so glaring that for all practical purposes he forced Truman's hand. Nonetheless, the dismissal badly wounded Truman's presidency and prompted increased criticism of his handling of the Korea issue.

Keenly aware of his deteriorating standing with American voters, Truman decided not to run for a second term in 1952. The Democratic nominee was instead Adlai Stevenson, but he was defeated by Republican Dwight D. Eisenhower. Truman and his wife Bess retired to his home in Independence after Eisenhower's inauguration in 1953. The Korean War ended with the signing of an armistice agreement several months later, in July 1953. Truman lived in Independence for the rest of his life, studying, writing his memoirs, and establishing the Truman Presidential Library. Truman died on December 26, 1972, in Kansas City, Missouri.

Sources

Ferrell, Robert H. *Harry S. Truman: A Life*. Columbia: University of Missouri Press, 1994.

Hamby, Alonzo L. *Man of the People: The Life of Harry S. Truman*. New York: Oxford University Press, 1995.

McCullough, David. *Truman*. New York: Simon and Schuster, 1992.

Pemberton, William E. *Harry S. Truman: Fair Dealer and Cold Warrior*. Boston: Twayne, 1989.

Schneider, Carl J., and Dorothy Schneider. *World War II: An Eyewitness History*. New York: Facts on File, 2003.

Thomas, Evan, and Walter Issacson. *The Wise Men: Six Friends and the World They Made*. New York: Simon & Schuster, 1988.

Truman, Harry S. *Memoirs*. 2 vols. Garden City, NY: Doubleday, 1955-1956.

PRIMARY SOURCES

The Truman Doctrine—President Harry S. Truman's Address before a Joint Session of Congress, March 12, 1947

In 1947, Great Britain informed the United States that it could no longer provide financial assistance to Greece and Turkey. The U.S. State Department received this news somberly. In Greece, economic and political conditions were deteriorating. In Turkey, a weak government faced pressure from the Soviet Union. A short time after the British announcement, Secretary of State Dean Acheson spoke before representatives from Congress and explained his view that if Greece and Turkey fell to Communism, then Communism would spread as far as Iran and India. U.S. legislators agreed to fund a financial aid package for Greece and Turkey, but they asked that President Truman explain the nature of the crisis to the American people.

On March 12, 1947, President Truman addressed a joint session of Congress and requested $400 million in economic aid for Greece and Turkey. During this address, which was broadcast across the nation on radio, he argued that "It must be the policy of the United States to support free peoples who are resisting attempted subjugation by armed minorities or by outside pressures." This policy, which became known as the Truman Doctrine, guided U.S. foreign policy for the next 40 years. The following are excerpts from President Truman's address:

Mr. President, Mr. Speaker, Members of the Congress of the United States:

The gravity of the situation which confronts the world today necessitates my appearance before a joint session of the Congress. The foreign policy and the national security of this country are involved.

One aspect of the present situation, which I wish to present to you at this time for your consideration and decision, concerns Greece and Turkey.

The United States has received from the Greek Government an urgent appeal for financial and economic assistance. Preliminary reports from the American Economic Mission now in Greece and reports from the American Ambassador in Greece corroborate the statement of the Greek Government that assistance is imperative if Greece is to survive as a free nation.

I do not believe that the American people and the Congress wish to turn a deaf ear to the appeal of the Greek Government.

Greece is not a rich country. Lack of sufficient natural resources has always forced the Greek people to work hard to make both ends meet. Since

1940, this industrious and peace loving country has suffered invasion, four years of cruel enemy occupation, and bitter internal strife.

When forces of liberation entered Greece they found that the retreating Germans had destroyed virtually all the railways, roads, port facilities, communications, and merchant marine. More than a thousand villages had been burned. Eighty-five per cent of the children were tubercular. Livestock, poultry, and draft animals had almost disappeared. Inflation had wiped out practically all savings.

As a result of these tragic conditions, a militant minority, exploiting human want and misery, was able to create political chaos which, until now, has made economic recovery impossible.

Greece is today without funds to finance the importation of those goods which are essential to bare subsistence. Under these circumstances the people of Greece cannot make progress in solving their problems of reconstruction. Greece is in desperate need of financial and economic assistance to enable it to resume purchases of food, clothing, fuel, and seeds. These are indispensable for the subsistence of its people and are obtainable only from abroad. Greece must have help to import the goods necessary to restore internal order and security, so essential for economic and political recovery.

The Greek Government has also asked for the assistance of experienced American administrators, economists and technicians to insure that the financial and other aid given to Greece shall be used effectively in creating a stable and self-sustaining economy and in improving its public administration.

The very existence of the Greek state is today threatened by the terrorist activities of several thousand armed men, led by Communists, who defy the government's authority at a number of points, particularly along the northern boundaries. A Commission appointed by the United Nations Security Council is at present investigating disturbed conditions in northern Greece and alleged border violations along the frontier between Greece on the one hand and Albania, Bulgaria, and Yugoslavia on the other.

Meanwhile, the Greek Government is unable to cope with the situation. The Greek army is small and poorly equipped. It needs supplies and equipment if it is to restore the authority of the government throughout Greek territory. Greece must have assistance if it is to become a self-supporting and self-respecting democracy.

172

The United States must supply that assistance. We have already extended to Greece certain types of relief and economic aid but these are inadequate.

There is no other country to which democratic Greece can turn.

No other nation is willing and able to provide the necessary support for a democratic Greek government.

The British Government, which has been helping Greece, can give no further financial or economic aid after March 31. Great Britain finds itself under the necessity of reducing or liquidating its commitments in several parts of the world, including Greece.

We have considered how the United Nations might assist in this crisis. But the situation is an urgent one requiring immediate action and the United Nations and its related organizations are not in a position to extend help of the kind that is required.

It is important to note that the Greek Government has asked for our aid in utilizing effectively the financial and other assistance we may give to Greece, and in improving its public administration. It is of the utmost importance that we supervise the use of any funds made available to Greece; in such a manner that each dollar spent will count toward making Greece self-supporting, and will help to build an economy in which a healthy democracy can flourish.

No government is perfect. One of the chief virtues of a democracy, however, is that its defects are always visible and under democratic processes can be pointed out and corrected. The Government of Greece is not perfect. Nevertheless it represents 85 per cent of the members of the Greek Parliament who were chosen in an election last year. Foreign observers, including 692 Americans, considered this election to be a fair expression of the views of the Greek people.

The Greek Government has been operating in an atmosphere of chaos and extremism. It has made mistakes. The extension of aid by this country does not mean that the United States condones everything that the Greek Government has done or will do. We have condemned in the past, and we condemn now, extremist measures of the right or the left. We have in the past advised tolerance, and we advise tolerance now.

Greece's neighbor, Turkey, also deserves our attention.

The future of Turkey as an independent and economically sound state is clearly no less important to the freedom-loving peoples of the world than the future of Greece. The circumstances in which Turkey finds itself today are considerably different from those of Greece. Turkey has been spared the disasters that have beset Greece. And during the war, the United States and Great Britain furnished Turkey with material aid.

Nevertheless, Turkey now needs our support.

Since the war Turkey has sought financial assistance from Great Britain and the United States for the purpose of effecting that modernization necessary for the maintenance of its national integrity.

That integrity is essential to the preservation of order in the Middle East.

The British government has informed us that, owing to its own difficulties, it can no longer extend financial or economic aid to Turkey.

As in the case of Greece, if Turkey is to have the assistance it needs, the United States must supply it. We are the only country able to provide that help.

I am fully aware of the broad implications involved if the United States extends assistance to Greece and Turkey, and I shall discuss these implications with you at this time.

One of the primary objectives of the foreign policy of the United States is the creation of conditions in which we and other nations will be able to work out a way of life free from coercion. This was a fundamental issue in the war with Germany and Japan. Our victory was won over countries which sought to impose their will, and their way of life, upon other nations.

To ensure the peaceful development of nations, free from coercion, the United States has taken a leading part in establishing the United Nations. The United Nations is designed to make possible lasting freedom and independence for all its members. We shall not realize our objectives, however, unless we are willing to help free peoples to maintain their free institutions and their national integrity against aggressive movements that seek to impose upon them totalitarian regimes. This is no more than a frank recognition that totalitarian regimes imposed on free peoples, by direct or indirect aggression, undermine the foundations of international peace and hence the security of the United States.

The peoples of a number of countries of the world have recently had totalitarian regimes forced upon them against their will. The Government of the United States has made frequent protests against coercion and intimidation, in violation of the Yalta agreement, in Poland, Rumania, and Bulgaria. I must also state that in a number of other countries there have been similar developments.

At the present moment in world history nearly every nation must choose between alternative ways of life. The choice is too often not a free one.

One way of life is based upon the will of the majority, and is distinguished by free institutions, representative government, free elections, guarantees of individual liberty, freedom of speech and religion, and freedom from political oppression.

The second way of life is based upon the will of a minority forcibly imposed upon the majority. It relies upon terror and oppression, a controlled press and radio, fixed elections, and the suppression of personal freedoms.

I believe that it must be the policy of the United States to support free peoples who are resisting attempted subjugation by armed minorities or by outside pressures.

I believe that we must assist free peoples to work out their own destinies in their own way.

I believe that our help should be primarily through economic and financial aid which is essential to economic stability and orderly political processes.

The world is not static, and the status quo is not sacred. But we cannot allow changes in the status quo in violation of the Charter of the United Nations by such methods as coercion, or by such subterfuges as political infiltration. In helping free and independent nations to maintain their freedom, the United States will be giving effect to the principles of the Charter of the United Nations.

It is necessary only to glance at a map to realize that the survival and integrity of the Greek nation are of grave importance in a much wider situation. If Greece should fall under the control of an armed minority, the effect upon its neighbor, Turkey, would be immediate and serious. Confusion and disorder might well spread throughout the entire Middle East.

Moreover, the disappearance of Greece as an independent state would have a profound effect upon those countries in Europe whose peoples are struggling against great difficulties to maintain their freedoms and their independence while they repair the damages of war.

It would be an unspeakable tragedy if these countries, which have struggled so long against overwhelming odds, should lose that victory for which they sacrificed so much. Collapse of free institutions and loss of independence would be disastrous not only for them but for the world. Discouragement and possibly failure would quickly be the lot of neighboring peoples striving to maintain their freedom and independence.

Should we fail to aid Greece and Turkey in this fateful hour, the effect will be far reaching to the West as well as to the East.

We must take immediate and resolute action.

I therefore ask the Congress to provide authority for assistance to Greece and Turkey in the amount of $400 million for the period ending June 30, 1948. In requesting these funds, I have taken into consideration the maximum amount of relief assistance which would be furnished to Greece out of the $350 million which I recently requested that the Congress authorize for the prevention of starvation and suffering in countries devastated by the war.

In addition to funds, I ask the Congress to authorize the detail of American civilian and military personnel to Greece and Turkey, at the request of those countries, to assist in the tasks of reconstruction, and for the purpose of supervising the use of such financial and material assistance as may be furnished. I recommend that authority also be provided for the instruction and training of selected Greek and Turkish personnel.

Finally, I ask that the Congress provide authority which will permit the speediest and most effective use, in terms of needed commodities, supplies, and equipment, of such funds as may be authorized.

If further funds, or further authority, should be needed for purposes indicated in this message, I shall not hesitate to bring the situation before the Congress. On this subject the Executive and Legislative branches of the Government must work together.

This is a serious course upon which we embark.

I would not recommend it except that the alternative is much more serious. The United States contributed $341 billion toward winning World War II. This is an investment in world freedom and world peace.

The assistance that I am recommending for Greece and Turkey amounts to little more than 1 tenth of 1 per cent of this investment. It is only common sense that we should safeguard this investment and make sure that it was not in vain.

The seeds of totalitarian regimes are nurtured by misery and want. They spread and grow in the evil soil of poverty and strife. They reach their full growth when the hope of a people for a better life has died. We must keep that hope alive.

The free peoples of the world look to us for support in maintaining their freedoms.

If we falter in our leadership, we may endanger the peace of the world—and we shall surely endanger the welfare of our own nation.

Great responsibilities have been placed upon us by the swift movement of events.

I am confident that the Congress will face these responsibilities squarely.

Source: Harry S. Truman. "Special Message to the Congress on Greece and Turkey: The Truman Doctrine," –3/12/47. Truman Public Papers, Truman Library. http://trumanlibrary.org/publicpapers/index. php?pid=2189&st=truman+doctrine&st1=

United Nations Security Council Resolution, June 25, 1950

On June 25, 1950, the United Nations Security Council issued a statement expressing "grave concern" about North Korea's invasion of South Korea and calling on the North Koreans to withdraw their forces back to their side of the 38th parallel. Following is the complete text of the June 25 Security Council resolution:

> *The Security Council,*
>
> *Recalling* the finding of the General Assembly in its resolution 293 (IV) of 21 October 1949 that the Government of the Republic of Korea is a lawfully established government having effective control and jurisdiction over that part of Korea where the United Nations Temporary Commission on Korea was able to observe and consult and in which the great majority of the people of Korea reside; and that this Government is based on elections which were a valid expression of the free will of the electorate of that part of Korea and which were observed by the Temporary Commission; and that this is the only such government in Korea,
>
> *Mindful* of the concern expressed by the General Assembly in its resolutions 195 (III) of 12 December 1948 and 293 (IV) 21 October 1949 about the consequences which might follow unless Member States refrained from acts derogatory to the results sought to be achieved by the United Nations in bringing about the complete independence and unity of Korea; and the concern expressed that the situation described by the United Nations Commission on Korea in its report menaces the safety and well-being of the Republic of Korea and of the people of Korea and might lead to open military conflict there,
>
> *Noting,* with grave concern the armed attack upon the Republic of Korea by forces from North Korea,
>
> *Determines* that this action constitutes a breach of the peace; and
>
> I. *Calls for* the immediate cessation of hostilities;
>
> *Calls upon* the authorities in North Korea to withdraw forthwith their armed forces to the 38th parallel;
>
> II. *Requests* the United Nations Commission on Korea:
>
> a. To communicate its fully considered recommendations on the situation with the least possible delay;

    b. To observe the withdrawal of North Korean forces to the 38th parallel; and

    c. To keep the Security Council informed on the execution of this resolution;

III. *Calls* upon all Member States to render every assistance to the United Nations in the execution of this resolution and to refrain from giving assistance to the North Korean authorities.

Source: United Nations. Security Council Resolution, June 25, 1950. http://www.un.org.

United Nations Security Council Resolution, June 27, 1950

On June 27, 1950, the United Nations Security Council passed a U.S.-sponsored resolution call-ing for military action against North Korea. The Soviet Union voluntarily abstained from the vote. Following is the complete text of the June 27 Security Council Resolution:

The Security Council,

Having determined, that the armed attack upon the Republic of Korea by forces from North Korea constitutes a breach of the peace,

Having called for an immediate cessation of hostilities,

Having called upon the authorities in North Korea to withdraw forthwith their armed forces to the 38th parallel,

Having noted from the report of the United Nations Commission on Korea that the authorities in North Korea have neither ceased hostilities nor withdrawn their armed forces to the 38th parallel, and that urgent military measures are required to restore international peace and security,

Having noted the appeal from the Republic of Korea to the United Nations for immediate and effective steps to secure peace and security,

Recommends that the Members of the United Nations furnish such assis-tance to the Republic of Korea as may be necessary to repel the armed attack and to restore international peace and security in the area.

Source: United Nations. Security Council Resolution, June 27, 1950. http://www.un.org.

Statement by President Harry S. Truman, June 27, 1950

In the wake of North Korea's surprise invasion of South Korea, U.S. President Harry S. Truman publicly condemned the invasion in strong terms. He also declared his belief that events on the Korean Peninsula showed that "Communism has passed beyond the use of subversion to conquer independent nations and will now use armed invasion and war." Following is the complete text of Truman's statement of June 27, 1950:

In Korea the Government forces, which were armed to prevent border raids and to preserve internal security, were attacked by invading forces from North Korea. The Security Council of the United Nations called upon the invading troops to cease hostilities and to withdraw to the 38th parallel. This they have not done, but on the contrary, have pressed the attack. The Security Council called upon all members of the United Nations to render every assistance to the United Nations in the execution of this resolution. In these circumstances, I have ordered United States air and sea forces to give the Korean Government troops cover and support.

The attack upon Korea makes it plain beyond all doubt that Communism has passed beyond the use of subversion to conquer independent nations and will now use armed invasion and war. It has defied the orders of the Security Council of the United Nations issued to preserve international peace and security. In these circumstances, the occupation of Formosa [now called Taiwan] by Communist forces would be a direct threat to the security of the Pacific area and to United States forces performing their lawful and necessary functions in that area.

Accordingly, I have ordered the Seventh Fleet to prevent any attack on Formosa. As a corollary of this action I am calling upon the Chinese Government on Formosa to cease all air and sea operations against the mainland. The Seventh Fleet will see that this is done. The determination of the future status of Formosa must await the restoration of security in the Pacific, a peace settlement with Japan, or consideration by the United Nations.

I have also directed that United States Forces in the Philippines be strengthened and that military assistance to the Philippine Government be accelerated.

I have similarly directed acceleration in the furnishing of military assistance to the forces of France and the Associated States in Indo China and the dispatch of a military mission to provide close working relations with those forces.

I know that all members of the United Nations will consider carefully the consequences of this latest aggression in Korea in defiance of the Charter of the United Nations. A return to the rule of force in international affairs would have far reaching effects. The United States will continue to uphold the rule of law.

I have instructed Ambassador Austin, as the representative of the United States to the Security Council, to report these steps to the Council.

Source: Harry S. Truman. "Statement by the President on the Situation in Korea," 06/27/50. Truman Public Papers, Truman Library. http://trumanlibrary.org/publicpapers/index.php?pid=800&st=&st1=

Secretary Pace Recalls the Korean War

Frank Pace Jr. served under six different U.S. presidents and was Secretary of the Army before and during the Korean War. Jerry N. Hess conducted five taped interviews with Pace between January 17 and June 26, 1972. They are available in their entirety at the Harry S. Truman Presidential library (www.trumanlibrary.org) and cover a wide variety of issues pertinent to Truman's administration. The excerpted portions below are relevant to the Korean War and policy decisions that were made in connection with that event.

From January 17, 1972

HESS: At the time of the Korean invasion, our armed forces had been greatly reduced and perhaps their effectiveness was reduced also. I believe the armed forces had been cut back to such a point to where they couldn't function effectively. Why were those cutbacks made?

PACE: Well, you know, in these matters you are talking about generalizations that are hard to specifically identify. I mean by that, I think Mr. Truman at this juncture in history, felt that the great requirement was social development internally in this country. The mood of this country was in that direction.

I don't believe that you will ever have what anyone would describe as adequate defense and therefore it becomes a matter of judgment how far you cut back. We had finished World War II, small wars had never occurred, we didn't realize that international leadership was very likely to bring us into contact with problems we hadn't faced before. Whenever a war comes you've always cut back too far. Nobody is ever going to be ready for any kind of a war. And so it is clear that we had cut back too far. But I have to say to you when a war comes, you've always cut back too far.

* * *

From January 22, 1972

HESS: At the time you came in as Secretary of the Army was there an awareness in the Pentagon and in the government as a whole, that the Communists might try to test our defenses in some part of the world?

PACE: I don't really think so. I think that frankly the only wars that America had engaged in and the recent memory of man had been total wars, World War I and World War II. Small wars had never been a part of our history. I don't think that any one thought that another world war was likely and I don't think people really thought in terms of small wars at that time.

* * *

[Below Hess asks about discussions between the President and his advisers after North Korea invaded South Korea.]

HESS: All right, now on Sunday evening after the President had returned there was a meeting held at the Blair House. What do you recall about that meeting?

PACE: Well, the President operated in his usual fashion, my recollection is that the people there were Mr. Acheson [Secretary of State] and Dean Rusk [Secretary of State for Far East Affairs], and I believe Louis Johnson [Secretary of Defense] had returned by that time, and the three service Secretaries, the Joint Chiefs of Staff—

HESS: That's right.

PACE:…were there, and I can't remember if anybody else was or not.

HESS: Yes, Dean Acheson and…

PACE: Dean Rusk.

HESS: Dean Rusk and Philip Jessup [Ambassador-at-large to South Korea].

PACE: Yes, Philip Jessup. Well…

HESS: And the others that you mentioned.

PACE: Well, the President asked each of us our opinion on what should be done.

HESS: What did you tell him?

PACE: Well, I think I told him very clearly that I felt we had to resist the attack. I told him that I felt that this was more than just a matter of Korea, that the Russians were testing, and if we allowed this test to go unchecked that they would undoubtedly take bigger steps and this would involve us in bigger problems. If we were going to stop this thrust, now was the time to do it and that we ought to undertake to do so.

HESS: Did he receive any advice in opposition to that viewpoint from anyone?

PACE: Not really, no. The feeling was very unanimous there. People expressed it in different ways. Some were a little more complex. I'm sure that a broader view of all the implications was made by Dean Acheson as Secretary of State, but the President had the comfort of really a unanimous assessment that this was the thing to do.

HESS: Was it discussed at that time that such a movement into Korea should be made through the United Nations, as it was done?

PACE: Yes, it was. That was suggested by Dean Acheson at that time and it was concurred in.

HESS: Was it discussed that if it could not have been done through the United Nations that we should go in unilaterally on our own anyway?

PACE: I don't believe that there was a sense that it could not be done through the United Nations. I don't believe that the issue that it could not be done really arose, and therefore, I don't think the alternative was discussed. I'm quite clear in my own mind that had it been discussed this group would have agreed we should have gone in unilaterally.

* * *

HESS: What were a few of the problems that the emergency brought up and how did you handle them during the first few days? Looking back into July of 1950 what were some of the problems that you were faced with and how did you handle them?

PACE: Well, in the early stages since the function was primarily Air and Navy, our role in the matter was largely that of planner and thinker. However it was only about three or four days before we had a critical telecom from General MacArthur, advising that the North Koreans were overwhelming the South Korean troops and that if we intended to make an effective stand in Korea that it was imperative that we agree to commit American ground troops.

* * *

From February 17, 1972

HESS: During those [Blair House] meetings, do you recall if it was discussed whether or not the Soviets might come in if we did take this move, if we went into Korea?

PACE: Oh, yes, that was thoroughly discussed, and it was the conclusion of most people involved that the Soviets would *not* come in. It was the conclusion of *all* people involved that the Soviets would not come in, but there were different shadings of concern about it. However, it was agreed that if the Soviets did come in this really was something that had to be faced and dealt with, because otherwise the impression would be left with the Soviets that they could undertake any kind of initiative anywhere in the world and we'd be afraid to counter it.

HESS: Do you recall if it was discussed at this early date whether or not the Chinese Communists would come in?

PACE: No, that was not discussed. As a matter of fact, at least it was not in my mind, and it was not a matter that was raised at all.

HESS: Some historians are of the opinion that the Soviets instigated matters in Korea as a diversionary matter to get our attention away from events in Europe?

PACE: No, I don't believe that's true. I believe that the Soviets did not think that we would react to this action. They had come to the conclusion that this was an isolated part of the world, that our basic interests were not there, and that they were in a position, using North Koreans, to go ahead and take over that whole area. I think there's a tendency often to ascribe to your opponents either an intelligence or a quality of planning that often isn't there. I think this was a very simple mistake on their part as to how we would react.

HESS: In your opinion, should the President have tried to get a joint-congressional resolution to support this decision, to share the load with Congress, in other words, such as was done in the Tonkin Gulf matter?

PACE: Yes, and I frankly said that to him.

HESS: What were the counter arguments, why wasn't that done?

PACE: I said this to him not at this meeting, but at a later time. He said, "Frank, it's not necessary. They are all with me."

I said, "Yes, Mr. President, but we can't be sure that they'll be with you over any period of time."

The matter never was raised as a matter of discussion at this larger meeting. It just so happened that I had a very strong feeling that here was a chance to very clearly get the support of the Congress at a time when it was very necessary.

HESS: Did any others of the President's advisers also feel that same way?

186

PACE: I have no idea. It was not brought up.

* * *

HESS: Moving on to a dual subject of the landing at Inchon. This took place on September 15. As you know, much has been written about this. There was a breakout of the Pusan perimeter from the column moving up to the north, took a little while to break out. There were good, valid reasons why good military men thought that an invasion at Inchon was ill advised: The mud flats, the island that's out in front of Inchon, the fact that there were other cities or other places where an invasion could have been made; but nevertheless, General MacArthur's position did win out, and it won out in glorious fashion. It's well-known that that's one of the things he will be known for, the success at Inchon. What were your views on that? Did you think that movement was a good idea?

PACE: Well, remember I came to the Defense Department in April of 1950. The Korean war broke out in June and this was quite early on. I was not a military expert in that sense, and therefore my views were really not important on that phase of it. I do recall that the Joint Chiefs of Staff, uniformly, thought it was a bad idea, and I think that they advised General MacArthur of that feeling. I think that all I can say is that after it was achieved, it made a very deep impression on me as to General MacArthur's capability as a commanding general.

HESS: Just in general, what was your opinion of his capabilities?

PACE: Well, again, I knew nothing of him other than through what I had read. His reputation, of course, was unique, and I accepted that. I must say that whatever I thought about him was enhanced by Inchon.

* * *

HESS: On October 7th of 1950 a resolution was passed within the United Nations authorizing the U.N. forces to move north of the 38th parallel to "insure conditions of stability throughout Korea." This was with General MacArthur moving in from Inchon and the forces that had broken out of the Pusan perimeter had moved north, retaken Seoul and now they had U. N. sanction to move north of the 38th parallel. As you will recall, the resolution of June 27, 1950, spoke only of repelling the invaders from the region south of the 38th parallel, South Korea, so the decision had now been made to move into North Korea. Did you attend any meetings in which it was decided

187

to change the scope of the war, which was very obviously done, and what were your views and recommendations?

PACE: Yes, there were a great many discussions on this. Again I don't remember any contrary opinions. If there were, I just don't recall. It seemed a very natural thing that in order to bring some sort of order to that area, it would be necessary to consolidate the successes that had been achieved at Inchon and to really try to restore some universality to Korea rather than leaving it as a divided land. The opinion of almost everybody [was] that if you did that, there was going to be constant trouble, an inability to grow and develop. I'm quite sure that I favored going north of the Han River, which as I recall, was the boundary line.

HESS: Reading just an excerpt from *The Korean War*, Matthew B. Ridgway's book. This is on page 44:

"The plan for crossing the 38th parallel to destroy all the hostile forces on the peninsula had of course required prior approval from Washington, for the implications of such a crossing were manifold. Red China had been threatening by radio almost daily that it would come into the war if North Korea were invaded…"

So now we have definite threats on the radio from the Communists, the Red Chinese, saying "If you do come north of the 38th parallel we will attack." Now, was this seriously discussed? Was this taken as a serious threat?

PACE: Not really, no. You've got to remember that the Red Chinese had been threatening throughout the period. General Ridgway merely emphasizes that they threatened at that time, but this was not something that started at that time. Quite frankly, I guess it's a case of crying "wolf" that often. I do not believe that at that time anybody seriously believed that the Red Chinese were going to enter the war. Certainly General MacArthur had very clear ideas that they would *not*, and I have to say that after Inchon I was very impressed with General MacArthur's capability to assess problems out there on the ground.

* * *

HESS: All right, not too long after these events, the Communist Chinese *did* come into the fighting. What was the feeling around the Pentagon at that time?

PACE: It was really a great shocker, just no question about it. Nobody had expected this at all. It was really a reflection on our total military planning. Much of the blame for it, I think, was properly placed on General

MacArthur who was on the ground, and his intelligence very clearly indicated that they would not participate, but it was a shocking thing, and we had troops trapped up there. There was both a shock and a pall of gloom in the Pentagon.

HESS: This was in November and then in December, our troops got pushed back down into the south. During that time General MacArthur was making various statements about wanting to bomb north of the Han river…

PACE: The Yalu River.

HESS: …the Yalu River, to move north of there. He had several different proposals to bomb industrial plants in China, to bomb military staging bases. What was your view of that? Should we have permitted General MacArthur to do more of what he wanted to do, to widen the war?

PACE: On this, the Joint Chiefs of Staff were unanimous. They believed it was a bad idea. First, they didn't think it would stop what was being done; and second, another point was the high degree to which we were vulnerable. We had a port at Pusan without any anti-aircraft protection. Their troops had been used to fighting with air interception; ours marched right down the middle of every road. And if in the process of doing this you also brought the Russians in, which was a possibility, we were infinitely more vulnerable—our whole supply line, our people—we were very, very vulnerable. General MacArthur had made an original mistake in judgment about whether they would come in. I think he compounded that or would have if he'd carried out his proposition of bombing north of the Yalu and in China.

* * *

HESS: The truce that was established in Korea, was established of course, after the Republicans came in. Do you think that it would have been possible for Mr. Truman to have reached somewhat the same agreements with the Communists before the election? Could he have ended the war on the same terms, or as favorable of terms, as General Eisenhower did?

PACE: I remember that there was a great deal of belief on the part of people who had served in the Defense Establishment that that was true, that Mr. Eisenhower had merely used the circumstance to achieve a settlement that Mr. Truman was not prepared to accept. I can't *honestly* say that that was true. Mr. Eisenhower came in with great prestige, he was the newly elected President, he was a new figure in old and unsatisfactory discussion of….

189

HESS: And during the campaign, he had used the phrase "If elected I will go to Korea."

PACE: That's right. That is correct. So, you're asking me a highly speculative question, I answer it in the vein that it is speculative, but my instinct is I *doubt* Mr. Truman could have achieved the same settlement. I would say to you that I am not sure that if the same settlement *could* have been achieved Mr. Truman would have accepted it.

Source: Pace, Frank Jr., interview by Jerry N. Hess, January 22, 1972-February 25, 1972, Harry S. Truman Library. http://www.trumanlibrary.org/oralhist/pacefj.htm.

United States Constitution, Article 1, Section 8

The United States Constitution is the document that defines the body of laws that the U.S. government and all U.S. courts must follow. In Article 1, Section 8, the Constitution grants Congress the power to declare war and to raise and support troops—powers which are not accorded to the President.

The Congress shall have power to lay and collect taxes, duties, imposts and excises, to pay the debts and provide for the common defense and general welfare of the United States; but all duties, imposts and excises shall be uniform throughout the United States;

To borrow money on the credit of the United States;

To regulate commerce with foreign nations, and among the several states, and with the Indian tribes;

To establish a uniform rule of naturalization, and uniform laws on the subject of bankruptcies throughout the United States;

To coin money, regulate the value thereof, and of foreign coin, and fix the standard of weights and measures;

To provide for the punishment of counterfeiting the securities and current coin of the United States;

To establish post offices and post roads;

To promote the progress of science and useful arts, by securing for limited times to authors and inventors the exclusive right to their respective writings and discoveries;

To constitute tribunals inferior to the Supreme Court;

To define and punish piracies and felonies committed on the high seas, and offenses against the law of nations;

To declare war, grant letters of marque and reprisal, and make rules concerning captures on land and water;

To raise and support armies, but no appropriation of money to that use shall be for a longer term than two years;

To provide and maintain a navy;

To make rules for the government and regulation of the land and naval forces;

To provide for calling forth the militia to execute the laws of the union, suppress insurrections and repel invasions;

To provide for organizing, arming, and disciplining, the militia, and for governing such part of them as may be employed in the service of the United States, reserving to the states respectively, the appointment of the officers, and the authority of training the militia according to the discipline prescribed by Congress;

To exercise exclusive legislation in all cases whatsoever, over such District (not exceeding ten miles square) as may, by cession of particular states, and the acceptance of Congress, become the seat of the government of the United States, and to exercise like authority over all places purchased by the consent of the legislature of the state in which the same shall be, for the erection of forts, magazines, arsenals, dockyards, and other needful buildings;—And

To make all laws which shall be necessary and proper for carrying into execution the foregoing powers, and all other powers vested by this Constitution in the government of the United States, or in any department or officer thereof.

Source: U.S. Constitution, art. 1, sec. 8. http://www.ourdocuments.gov/doc.php?doc=9&page=transcript.

CIA Analysis of the Invasion of South Korea

Early in the Korean War, as the Truman administration was considering the possibility of a greater conflict with the Soviet Union, the Central Intelligence Agency (CIA) investigated and analyzed the issue. The following documents are excerpts from CIA Memoranda Nos. 302 and 304 issued in July 1950. The memoranda illustrate the perceptions of the threat of the overall Communist agenda in Asia and the world at large. They also discuss possible Truman adminis-tration responses to the perceived threat.

Intelligence Memorandum No. 302
July 8, 1950
Subject: Consequences of the Korean Incident

I. Soviet Purposes in Launching the Northern Korean Attack

A. Apart from immediate strategic advantages, the basic Soviet objectives in launching the Northern Korean attack probably were to: (1) test the strength of U.S. commitments implicit in the policy of containment of Com-munist expansion; and (2) gain political advantages for the further expansion of Communism in both Asia and Europe by undermining the confidence of non-Communist states in the value of U.S. support.

B. The Soviet estimate of the reaction to the North Korean attack was probably that: (1) U.N. action would be slow and cumbersome; (2) the U.S. would not intervene with its own forces; (3) South Korea would therefore collapse promptly, presenting the U.N. with a fait accompli; (4) the episode would therefore be completely localized; and (5) the fighting could be por-trayed as U.S.-instigated South Korean aggression and the Northern Korean victory as a victory of Asiatic nationalism against Western colonialism.

II. Probable Developments from the Korean Incident

There are at present four major alternative courses of action open to the U.S.S.R. They are not mutually exclusive courses of action. In particular, it is estimated that the U.S.S.R. is very likely to try to prolong the fighting in Korea (alternative "B" below) for the short run and then within a few weeks or months, if conditions appear favorable to Soviet leaders, shift them to the more aggressive course of creating similar incidents elsewhere (alternative

"C" below). The alternatives are examined not in order of probability, but in order of increasing risk of global war and increasing expenditure of effort on the part of the U.S.S.R.:

Alternative A: The U.S.S.R. may localize the Korean fighting, permitting U.S. forces to drive the North Koreans back to the 38th Parallel and refrain from creating similar incidents elsewhere. In the meantime, the U.S.S.R. would remain uncommitted in Korea and would develop the propaganda themes of U.S. aggression and imperialistic interference in domestic affairs of an Asiatic nation.

1. This alternative is the most cautious course for the U.S.S.R. to take. Its adoption would indicate complete surprise at the U.S. reaction to the Korean incident and would suggest strongly that the U.S.S.R. was unwilling to run even a minimum risk of provoking a global conflict involving the U.S. and the U.S.S.R.

2. U.S. prestige and political influence would be substantially augmented, particularly with Western European allies and other nations aligned with the U.S.

3. Soviet prestige and influence would be damaged, but there would be compensations in the form of secondary political gains that would accrue as a result of:

    (a) promoting the "peace campaign" and portraying the U.S. as military aggressor;

    (b) exploiting the theme of Asian nationalism versus Western imperialism;

    (c) maintaining the North Koreans and Chinese Communist threat to South Korea as an embarrassment to development of a constructive U.S. or U.N. policy in Korea.

4. This alternative course of action is unlikely; Soviet advantages would be secondary, comparatively long range, and intangible, while Soviet disadvantages would be immediate.

Alternative B: The U.S.S.R. may localize the Korean fighting, still refrain from creating similar incidents elsewhere, but in order to prolong U.S. involvement in Korea, give increasing material aid to the North Koreans, perhaps employing Chinese Communist troops, either covertly or overtly. The

194

U.S.S.R. would remain uncommitted in Korea and would develop the propaganda themes of U.S. aggression and imperialistic interference in domestic affairs of an Asiatic nation.

1. This alternative is a moderately cautious course for the U.S.S.R. to take. The U.S.S.R. would probably consider that its adoption would involve only a slight risk of provoking a global conflict involving the U.S. and the U.S.S.R.

2. U.S. prestige would be seriously damaged if the U.S.S.R. succeeded in prolonging the incident in this way. Western European allies and other nations aligned with the U.S. would question the immediate military value of U.S. commitments even though expecting them to be honored.

3. Soviet prestige would be augmented if the fighting in Korea were prolonged without an open Soviet commitment.

4. The U.S.S.R. would obtain appreciable secondary, comparatively long-range gains in political influence as a result of promoting the "peace-campaign" and portraying U.S. as imperialistic Western aggressor in Asia, unless successfully countered by a U.S. "Truth" campaign.

5. Deep involvement of U.S. military forces in Korea would seriously limit U.S. capabilities to support similar commitments elsewhere. Moreover, the Western European allies of the U.S. would feel dangerously exposed for some time (even if the U.S. began a partial mobilization for war.)

6. The U.S.S.R. probably will adopt this alternative course of action at least for the short run, since there would be few Soviet disadvantages or risks and the Soviet gains would be appreciable.

7. This alternative will appear especially attractive to the U.S.S.R. because at any time, if conditions appeared favorable to Soviet leaders, the U.S.S.R. could shift to the more ambitious program (alternative "C," immediately below,) in which alternative "B" would merely be a first phase.

Alternative C: The U.S.S.R., while attempting to prolong the fighting in Korea as in alternative "B," may also attempt to disperse and perhaps over-strain U.S. military forces-in-readiness by creating a series of incidents similar to the Korean affair. Without directly and openly involving Soviet forces, such incidents could be created in Formosa, Indochina, Burma, Iran,

195

Yugoslavia, and Greece. The effects of such incidents could be aggravated by renewed pressure on Berlin and, possibly, Vienna.

1. This alternative would be a comparatively aggressive course for the U.S.S.R. to take. Its adoption would indicate willingness to run an appreciable risk of provoking a global conflict because of the possible U.S. reaction. The U.S.S.R. could easily turn to this alternative at any time, but it is not likely to turn to it until the U.S.S.R. has fully analyzed the implications of the U.S. commitment in Korea.

2. Having employed its armed forces in support of its commitment in Korea, the U.S. will have to honor similar commitments or lose most of the advantages of the policy of supporting the Korean commitment.

3. The U.S. does not have the military forces-in-readiness to honor its commitments with U.S. military forces and equipment in many areas other than Korea (perhaps none) without a substantial increase in U.S. military forces and industrial productivity in the military field, bringing about what would amount to at least a partial (as distinguished from a general) mobilization for war.

4. Deep involvement of U.S. military forces in the Far East or Near East would leave Western Europe even more dangerously exposed than at present.

5. At some point further Korean-style incidents (requiring the commitment of U.S. forces to stabilize the situation) presumably would force the U.S. to adopt one of the following alternatives:

   (a) revise the policy of general containment by limiting U.S. commitments and by planning to combat Soviet aggression only at those selected points where existing U.S. military strength would permit;

   (b) begin partial military and industrial mobilization in an attempt to enable the U.S. to combat any further Soviet-sponsored aggression anywhere in the world; or

   (c) begin total mobilization to enable the U.S. to threaten to meet any Soviet or Soviet-sponsored aggression with war against the U.S.S.R.

6. The U.S.S.R. probably will adopt alternative "C" sooner or later if Soviet leaders do not estimate the risk of global war involved to be substantial or are prepared for a global war if it develops.

7. If Soviet development of this alternative course of action leads to a general U.S. mobilization, it appears at this time that the U.S.S.R. probably would in that event continue limited aggressions, accompanied by the customary "peace" propaganda, discounting actual U.S. initiation of a general war and perhaps estimating that the political and economic strains of mobilization would weaken or discredit the U.S. and its foreign policy. The U.S.S.R., however, may:

   (a) desist from further aggression of the Korean type, fearing a global war and taking mobilization as an indication of greater risk than Soviet leaders had anticipated in choosing this course of action; or

   (b) expecting U.S.-initiated global war, attempt to seize the initiative by immediately attacking the U.S. (in effect turning to alternative "D," below.)

Alternative D: The U.S.S.R. may consider U.S. intervention in Korea either as the prelude of an inevitable global war or as justification for beginning a global war for which it is prepared — in either case immediately attacking the U.S. and its allies.

1. Nothing in the Korean situation as yet indicates that the U.S.S.R. would deliberately decide to employ Soviet forces in direct military action precipitating global war. Such a decision is unlikely if, as now seems probable, Soviet leaders believe that:

   (a) there are continuing opportunities to expand Soviet influence by the comparatively cheap and safe means of Soviet-controlled Communist revolutionary activity (including propaganda, sabotage, subversion, guerrilla warfare, and organized military action by local Communist troops—as in Korea,) which can be supported by Soviet diplomacy and the mere threat of Soviet military strength-in-readiness; and

   (b) there is substantial risk involved for the U.S.S.R. in the global war that almost certainly would ensue from direct military action by Soviet forces.

2. The U.S.S.R. would appear to have little reason to be pessimistic about gains by methods short of global war, particularly by adopting the courses of action described in Alternatives "B" and "C" above.

3. The U.S.S.R. is unlikely to choose the alternative of deliberately provoking global war at this time in view of: (a) the general superiority of the U.S. and its allies in total power-potential; and (b) the fact that the present Soviet atomic capability is insufficient to neutralize U.S. atomic retaliatory capabilities and to offset the generally superior power-potential of the U.S. and its allies by interfering with the U.S. military and industrial mobilization.

III. Effects of a Failure of U.S. Forces to Hold South Korea

A. The immediate consequences of a failure to hold South Korea would be a damaging blow to U.S. prestige with loss in political influence greater than the loss that would have been incurred if the U.S. had not undertaken to support its moral containment in South Korea.

B. The U.S. would be confronted with a choice between two undesirable alternatives: (1) accepting the loss of U.S. prestige; or (2) attempting to regain as much prestige as possible by committing substantial U.S. military resources in a different and costly invasion of an area which is not of primary strategic importance to the over-all U.S. military position. In either case U.S. foreign policy and military capabilities would be discredited at home and abroad.

C. If U.S. forces were expelled from Korea, the U.S.S.R. would probably adopt alternative "C" as described above (Section II.) It might be tempted, however, to postpone further aggressive action elsewhere until it had determined whether, as a result of the loss of world confidence in the effectiveness of U.S. aid, other areas might not be brought within its sphere of influence through intimidation alone.

Intelligence Memorandum No. 304
July 10, 1950
Subject: Effects of a Voluntary Withdrawal of U.S. Forces from Korea

CONCLUSIONS

Voluntary withdrawal of U.S. forces from Korea would be a calamity, seriously handicapping efforts to maintain U.S. alliances and build political influence among the nations on whose strength and energetic cooperation the policy of containment of Soviet-Communist expansion depends. It would discredit U.S. foreign policy and undermine confidence in U.S. military capabilities. Voluntary withdrawal would be more damaging than a failure to send U.S. troops to Korea in the first place or than a failure of U.S. forces to hold Korea. Not only would U.S. commitments be shown to be unreliable when put to a severe test, but also considerable doubt would be cast on the ability of the U.S. to back up its commitments with military force.

DISCUSSION

1. U.S. withdrawal from intervention in Korea on behalf of the U.N., especially since U.N. action resulted mainly from U.S. initiative, would disillusion all nations heretofore hopeful that U.S. leadership within the framework of the U.N. could preserve world peace. As a voluntary act of the U.S., a withdrawal would damage U.S. standing in U.N. affairs and would undermine the effectiveness of the U.N. as a device for mobilizing Western resistance to Soviet-Communist aggression.

2. The Western European allies and other nations closely aligned with the U.S. would lose confidence in the military value of U.S. commitments to assist them against armed aggression. This lack of confidence would militate against energetic measures to oppose the expansion of Soviet-Communism through NATO and MDAP programs. Although some slight credit still might accrue to the U.S. for initially attempting to honor its commitment in South Korea, most of the nations allied or aligned with the U.S. are more concerned about U.S. ability to counter threats of Soviet aggression than about U.S. intentions to do so.

3. Pro-U.S. governments, particularly in areas where the U.S.S.R. could initiate limited military aggressions without openly using Soviet forces, would suffer serious losses of prestige. In some cases they might lose political control of the country or feel compelled to seek an accommodation with the U.S.S.R. (for example, Indochina, Iran.)

4. Whether or not U.S. forces withdraw from Korea, the U.S.S.R. has the capability of creating a series of incidents generally similar to the Korean affair, each one threatening either to bankrupt the U.S. policy of containing Soviet expansion or to disperse and overstrain U.S. military forces-in-readiness. Without directly and openly involving Soviet forces, such incidents could be created in Formosa, Indochina, Burma, Iran, Yugoslavia, Greece, and Turkey. The U.S.S.R. will proceed with limited aggressions similar to the Korean incident if it does not estimate the risk of global war to be substantial or is prepared for a global war if it develops. Voluntary U.S. withdrawal from Korea probably would encourage rather then discourage Soviet initiation of limited wars in other areas.

5. Upon withdrawal from Korea or certainly after another Korean-style incident, the U.S. presumably would be forced to adopt one of the three following alternatives:

(a) Drastically revise the policy of general containment by reducing or limiting U.S. commitments and by planning to combat Soviet-inspired aggression only at selected points where existing military strength would be adequate for the task;

(b) Begin partial military and industrial mobilization in an attempt to enable the U.S. to combat any further Soviet-inspired aggression anywhere in the world; or

(c) Begin total mobilization to enable the U.S. to threaten to meet any Soviet or Soviet-sponsored aggression with war against the U.S.S.R.

6. If the U.S., under the pressure of Soviet-sponsored aggressions, did not drastically revise the policy of general containment but began mobilization on a fairly large scale, it would be politically and psychologically more advantageous for the U.S. to mobilize in support of U.S. and U.N. intervention in Korea rather than to mobilize after a voluntary withdrawal from Korea.

(a) U.S. mobilization after a voluntary withdrawal of U.S. forces from Korea would do little to reduce the disillusion and defeatism that would spread in the Western world as a consequence of the withdrawal itself. While this disillusion and defeatism might not be fatal, it would seriously handicap military, political, and economic efforts to strengthen the North Atlantic community.

(b) If the U.S. should withdraw its forces from Korea and then begin partial mobilization, Soviet leaders would be more likely to anticipate war aimed directly at the U.S.S.R. than if the mobilization were begun in support of the U.N. intervention in Korea. It is possible that the U.S.S.R., if it should anticipate global war, would try to seize the initiative by attacking the U.S.

Source: Central Intelligence Agency. "Intelligence Memorandum No. 302: Consequences of the Korean Incident," 07/08/50, and "Intelligence Memorandum No. 304: Effects of a Voluntary Withdrawal of US Forces from Korea," 07/10/50. http://www.cia.gov/csi/books/coldwaryrs/5563bod4.pdf (pp. 25-29, 30-32).

Troop Recollections from the Early Days of the War

Captain Russell A. Gugeler was directed by the U.S. Army Chief of Military History to talk to military personnel and to write an easy-to-read account of combat actions based on the accounts from foot soldiers, including correspondence, interviews, and reports. The following excerpt is based on the recollections of two sergeants from the 24th Infantry Division, Zack C. Williams and Roy E. Collins, who recalled the early days of the war.

Korean summers are wet. It was raining and unseasonably cold during the dark early morning hours of July 5, 1950, when the 1st Battalion, 34th Infantry, reached Pyongtaek. Approximately 40 miles south of Seoul, the village was near the west coast of Korea on the main road and railroad between the capital city and Taejon, Taegu, and Pusan to the south. Pyongtaek was a shabby huddle of colorless huts lining narrow, dirt streets.

The infantrymen stood quietly in the steady rain, waiting for daylight. They grumbled about the weather but, in the sudden shift from garrison duties in Japan, few appeared to be concerned about the possibility of combat in Korea. None expected to stay there long. High-ranking officers and riflemen alike shared the belief that a few American soldiers would restore order within a few weeks.

"As soon as those North Koreans see an American uniform over here," soldiers boasted to one another, "they'll run like hell." American soldiers later lost this cocky attitude when the North Koreans overran their first defensive positions. Early overconfidence changed to surprise, then to dismay, and finally to the grim realization that, of the two armies, the North Korean force was superior in size, equipment, training, and fighting ability....

[While Colonel Brad Smith's group was being attacked at Osan] only a few miles away, men of Company A at Pyongtaek finished digging their defensive positions or sat quietly in the cold rain. In spite of the fact that a column of tanks had overrun the Osan position and was then not more than six miles from Pyongtaek, the infantrymen did not know about it. They continued to exchange rumors and speculations. One of the platoon leaders called his men together later that afternoon to put an end to the growing anxiety over the possibility of combat. "You've been told repeatedly," he explained, "that this is a police action, and that is exactly what it is going to be." He assured them that the rumors of a large enemy force in the area were false, and that they would be back in Sasebo within a few weeks. He directed them to put out only the normal guard for the night.

Up on the hill, Sergeant Collins was eating a can of beans. He had eaten about half of it when he heard the sound of engines running. Through the fog he saw the faint outline of several tanks that had stopped just beyond the bridge…. At the same time, through binoculars, Collins could see two columns of infantrymen moving beyond the tanks, around both ends of the bridge, and out across the rice paddies. He yelled back to his platoon leader (Lt. Robert R. Ridley), "Sir, we got company." Lieutenant Ridley, having been warned that part of the 21st Infantry might be withdrawing down this road, said it was probably part of that unit. "Well," said Collins, "These people have tanks and I know the 21st hadn't any." The battalion commander arrived at Captain Osburn's command post just in time to see the column of enemy infantrymen appear. Deciding it was made up of men from the 21st Infantry, the two commanders watched it for several minutes before realizing it was too large to be friendly troops. They could see a battalion-size group already, and others were still coming in a column of fours. At once, the battalion commander called for mortar fire. When the first round landed, the enemy spread out across the rice paddies on both sides of the road but continued to advance. By this time Collins could count 13 tanks …to the point where the column disappeared in the early morning fog.

Within a few minutes the men from the enemy's lead tank returned to their vehicle, got in, closed the turret, and then swung the tube until it pointed directly toward Company A.

"Get down!" Sergeant Collins yelled to his men. "Here it comes!"

The first shell exploded just above the row of foxholes, spattering dirt over the center platoon. The men slid into their holes. Collins and the two other combat veterans of World War II began shouting to their men to commence firing. Response was slow although the Americans could see the North Korean infantrymen advancing steadily, spreading out across the flat ground in front of the hill. In the same hole with Sergeant Collins were two riflemen. He poked them. "Come on," he said. "You've got an M1. Get firing."

After watching the enemy attack for a few minutes, the battalion commander told Captain Osburn to withdraw Company A.

Source: Gugeler, Russell A. *Combat Actions in Korea*. Army Historical Series. Washington, DC: Center of Military History, United States Army, U.S. Government Printing Office, 1987.

Supply Difficulties during the Korean War

During the Korean War, keeping supply lines open was a difficult task. In addition to arms and ammunition, troops needed appealing food, clean clothing, and showers, all of which were important to soldiers' morale. The following includes excerpts from three reports published in John G. Westover's Combat Support in Korea. All three pieces were written either by or for the quartermasters, the officers in charge of quarters (lodgings), food, and clothing. Together, these excerpts give some very different views of the challenges of life on the front lines.

In the following excerpt, taken from an oral report dated April 25, 1951, Major Lawrence Dobson shares his observations about combat meals, also known as combat rations or C rations.

The troops in Korea are fed two hot meals a day whenever it is tactically possible. It is desirable, of course, to have three hot meals, but we say a minimum of two: normally, breakfast and supper. Noon meals are an operational ration. Hot meals were started by necessity because of a shortage of operational rations. Today we have plenty of rations, but the troops and the leaders appreciate the benefit of kitchen-prepared meals. It is a terrific morale builder among the forward elements....

The C ration is the most acceptable ration we have to use in Korea. Everyone likes it. The relative acceptance ratings of the meat items are: (1) beans and frankfurters; (2) beans and pork; (3) meat and beans; (4) ham and lima beans; (5) spaghetti and meat; (6) hamburgers with gravy; (7) pork sausage patties with gravy; (8) meat and noodles; (9) chicken and vegetables; (10) beef stew; and (11) corned-beef hash.

This ration is a combat ration, and one of its characteristics is its capability of being consumed hot or cold. The reaction of the men was that the only items acceptable cold were the three bean items. The principal complaints were against the meat-and-spaghetti and the meat-and-noodle combinations. Both items were too dry, and when heated they would burn. The hamburgers and the sausage patties had too much fat and too much gravy. It is difficult to determine the acceptance of the chicken and vegetables. In the C-4 and the C-6 we had a chick-and-vegetables combination. The men disliked it. We had previously received reports on this, and in the C-7 we have a product of the same name but from a different formula. The men interviewed who have eaten the C-7 reported that the acceptance on the chicken-and-vegetables was very high. It is a very good product....

It had been reported previously that there was too much meat in the C ration. I found that for those men in the rear areas—those who used the ration only when they were making a movement—there may be too much meat. But we must remember that this ration was designed for the fighting man. He is a very young man—old men cannot climb hills. Fighters work hard [and] they will eat practically all you can carry up to them.

When talking to them, I asked, "Is there too much meat?"

"No."

"Is there too much in the ration?"

"No; we will eat it all."

Even the cocoa disc and the coffee. If they cannot prepare them at the time they are eating the ration, they will save them for later. An interesting comment was that they liked the cocoa but sometimes do not have the fire to heat the water. So the cocoa is being eaten as a chocolate bar. They wondered if we could not improve the eating quality of the cocoa disc and still save its quality for reconstituting it into cocoa....

When I asked, "What do you think of the individual combat ration?" the first thing said was, "Where is the spoon in the C-6?" And the next thing: "The C-7 is a lot better ration; it has a spoon."

As I mentioned before, the men carry nothing. Mess kits are kept in kitchen trucks. Soldiers are stripped down—no packs—just the clothes they wear. We also used to think a man would never lose his eating utensils. That is not so. They lose them, and unit commanders cannot have them resupplied as fast as they are needed. In many cases knives, forks, and spoons are kept in the kitchen. At first the C ration came without spoons, and we got reports of men eating beans with their fingers. One Marine colonel cut his finger trying to make a spoon from the top of a can. I would say—and I am stating the opinion of everyone I interviewed—that plastic spoons are a *must* in the operational rations.

In the past we included a can opener in each accessory pack. Every soldier I saw had a can opener in his pocket or on his dogtag chain. He was afraid he would not have a can opener when he wanted to eat. If he had a can opener and got hold of another, he saved it. My prize example is a colonel who had one can opener on his dogtag chain and nine in his pack. So my recommendation is that the can openers be reduced to either two or three per case and that they no longer be packed in the accessory pack, but be placed on top.

I am sure you have been told before of the method of feeding forward elements in Korea. The meals are cooked in the battalion areas, then carried forward in jeeps as far as possible, and finally packed by the Korean bearers using carrier straps or A-frames. Now, there are problems involved. Bearers cannot carry water up to the top of the hill except for drinking, and they cannot carry a stove to heat mess-kit water [for washing up], so no one on the hill keeps his mess kit. The kits are all kept back in the kitchen and are carried forward with the food. This is a problem, since the meat ones do not nest very well. Fifty mess kits to take care of an average platoon will fill a foot locker, so the mess kits are carried forward in foot lockers, boxes, or duffel bags. They are washed first in the kitchen, but they become dusty on the trip forward.

* * *

In this undated excerpt, Lieutenant Colonel Kenneth G. Schelberg discusses clothing exchanges.

We learned that the quartermaster's shower and clothing exchange was a great economy in spite of the additional equipment necessary to allow the men to bathe and to launder their clothing.

The 7th Infantry Division began its clothing exchange in February 1951. Before that each man wore and carried two sets of clothing, and reserve supplies in the division held at least one complete uniform per man. When the clothing exchange began, we collected all the duffel bags and limited each soldier to the clothing on his back plus a change of underclothing and socks. Clothing at the shower points and laundry equaled one half uniform per soldier. Thus the total number of uniforms per man dropped from three sets to one and a half....

There were many advantages to the clothing exchange system. It cut down the weight the soldier had to carry; it also eliminated duffel bags and the 30-man detail in each regiment to guard and handle them. This increased our mobility. The cleaner clothing improved the hygiene of the troops, and the automatic exchange of clothing eliminated all requisitions below division. Exchange made possible early repair before shirts and trousers became unsalvageable, and it eliminated the old practice of mutilating Government property in order to get the supply sergeant to issue a new item. Reduced stocks also lessened the possibility of the enemy's capturing valuable supplies.

We learned that in combat there is no need to publish a shower schedule because company commanders preferred to send men to get showers whenever the tactical situation permitted. From experience we learned that the shower units could not be moved farther forward than regiment....

The shower and clothing exchange was a great morale builder for the men. After an attack in which a regiment was unable to release men to get showers, we would augment its bathing facilities and see that every man could bathe and change within four days. Normally, however, the men had a shower once a week.

Company commanders watched their men for signs of excessive fatigue and sent them to the showers when a relief seemed necessary. Often a shower and a hot meal at regiment was enough to restore a soldier's efficiency. If the fatigue were dangerous, the soldier could be sent to the regimental rest camp for a day or two of sleep, hot meals, and regular baths. This was an excellent way to prevent combat fatigue.

* * *

In this excerpt from a statement written November 15, 1950, Major James W. Spellman discusses the ways in which support services failed the troops.

From the first day they spent in Korea, members of the 24th Division's quartermaster section have had mixed feelings about quartermaster support. We remember with pride the difficult things being done immediately, and the impossible taking a little longer. Then we shudder as we recall how often we failed in those hectic days of defeat, victory, and stalemate. We don't like to remember how many times we have had to turn down requests. "How about the mantle for my Coleman lantern?" "How about a generator for my field range?" "How about ..." stencil paper, GI soap, trousers, tent poles, paper clips, underwear, cigarettes?

We seldom had to make excuses for lack of rations or gasoline. But yeast, baking powder, shoestrings, toilet paper, and forks were not available. It has been weeks since many of the small but very important items have been received. Shoes are tied with scraps of cord and kitchens are using toilet soap received from home by mail. I do not doubt that hundreds of soldiers are writing home for items of quartermaster issue because they are not available, or because they come more quickly by mail....

From the tragic days in Taejon we have sensed a passive indifference to our requirements for individual and unit equipment. In the heat of summer we begged for even salvaged fatigue jackets and trousers to be shipped from Japan to cover our semi-naked soldiers, for salt tablets, and for mess kits to replace those lost by our troops as they withdrew over the mountains, carrying only their rifles.

It was understandable that supply confusion should exist at first. But I do not understand why the supply authorities should resist our legitimate requests with criticisms that we were using too much. How *were* we using too much? What known yardstick of modern U.S. logistics could be applied to this long series of defeats and withdrawals?

From the first telephone request—ignored—for minimum clothing and equipment, through the present requirement of six copies of every requisition, we have felt the antagonistic unsympathetic reaction on the part of Eighth Army's minor quartermaster personnel. They have minutely questioned every item of even emergency requirements, and deliberately delayed supplies while they checked and rechecked requests against noncombat-type statistical reports. There has been an almost comical questioning of requirements, delving into the microscopic details of why a company, outnumbered 30 to 1, did not evacuate kitchen equipment under small arms fire....

So long as Pusan remained within truck distance, it was possible to bypass approving authorities and go directly to the mountains of supplies in the port. Often we obtained supplies in Pusan that were impossible to get through the red-tape maze of proper channels. Personnel in charge of warehouse operations frequently begged us to take supplies so they could make room for those being unloaded from ships....

Even now, if a unit is willing to send its trucks 230 miles to Ascom City, or 400 miles to Pusan, supplies can be obtained. But the price in broken springs and deadlined trucks is prohibitive.

As the drive passed Kaesong, Pyongyang, and points north, frantically worded requests to Pusan awaited the opening of a shaky rail system for delivery. On 10 November, the 24th Division had just completed a 40-mile withdrawal of its forward elements. The quartermaster section, then at Sukchon, received a placid notification of a boxcar of class II and class IV supplies—complete with car, engine and train numbers, and hour of departure from Pusan on 9 November—destined for "24th Division, Waegwan." Our rear echelons had cleared Waegwan nearly two months earlier.

A long time would be required to list the major deficiencies in our supply line. In the prosecution of a war the lack of a generator for a field range is not vital. But the result of poor meals is lowered morale—which is vital. When repeated supply failures occur, when indifference is shown, troops often become discouraged and indifferent. Supply failures at this level cost men their lives.

Source: Westover, John G. *Combat Support in Korea*. U.S. Army in Action Series. Washington, DC: Center of Military History, United States Army, U.S. Government Printing Office, n.d.

Defeat at Chosin Reservoir

Captain Russell A. Gugeler was directed by the U.S. Army Chief of Military History to talk to military personnel and to write an easy-to-read report of combat actions based on accounts from foot soldiers, including correspondence, interviews, and reports. The following excerpt is from his book Combat Actions in Korea. *This excerpt is based primarily on the account by U.S. Army historian Captain Martin Blumenson, who describes the experiences of a group of soldiers—the 1st Battalion, 32nd Infantry—during the defeat of X Corps at the Chosin Reservoir in late November 1950.*

It was bitter cold. The temperature was below zero. Snow fell—a snow so dry that dust from the road mixed with it in yellowish clouds that swirled about the column of trucks. Tundra-like, bleak, and without vegetation in most places, the land was depressing.

Huddled together in the back of the trucks, the men of the 1st Battalion, 32d Infantry, stomped their feet on the truck beds in futile attempts to keep their limbs from becoming stiff and numb. Most of them wore long woolen underwear, two pairs of socks, a woolen shirt, cotton field trousers over a pair of woolen trousers, shoepacs, pile jacket, wind-resistant reversible parka with hood, and trigger-finger mittens of wool insert and outer shell. To keep their ears from freezing they tied wool scarves around their heads underneath their helmets. Still, the cold seeped through. Occasionally the entire column ground to a halt to permit the men to dismount and exercise for a few minutes.

Lieutenant Colonel Don C. Faith commanded the 1st Battalion, 32d Infantry. As part of the 7th Infantry Division and of X Corps, the battalion was moving from Hamhung north to relieve Marines on the east shore of Chosin Reservoir and then to continue the attack to the Yalu River. A man could take even stinging, stiffening cold if it meant the end of a war. And that was just how things looked on this 25th day of November 1950. In fact, just before Faith's battalion left Hamhung, some of the men had listened to a news broadcast from Tokyo describing the beginning of a United Nations offensive in Korea designed to terminate the war quickly. Originating in General of the Army Douglas MacArthur's headquarters, the report predicted that U.S. divisions would be back in Japan by Christmas. It had been cheering news....

One regiment of the 7th Division—the 17th Infantry—had gone more than 100 miles north of Hungnam and had reached the Yalu River on November 21. Other units of that division were separated by straight-line distances

210

of 70 or 80 miles. Road distances, tortuously slow, were much longer. North Koreans had offered only slight resistance against X Corps advances, but the obstacles of terrain and weather were tremendous....

At least one or two men from each company were frostbite casualties late that afternoon [November 25] when the battalion closed into defensive positions [at the south end of Chosin Reservoir]. The night was quiet. There were warm-up tents behind the main crests of the hills and the men spent alternate periods manning defensive positions and getting warm....

As night fell on November 27, the first order of business was defense, [and] a continuation of the northward drive the Marines had begun was planned for the next day. Lending greater force to common knowledge that the Chinese forces in undetermined strength were roaming the mountains in the vicinity of Chosin Reservoir, the Marines had told Colonel Faith that on the day before several Chinese prisoners had revealed the presence of three fresh divisions operating in the area of the reservoir. Their mission, the prisoners had said, was to sever the American supply route. The Marines also told Faith's men that on the previous night, in this same location, a Chinese patrol had pulled a Marine from his foxhole, disarmed him, and beaten him....

The enemy attacked [on November 27, while the command meeting] was in progress. Probing patrols came first.... A few minutes after midnight the patrolling gave way to determined attack....

The defensive perimeter began to blaze with fire. In addition to directing steady mortar and small-arms fire against Colonel Faith's battalion, the Chinese kept maneuvering small groups around the perimeter to break the line. As one enemy group climbed a steep ridge toward a heavy machine gun operated by Corporal Robert Lee Armentrout, the corporal discovered he could not depress his gun enough to hit the enemy. He then picked up his weapon, tripod and all, cradled it in his arms, and beat off the attack....

Similar attacks had fallen against the perimeter enclosing Colonel MacLean's force four miles to the south of Faith's battalion. Chinese had overrun two infantry companies during the early morning and got back to artillery positions before members of two artillery batteries and of the overrun companies stopped them. After confused and intense fighting during the hours of darkness, the enemy withdrew at first light. Both sides suffered heavily....

Sixty or more casualties gathered at the battalion aid station during the day. By evening about 20 bodies had accumulated in front of the two-room farm house in which the aid station was operating. Inside, the building was crowded with wounded; a dozen more wounded, some wearing bandages, stood in a huddle outside....

That afternoon Colonel MacLean came forward to Colonel Faith's battalion. Toward evening, however, when he attempted to leave, he was stopped by a Chinese roadblock between the two battalions, thus confronting him with the grim realization that the enemy had surrounded his position. He remained at the forward position.

Just before dark, between 5:00 and 5:30 p.m., November 28, planes struck what appeared to be a battalion-sized enemy group that was marching toward the battalion perimeter from the north, still two or three miles away. The tactical situation, even during the daytime, had been so serious that many of the units did not take time to carry rations to the front line. When food did reach the soldiers after dark, it was frozen and the men had no way to thaw it except by holding it against their bodies. By this time most of the men realized the enemy was mounting more than light skirmishes, as they had believed the previous evening.

"You'd better get your positions in good tonight," one platoon leader told his men that evening, "or there won't be any positions tomorrow." As darkness fell on November 28, Colonel Faith's battalion braced itself for another attack.

[While the fighting was taking place, General Ned Almond received orders for X Corps to withdraw and consolidate forces and for Colonel Faith and Colonel MacLean to combine their troops.]

Because of the enemy roadblock separating the two elements of his task force, Colonel MacLean ordered Faith to abandon as much equipment as necessary in order to have enough space on the trucks to haul out the wounded, and then to attack south. All wounded men—about 100 by now—were placed on trucks that formed in column on the road. Because of the necessity of maintaining blackout, it was not practical to burn the vehicles, kitchens, and other equipment left behind.

When the withdrawal order reached the rifle platoons, the plan for withdrawing the battalion segment by segment collapsed as the men abruptly broke contact with the Communists, fell back to the road, and assembled for the march. Enemy fire picked up immediately since the movement and the abrupt end of the firing made it obvious to the Chinese that the American were leaving.

Colonel Faith directed two companies to provide flank security by preceding the column along the high ground that paralleled the road on both sides for about two miles. Movement of the 1st Battalion column got underway about an hour before dawn, November 29.... The column moved without opposition until, at the first sign of daylight, it reached the point where the road, following the shoreline [of the reservoir], turned northeast to circle a long finger of ice. The Chinese roadblock was at the end of the narrow strip, and here enemy fire halted the column. The battalion's objective, the perimeter of the rest of MacLean's task force, was now just across the strip of ice and not much farther than a mile by the longer road distances....

Colonel Faith's column suddenly received fire from the vicinity of the friendly units across the finger of ice. Believing that the fire was coming from his own troops, Colonel MacLean started across the ice to make contact with them and halt the fire. He was hit four times by enemy fire—the men watching could see his body jerk with each impact—but he continued and reached the opposite side. There he disappeared and was not seen again.

It now became evident that the fire was Chinese. Colonel Faith assembled as many men as he could and led them in a skirmish line directly across the ice. As it happened, a company-sized enemy force was preparing to attack ...when Faith's attack struck this force in the rear. Disorganized, the Chinese attack fell part. Faith's men killed about 60 Chinese and dispersed the rest. In the meantime, the two rifle companies approached the enemy force manning the roadblock. Now surrounded itself, the roadblock force also fell apart and disappeared into the hills. With the road open, the column of vehicles entered the perimeter of the other friendly forces.

After a search for Colonel MacLean failed to discover any trace of him, Colonel Faith assumed command and organized all remaining personnel into a task force. Friendly forces, although consolidated, still occupied a precarious position. During the afternoon Faith and his commanders formed a perimeter defense of an area about 600 by 2,000 yards.... This perimeter, around a pocket of low, slight sloping ground, was particularly vulnerable to attack. Except for the area along the reservoir, Colonel Faith's task force was surrounded by ridgelines, all of which belonged to the Chinese.... Rations were almost gone. Ammunition and gasoline supplies were low. The men were numbed by the cold. Even those who had managed to retain their bedrolls did not dare fall asleep for fear of freezing. The men had to move their legs and change position occasionally to keep their blood circulating. Automatic weapons had to be tried every 15 to 30 minutes to keep them in working order....

Ten miles above Hagaru-ri, Colonel Faith's task force beat off enemy probing attacks that harassed his force during the night of November 29-30.... There were no determined attacks, however, and the perimeter was still intact when dawn came. It was another cold morning. The sky was clear enough to permit air support. Inside the perimeter, soldiers built fires to warm themselves and the fires drew no enemy fire. Hopefully, the men decided they had withstood the worst part of the enemy attack. Surely, they thought, a relief column would reach the area that day.

A litter-bearing helicopter made two trips to the area on November 30, carrying out four seriously wounded men. Fighter planes made a strike on high ground around Task Force Faith, and cargo planes dropped more supplies, some of which again fell to the enemy. As the afternoon wore on, it became apparent that no relief column was coming that day.... As darkness settled for another 16-hour-long night, commanders tried to encourage their troops: "Hold out one more night and we've got it made."

On November 30, again beginning about 10:00 p.m., the Chinese made another of their dishearteningly regular attacks. From the beginning it showed more determination than those of the two previous nights.... Soon after midnight, when the enemy attack was most intense, a small group of Chinese broke into the perimeter at one end. Faith sent his counterattack force to patch up the line. From then until morning there were five different penetrations, and as many counterattacks....

[On the morning of December 1] The aid-station squad tent was full; about 50 patients were inside. Another 35 wounded were lying outside in the narrow-gauge railroad cut where the station was located.... Colonel Faith appeared at the aid station, asked all men who could possibly do so to come back on line.

"If we can hold out 40 minutes more," the Colonel pleaded, "we'll get air support."

There was not much response. Most of the men were seriously wounded.

"Come on, you lazy bastards," Faith said, "and give us a hand."

That roused several men, including [Lieutenant Campbell, who had been hit by a mortar shell]. Because he could not walk, he crawled 20 yards along the railroad track and found a carbine with one round in it. Dragging the carbine, Campbell continued to crawl to the west. He collapsed into a foxhole before he reached the lines, and waited until someone helped him back to the aid station. This time he got inside for treatment. The medical personnel had no more bandages. There was no more morphine. They cleansed his wounds with disinfectant, and he dozed there for several hours....

Most of the surgical equipment was gone. Aid men improvised litters from ponchos and field jackets. One splint set was on hand, however, and there was plenty of blood plasma. When bandages were gone, aid men used personal linens, handkerchiefs, undershirts, and towels. They gathered up parachutes recovered with the airdropped bundles, using white ones for dressings and colored ones to cover the wounded and keep them warm. Sergeant Leon Pugowski of the Headquarters Company kitchen had managed to save two stoves, coffee, and some cans of soup. He set the stoves up in the aid station, and the seriously wounded got hot soup or coffee.

Task Force Faith had been under attack for 80 hours in sub-zero weather. None of the men had washed or shaved during that time, nor eaten more than a bare minimum. Frozen feet and hands were common. Worst of all, the weather appeared to be getting worse, threatening air support and aerial resupply. Few men believed they could hold out another night against determined attacks.

Captain Seever (CO, Company C) sat on the edge of a hole discussing the situation with Major Curtis (Battalion S3). An enemy mortar shell landed 10 to 15 feet away and exploded without injuring either of them. Seever shrugged his shoulders.

"Major," he said, "I feel like I'm a thousand years old."...

Colonel Faith decided to try to break out of the perimeter and reach Hagaru-ri in a single dash rather than risk another night where he was. He planned to start the breakout about 1:00 p.m. so it would coincide with the air strike. He ordered the artillery batteries and the Heavy Mortar Company to shoot up all remaining ammunition before that time and then to destroy their weapons.... To minimize danger from enemy attack, Colonel Faith wanted the column to be as short as possible—only enough vehicles to haul out the wounded. All other men would walk. Vehicles, equipment, and supplies that could not be carried, or that were not necessary for the move, he ordered destroyed. The men selected 22 of the best vehicles … and lined them up on the road. They drained gasoline from the other vehicles and filled the tanks of the ones they were going to take.

About noon someone roused Lieutenant Campbell and said, "We're going to make a break for it."

He and the other wounded men—several hundred of them by this time—were placed in the vehicles. They lay there for about an hour while final preparations for the breakout attempt were made. Enemy mortar shells began dropping in the vicinity.

Colonel Faith selected Company C, 32d Infantry, as advance guard for the column. Lieutenant Mortrude's platoon, the least hurt, was to take the point position…. Company A, followed by Company B, would act as flank security east of the road. There was no danger at the beginning of the breakout from the direction of the reservoir, which was to the west.

Friendly planes appeared overhead. Mortrude moved his platoon out about 1:00 p.m. Lieutenant Smith led out Company A. The men of these units had walked barely out of the area that had been their defensive perimeter when enemy bullets whistled past or dug into the ground behind them. At almost the same time, four friendly planes, in close support of the breakout action, missed the target and dropped napalm bombs on the lead elements. The halftrack in which Mortrude planned to ride was set ablaze. Several men were burned to death immediately. About five others, their clothes afire, tried frantically to beat out the flames. Everyone scattered. Disorganization followed.

Up to this point, units had maintained organizational structure, but suddenly they began to fall apart. Intermingling in panic, they disintegrated into leaderless groups of men. Most of the squad and platoon leaders and the commanders of the rifle companies were dead or wounded…. No one had slept for several days. One thought drove the men: they had to keep moving if they were to get out. Even those who were not wounded were strongly tempted to lie down and go to sleep; but they knew they would be lost if they did.

Lieutenant Mortrude gathered ten men around him and proceeded to carry out his orders. Firing as they advanced, they dispersed 20 or more enemy sol-

216

diers who fled. As they ran down the road screaming obscenities at the enemy, Mortrude and his men encountered several small Chinese groups, which they killed or scattered…. Out of breath and hardly able to walk on his wounded leg, Mortrude and those men still with him reached a blown-out bridge two miles or more south of the starting point. Attracting no enemy fire, they stopped there to rest and wait for the column…. Enemy fire came in from the high ground to the northeast. Most of the men fell to the ground to take cover. Lieutenant Mortrude wondered why the vehicles were not coming down the road, since he had expected the column to follow closely. As he lay on the slope of the ridge, a bullet struck him in the head and knocked him unconscious….

When Lieutenant Mortrude regained consciousness on the slope of the ridge, he noticed friendly troops moving up the hill in the area south of the blown-out bridge. An aid man (Corporal Alfonso Camoesas) came past and bandaged his head. Then Mortrude stumbled across the ridgeline, passing many American dead and wounded on the slope. Dazed and in a condition of shock, he followed a group of men he could vaguely see ahead of him. The group went toward the reservoir and walked out on the ice.

While all this was taking place, another enemy roadblock halted the lead trucks in the column at a hairpin curve a half-mile beyond the blown-out bridge. At least two machine guns and enemy riflemen kept the area under fire. Colonel Faith, a blanket around his shoulders, walked up and down the line of trucks as he organized a group to assault the enemy who were firing from positions east of the road…. Darkness was not far off. Colonel Faith was desperately anxious to get his column moving and the wounded men out before the Chinese closed in on them. He got some wounded into the ditch to form a base of fire and then organized several groups to assault the enemy positions. One group of men …was to clear out the area between the road and the reservoir. Colonel Faith instructed [another group under Major Robert E. Jones] to gather all available men and move them onto the high ground south of the hairpin curve, while he himself organized another group to move onto the high ground just north of the roadblock at the hairpin curve. They would then attack from opposite directions at the same time.

It was almost dark when Major Jones and Colonel Faith, each with 100 men or less, launched their attacks against the roadblock and knocked it out. Colonel Faith, hit by grenade fragments, was mortally wounded. A man next to him, hit by fragments of the same grenade, tried to help him down to the road, but was unable to do so. Some other men came by, carried him down to the road, and put him in the cab of a truck.

Colonel Faith's task force, which had started to break up soon after it got under way that afternoon, now disintegrated completely because those men who had commanded the battalions, companies, and platoons were either dead or wounded so seriously they could exercise no control. The task force crumbled into individuals, or into groups of two or 10 or 20 men. Major Jones, with the help of several others, took charge of the largest group of men remaining—those who stayed to help with the trucks carrying the wounded. Enemy fire had severely damaged the truck column. Several trucks were knocked out and blocked the column, and others had flat tires. The time was about 5:00 p.m., December 1, and it was almost dark.

Those who were able, now removed all wounded men from the three destroyed 2½-ton trucks which blocked the column, carried the wounded to other trucks, and then pushed the destroyed vehicles over the cliff toward the reservoir. Someone shouted for help to gather up all men who had been wounded during the roadblock action. For half an hour the able-bodied men searched both sides of the road. When the column was ready to move again the wounded were piled two deep in most of the trucks. Men rode across the hoods and on the bumpers, and six or eight men hung to the sides of each truck. After re-forming the truck column with all operating vehicles, Major Jones organized as many able-bodied and walking wounded men as he could—between 100 and 200 men—and started south down the road. The trucks were to follow....

It was a ragged and desperate-looking column of men and vehicles. Those following Major Jones had little semblance to a military unit. Without subordinate leaders, without formation or plan, they were a mixture of the remnants of all units, a large percentage being walking wounded. About 15 of the original 22 trucks were left.

[By about 9:00 p.m. the truck column had covered about half of the approximately 10 miles between the last defensive perimeter and Hagaru-ri, where UN troops had established a perimeter. The truck column approached a village, Hudong-ni. Soon Chinese troops there began firing on the lead truck, killing the driver. Major Jones and a few men decided to get away from the road and follow the railroad tracks instead. The rest of the column waited for a while near the village, assuming that word of their situation had gotten to Hagaru-ri and that help would be sent. But reinforcements failed to arrive, and when the column began to take heavy fire from the enemy, the men decided to make a run for it.]

As the column proceeded through the village, moving slowly, enemy fire killed the drivers of the first three trucks. The column halted and an enemy machine gun immediately raked it at point-blank range. Jumping off the tailgate of the third truck, Lieutenant Campbell scrambled for the right side of the road…. Leaning against the embankment, he fired his carbine at the machine gun's flashes. A body, an arm torn off, lay nearby on the road. The overturned truck, its wheels in the air, rested in the small field below the road. Someone pinned under it kept pounding on the truck's body. Wounded men, scattered nearby, screamed either in pain or for help. Up on the road someone kept yelling for men to drive the trucks through. Chinese soldiers closed in on the rear of the column. Campbell saw a white phosphorous grenade explode in the rear of a truck at the end of the column.

"This is the end of the truck column!" he said to himself.

Someone yelled, "Look out!"

Campbell turned in time to see a 3/4-ton truck coming over the embankment toward him. As he scrambled to one side, the truck ran over his foot, bruising the bones. Someone had tried to get the lead vehicles off the road. Pushed by the fourth, the first three trucks, without their drivers, jammed together, rolled off the embankment, and overturned. Wounded men inside were spilled and crushed. The frantic screams of these men seemed to Lieutenant Campbell like the world gone mad. He fired his last three rounds at the enemy machine gun, headed for the railroad track on the opposite side of the tiny field, and dived into a culvert underneath the railroad. It began to snow again—a fine, powdery snow….

Lieutenant Campbell crawled through the culvert. He found a man, wounded in the leg, who could not walk. Two other soldiers came over the embankment and joined him. Dragging the wounded man, the group walked in a crouch across the rice paddy to a large lumber pile in the middle of the field…. [As others joined them], the men walked on the reservoir ice. Campbell was not sure where Hagaru-ri was….

Lieutenant Campbell thought he recognized the road. He led off, and the rest followed. By then, he had 17 men with him, of whom three were armed.

Two miles down the road, the group reached a Marine tank outpost, and the tankers directed them to the nearest command post, where a truck took them to a Marine hospital in Hagaru-ri. Lieutenant Campbell arrived there at 5:30 a.m., December 2. The shell fragment in the roof of his mouth began to bother him.

Individuals and other groups straggled into Hagaru-ri for several days beginning on the night of December 1.... The men who went with Major Jones, after following the railroad tracks for some distance, had been fired on by an enemy machine gun. Many of the men took off toward the reservoir and began arriving at the Marine perimeter soon after midnight.

Most of the men who had served with Task Force Faith were left where the truck column stopped near the lumber village of Hudong-ni, or were strewn along the road from there to the northernmost position. When those few men who could move had left, the others were either captured or frozen.

Private First Class Glenn J. Finfrock (a machine gunner from Company D) became unconscious from loss of blood about the time the truck column came to its final halt. It was daylight on the morning of December 2 when he regained consciousness again. He moved down the road a short distance until he found several wounded men trying to build a fire by one of the trucks—the one in which Colonel Faith had been placed the previous evening. His frozen body was still in the cab. Since the truck appeared to be in good order, Finfrock and another man tried unsuccessfully to start it. As they were working on the truck some Chinese walked toward them from the village, and several of the men ran toward the ice. Others were captured. The Chinese gave morphine to several men, bandaged their wounds, and, after caring for them for several days, freed them.

Lieutenant Mortrude, wounded in the knee and in the head, walked to Hagaru-ri from the blown-out bridge. It was 3:30 a.m. on December 2 when he reached friendly lines....

All day other men made their way back to friendly lines. On December 4, when most of its survivors had returned, the 1st Battalion, 32d Infantry, counted only 181 officers, men, and attached Republic of Korea troops, of the original 1,053 that had begun the operation. The other battalions in the perimeter had suffered equal losses.

This was not the immediate end of trouble, since the enemy still controlled much of the road between Hagaru-ri and the port city of Hungnam.

But at Hagaru-ri the 1st Marine Division had a solid perimeter that included the airstrip, and there were food and ammunition and medical supplies. From Hungnam the more seriously wounded were evacuated by plane. For the others, 10 days of fighting lay ahead.

Source: Gugeler, Russell A. *Combat Actions in Korea*. Army Historical Series. Washington, DC: Center of Military History, United States Army, U.S. Government Printing Office, 1987.

President Truman's Radio Report to the American People on Korea and on U.S. Policy in the Far East

After dismissing General MacArthur on April 11, 1951, President Truman gave a radio address to the American people in which he explained his rationale for firing MacArthur. He also reiterated his belief that U.S. involvement in Korea was to prevent a third world war, to defeat aggression, and to contain Communism. Following is the full text of that address:

April 11, 1951
[Broadcast from the White House at 10:30 p.m.]

My fellow Americans:

I want to talk to you plainly tonight about what we are doing in Korea and about our policy in the Far East.

In the simplest terms, what we are doing in Korea is this: We are trying to prevent a third world war.

I think most people in this country recognized that fact last June. And they warmly supported the decision of the Government to help the Republic of Korea against the Communist aggressors. Now, many persons, even some who applauded our decision to defend Korea, have forgotten the basic reason for our action.

It is right for us to be in Korea now. It was right last June. It is right today.

I want to remind you why this is true.

The Communists in the Kremlin are engaged in a monstrous conspiracy to stamp out freedom all over the world. If they were to succeed, the United States would be numbered among their principal victims. It must be clear to everyone that the United States cannot—and will not—sit idly by and await foreign conquest. The only question is: What is the best time to meet the threat and how is the best way to meet it?

The best time to meet the threat is in the beginning. It is easier to put out a fire in the beginning when it is small than after it has become a roaring blaze. And the best way to meet the threat of aggression is for the peace-loving nations to act together. If they don't act together, they are likely to be picked off, one by one.

If they had followed the right policies in the 1930s—if the free countries had acted together to crush the aggression of the dictators, and if they had acted in the beginning when the aggression was small—there probably would have been no World War II.

If history has taught us anything, it is that aggression anywhere in the world is a threat to the peace everywhere in the world. When that aggression is supported by the cruel and selfish rulers of a powerful nation who are bent on conquest, it becomes a clear and present danger to the security and independence of every free nation.

This is a lesson that most people in this country have learned thoroughly. This is the basic reason why we joined in creating the United Nations. And, since the end of World War II, we have been putting that lesson into practice—we have been working with other free nations to check the aggressive designs of the Soviet Union before they can result in a third world war.

That is what we did in Greece, when that nation was threatened by the aggression of international communism.

The attack against Greece could have led to general war. But this country came to the aid of Greece. The United Nations supported Greek resistance. With our help, the determination and efforts of the Greek people defeated the attack on the spot.

Another big Communist threat to peace was the Berlin blockade. That too could have led to war. But again it was settled because free men would not back down in an emergency.

The aggression against Korea is the boldest and most dangerous move the Communists have yet made.

The attack on Korea was part of a greater plan for conquering all of Asia.

I would like to read to you from a secret intelligence report which came to us after the attack on Korea. It is a report of a speech a Communist army officer in North Korea gave to a group of spies and saboteurs last May, one month before South Korea was invaded. The report shows in great detail how this invasion was part of a carefully prepared plot. Here, in part, is what the Communist officer, who had been trained in Moscow, told his men: "Our forces," he said, "are scheduled to attack South Korean forces about the middle of June.... The coming attack on South Korea marks the first step toward the liberation of Asia."

Notice that he used the word "liberation." This is Communist double-talk meaning "conquest."

I have another secret intelligence report here. This one tells what another Communist officer in the Far East told his men several months before the invasion of Korea. Here is what he said: "In order to successfully undertake the long-awaited world revolution, we must first unify Asia…. Java, Indochina, Malaya, India, Tibet, Thailand, Philippines, and Japan are our ultimate targets…. The United States is the only obstacle on our road for the liberation of all the countries in southeast Asia. In other words, we must unify the people of Asia and crush the United States." Again, "liberation" in "commie" language means conquest.

That is what the Communist leaders are telling their people, and that is what they have been trying to do.

They want to control all Asia from the Kremlin.

This plan of conquest is in flat contradiction to what we believe. We believe that Korea belongs to the Koreans, we believe that India belongs to the Indians, we believe that all the nations of Asia should be free to work out their affairs in their own way. This is the basis of peace in the Far East, and it is the basis of peace everywhere else.

The whole Communist imperialism is back of the attack on peace in the Far East. It was the Soviet Union that trained and equipped the North Koreans for aggression. The Chinese Communists massed 44 well-trained and well-equipped divisions on the Korean frontier. These were the troops they threw into battle when the North Korean Communists were beaten.

The question we have had to face is whether the Communist plan of conquest can be stopped without a general war. Our Government and other countries associated with us in the United Nations believe that the best chance of stopping it without a general war is to meet the attack in Korea and defeat it there.

That is what we have been doing. It is a difficult and bitter task.

But so far it has been successful.

So far, we have prevented world war III.

So far, by fighting a limited war in Korea, we have prevented aggression from succeeding, and bringing on a general war. And the ability of the whole free world to resist Communist aggression has been greatly improved.

224

We have taught the enemy a lesson. He has found that aggression is not cheap or easy. Moreover, men all over the world who want to remain free have been given new courage and new hope. They know now that the champions of freedom can stand up and fight, and that they will stand up and fight.

Our resolute stand in Korea is helping the forces of freedom now fighting in Indochina and other countries in that part of the world. It has already slowed down the timetable of conquest.

In Korea itself there are signs that the enemy is building up his ground forces for a new mass offensive. We also know that there have been large increases in the enemy's available air forces.

If a new attack comes, I feel confident it will be turned back. The United Nations fighting forces are tough and able and well equipped. They are fighting for a just cause. They are proving to all the world that the principle of collective security will work. We are proud of all these forces for the magnificent job they have done against heavy odds. We pray that their efforts may succeed, for upon their success may hinge the peace of the world.

The Communist side must now choose its course of action. The Communist rulers may press the attack against us. They may take further action which will spread the conflict. They have that choice, and with it the awful responsibility for what may follow. The Communists also have the choice of a peaceful settlement which could lead to a general relaxation of the tensions in the Far East. The decision is theirs, because the forces of the United Nations will strive to limit the conflict if possible.

We do not want to see the conflict in Korea extended. We are trying to prevent a world war—not to start one. And the best way to do that is to make it plain that we and the other free countries will continue to resist the attack.

But you may ask why can't we take other steps to punish the aggressor. Why don't we bomb Manchuria and China itself? Why don't we assist the Chinese Nationalist troops to land on the mainland of China ?

If we were to do these things we would be running a very grave risk of starting a general war. If that were to happen, we would have brought about the exact situation we are trying to prevent.

If we were to do these things, we would become entangled in a vast conflict on the continent of Asia and our task would become immeasurably more difficult all over the world.

What would suit the ambitions of the Kremlin better than for our military forces to be committed to a full-scale war with Red China?

It may well be that, in spite of our best efforts, the Communists may spread the war. But it would be wrong—tragically wrong—for us to take the initiative in extending the war.

The dangers are great. Make no mistake about it. Behind the North Koreans and Chinese Communists in the front lines stand additional millions of Chinese soldiers. And behind the Chinese stand the tanks, the planes, the submarines, the soldiers, and the scheming rulers of the Soviet Union.

Our aim is to avoid the spread of the conflict.

The course we have been following is the one best calculated to avoid an all-out war. It is the course consistent with our obligation to do all we can to maintain international peace and security. Our experience in Greece and Berlin shows that it is the most effective course of action we can follow.

First of all, it is clear that our efforts in Korea can blunt the will of the Chinese Communists to continue the struggle. The United Nations forces have put up a tremendous fight in Korea and have inflicted very heavy casualties on the enemy. Our forces are stronger now than they have been before. These are plain facts which may discourage the Chinese Communists from continuing their attack.

Second, the free world as a whole is growing in military strength every day. In the United States, in Western Europe, and throughout the world, free men are alert to the Soviet threat and are building their defenses. This may discourage the Communist rulers from continuing the war in Korea—and from undertaking new acts of aggression elsewhere.

If the Communist authorities realize that they cannot defeat us in Korea, if they realize it would be foolhardy to widen the hostilities beyond Korea, then they may recognize the folly of continuing their aggression. A peaceful settlement may then be possible. The door is always open.

Then we may achieve a settlement in Korea which will not compromise the principles and purposes of the United Nations.

I have thought long and hard about this question of extending the war in Asia. I have discussed it many times with the ablest military advisers in the country. I believe with all my heart that the course we are following is the best course.

I believe that we must try to limit the war to Korea for these vital reasons: to make sure that the precious lives of our fighting men are not wasted; to see that the security of our country and the free world is not needlessly jeopardized; and to prevent a third world war.

A number of events have made it evident that General MacArthur did not agree with that policy. I have therefore considered it essential to relieve General MacArthur so that there would be no doubt or confusion as to the real purpose and aim of our policy.

It was with the deepest personal regret that I found myself compelled to take this action. General MacArthur is one of our greatest military commanders. But the cause of world peace is much more important than any individual.

The change in commands in the Far East means no change whatever in the policy of the United States. We will carry on the fight in Korea with vigor and determination in an effort to bring the war to a speedy and successful conclusion. The new commander, Lt. Gen. Matthew Ridgway, has already demonstrated that he has the great qualities of military leadership needed for this task.

We are ready, at any time, to negotiate for a restoration of peace in the area. But we will not engage in appeasement. We are only interested in real peace.

Real peace can be achieved through a settlement based on the following factors:

One: The fighting must stop.

Two: Concrete steps must be taken to insure that the fighting will not break out again.

Three: There must be an end to the aggression.

A settlement founded upon these elements would open the way for the unification of Korea and the withdrawal of all foreign forces.

In the meantime, I want to be clear about our military objective. We are fighting to resist an outrageous aggression in Korea. We are trying to keep the Korean conflict from spreading to other areas. But at the same time we must conduct our military activities so as to insure the security of our forces. This is essential if they are to continue the fight until the enemy abandons its ruthless attempt to destroy the Republic of Korea.

227

That is our military objective—to repel attack and to restore peace.

In the hard fighting in Korea, we are proving that collective action among nations is not only a high principle but a workable means of resisting aggression. Defeat of aggression in Korea may be the turning point in the world's search for a practical way of achieving peace and security.

The struggle of the United Nations in Korea is a struggle for peace.

Free nations have united their strength in an effort to prevent a third world war.

That war can come if the Communist rulers want it to come. But this Nation and its allies will not be responsible for its coming.

We do not want to widen the conflict. We will use every effort to prevent that disaster. And in so doing, we know that we are following the great principles of peace, freedom, and justice.

Source: Harry S. Truman. "Radio Report to the American People on Korea and on U.S. Policy in the Far East," 04/11/51. Truman Public Papers, Truman Library. http://trumanlibrary.org/publicpapers/index.php?pid=290&st=&st1=

One U.S. Soldier's POW Experience

Akiro Chikami was a U.S. soldier of Japanese descent who served in both World War II and the Korean War, where he became a prisoner of war (POW). He was imprisoned in Camp Twelve, near Pyongyang, a re-education camp for prisoners who the Chinese hoped would cooperate. Like many other POWs, Chikami refused to cooperate with his captors. Nonetheless, after returning to the United States, he was investigated for three years before being cleared of all allegations of collaboration. In the excerpt below, Chikami describes his experiences as a captured soldier.

I was born March 19, 1927, of Japanese immigrant parents in La Junta, Colorado, but I grew up in Reno, Nevada, where I joined the Army. I got out of the service after World War II ended and became a professional boxer. There was a lot of discrimination when I used to fight on the West Coast, so they would call me an Indian, a Korean, or whatever. But I hurt my hand and had to quit. I thought I'd go back to Colorado and work in the lead mines to strengthen my hands and shoulders. I passed the physical, but when they looked at my papers and found out I was a Japanese American, they wouldn't hire me. They were very discriminatory, even though I had an honorable discharge. In the meantime, I saw a newsreel of the 1st Marine Division getting kicked out of the Chosin Reservoir. I got all excited. I had never seen combat so I thought, "Gee, That's where I want to go." I also had two older brothers who were with the 42nd Regimental Combat Team in World War II. I went to a recruiting office in Denver and asked the sergeant if I went back into the Army could I go to Korea. He said, "Sure thing." He signed me up and gave me a ticket to Fort Riley, Kansas, where they gave me a two day refresher course. The first day I took my M-1 apart and then put it back together. The second day I went through the infiltration course. That was my refresher course. This was December 1950. In January I was in the infantry with the 2nd Division on the frontlines in Korea, less than two months after I reenlisted.

I never had any regrets, at least not until I got captured by North Koreans in August 1951. At the time we were in the punchbowl and my company was out front as a kind of decoy but also in a blocking position, trying to get the enemy to attack us so we could call in artillery on them. We were only supposed to stay out there three days, but we got into the eighth and ninth days. I knew we were in trouble because I'd been in combat long enough to know we shouldn't be out there that long. Every night the enemy had been probing to find out where our automatic weapons were. Sure enough, on the morning of August 27 our company was overrun. We lost over 50 percent of our company that day.

We started to retreat and I got hit in the leg. My first reaction was, "Well, it's not too bad. Maybe it will be good enough to get me a trip to Japan." My company commander came by and said, "Sorry, I'm going to have to leave you." And he did [laughs]. Our medic stopped and helped bandage me up. Then two other guys came along and said, "Come on, Sarge, we'll help you." They picked me up between them and tried to carry me, but a machine gun opened up. They were both killed and fell into a stream. I started crawling, but I looked up and there was a young North Korean soldier staring at me. He was just a kid, but he had a burp gun. I still had a 45 on me. I didn't know whether to reach for it or not. I decided not to, and I was a prisoner. He immediately took what I had: a watch, a ring, and a bracelet and then turned me over to another group where they had assembled other prisoners.

The North Koreans herded us toward our own lines where the fighting was still going on. I couldn't figure out why they were taking us in that direction, instead of to the rear. When we came to a bend in the road where our machine guns were raking the area, I realized, "They're going to make us commit suicide by marching us right into our own fire." But the shooting suddenly stopped. I guess our guys recognized we were Americans.

By then there were some 35 of us, and they moved us into a little ravine where it became clear they were going to use us to carry their wounded to the rear. Then, I saw one of our spotter planes we used to call in artillery. Sure enough, I heard a couple of incoming rounds, and I knew our own troops were zeroing in on us. Five rounds came in right on top of us. The guy in front of me was hit, which saved me because I was right behind him. He caught a piece of shrapnel in his chest so big I could stick my whole fist in it. When it was over, there were only about four or five of us who weren't wounded. It was getting dusk and the North Koreans were going to move us out. This American lieutenant came up to me and asked, "Sarge, are you going to go?" I told him I was. This lieutenant decided to fake an injury and say he couldn't move. There were four of our guys who stayed behind. As I moved out over the hill, I heard a burp gun go off, and I knew the North Koreans had shot them. I found out some 20 years later that the lieutenant survived, although he was the only one of the four who did. One of our patrols picked him up the next day. He was all shot up, but he lived.

I was able to walk with somebody helping me. I had to. I knew if I didn't walk they were going to shoot me. The bullet that struck me hadn't hit a bone, which was lucky. It went right through my leg. Later I picked up a tree branch to use as a crutch, so I was able to walk.

They moved us to the rear that first night. The next day we had to cross a river that was flooding and I thought maybe I would get swept away because of my leg. But I made it. They then took us into this huge cave in a mountain that was their headquarters. They tried to interrogate us, but they didn't have an English-speaking person and none of us could understand them. I was the ranking man, and they were surprised to find an Oriental. They were very curious about me because they were afraid that Japan was going to send in troops. So they interrogated me pretty closely. When they went through my wallet, they were amazed to find photos of Caucasian girls. They would look at me and then at the pictures and they would yack, yack, yack. I could only imagine what they were saying. I more or less became a spokesman for our group of POWs for what little I could communicate.

You talk about tactics. The first interrogator treated me real rough. He threatened to push me over a cliff and all that kind of stuff. Then he went away and another guy took his place. He offered me a cigarette and tried to explain that the other guy was very bitter because he had lost his family in the war. He was a little more compassionate. He told me, "I know you're just a soldier." Then he wanted to know what outfit I was in, why we were there, and things like that. They were pretty shrewd and they could get to you pretty fast. One of our guys was all shook up. He had just been married and his wife was pregnant, so he was thinking, "How am I going to tell my wife I'm a prisoner?" Someone like him became an easy target for indoctrination, and they completely broke him down. I don't know if you call it brainwashing, but men like him became easily manipulated. Of course, the North Koreans already knew who we were. I mean they knew everything. There was nothing we could tell them that they didn't already know.

They moved us out the next day farther and farther to the rear. We walked mostly at night or in the evening. In the morning we would hole up in some village or they would put us into some kind of shack. The little kids in these villages would see me and holler something that I later found out meant "half-breed." They were fascinated by me because I was an Oriental. I would be lying on the side of the road trying to rest or sleep, and these kids

231

would pick up little rocks and throw them at me. The braver ones would poke me with sticks so they could see my face. I was an oddity to them.

About the 10th or 11th day after we were captured, the guards wanted to know who was going to represent our group. I was the ranking sergeant so I was selected by the other prisoners. Early the next day they took me and this other prisoner, Sergeant Nehrbas, put us in a jeep, and took us directly to Camp Twelve, which was on the outskirts of the North Korean capital of Pyongyang. When we arrived a prisoner who identified himself as Colonel Fleming asked us how the peace talks were going. He wasn't concerned about our welfare so I was a little turned off. Fleming was one of the few prisoners to be court-martialed and convicted after the war.

Camp Twelve consisted of about 50 or 60 prisoners, both officers and enlisted men. We got a real cool reception from the GIs who were already there. I couldn't understand this; it was like they didn't trust us. I had no idea what was going on. After I was released, I learned that the North Koreans had told the other prisoners they were bringing some sergeants who had voluntarily surrendered. No wonder they viewed us so suspiciously.

The camp commander was a North Korean by the name of Colonel Pak, but not the Pak who was in charge of the notorious Pak's Palace [another North Korean prison camp]. He was a spick-and-span officer and wore the cleanest clothes and the shiniest boots I had ever seen. He flat-out told us, "The only reason you're alive is because I'm a soldier. If I had my way, I would take you all out and shoot you because you murdered our people. But because I'm a soldier I have to take care of you and see that you stay alive." He meant it when he said he wanted to shoot us all.

The North Koreans selected us for Camp Twelve because it was a center for propaganda, and they hoped we might become Progressives and be willing to cooperate with them. Col. Paul Liles was the ranking officer in the camp. He was a West Point graduate who was also court-martialed after returning home. The North Koreans took Nehrbas and me to Camp Twelve because we were the ranking NCOs in our group of prisoners and because I had been voted to represent the men and could communicate with our captors. The North Koreans also hated the Second Division. They wanted to wipe us out because we fought so many bloody battles with them.

Within 200 yards of Camp Twelve was another compound called the Central Peace Committee. It consisted of four or six guys who were definitely cooperative. In fact, one of them was a British cartoonist named Ronald Cox who was a card-carrying Communist when he went into the British Army. He was an excellent artist and drew cartoons for the Chinese propaganda publications, one of which was a newsletter called Towards Truth and Peace. It originated in Camp Twelve with the Central Peace Committee, and then circulated to the other prison camps.

The North Koreans wanted to get some of us to make propaganda broadcasts over the Radio Pyongyang. Through intimidation and threats, they forced four of us sergeants to do so. When I was scheduled to go, I didn't know what to do, so I asked Colonel Liles how to keep from going to Pyongyang, which was about a day's walk from Camp Twelve. He told me, "Tell them that your leg hurts and you can't make the trip." So I complained about my leg, which did actually still hurt, and they sent me to a field hospital for two weeks. A black sergeant named Clarence Covington was sent to Pyongyang to make a broadcast in my name. He said, "This is Sergeant Chikami."

Being in a Chinese field hospital was a strange experience. I was in a tent hospital with all these wounded Chinese and North Koreans. They knew I was a prisoner, but they didn't pay too much attention to me, maybe because I looked like them. I got the same kind of food they did, and I got my bandage changed every day. My leg had never really healed. The only thing that had really saved my leg was I got maggots in it about six days after I got captured. I could feel this pain, and I thought for sure I had gangrene, but when I opened up the bandage a big, fat maggot fell out. My medic, Bill Middleton from Texas, cleaned them out for me, but I knew they were good because I had read stories about how Western cowboys during the Indian wars had put maggots on their wounds to clean them.

Howard Adams was in Camp Twelve, and I knew him quite well. He later became one of the 21 who chose to go to China instead of coming home. He had been in World War II and received a Bronze Star. I knew him so well because we were both disabled. So when the rest of the camp went out on work details, he and I stayed back in the camp grinding soy beans. We used to sit there, grind beans, and talk. I thought he was a pretty good guy. He wasn't political at all. He never tried to indoctrinate anybody, and he never talked politics to me. I also knew Richard Corden slightly when I was later in Camp Five. He was another of the 21. He also was not political so I never understood why these guys were so vilified. It is hard to figure what made these guys decide to stay behind. Some people say you get brainwashed, but I have no idea what people mean by "brainwashed." What does that really mean? Were we brainwashed because we had to sit there in a class listening to people talk about germ warfare, an unjust war, and all this kind of nonsense? That doesn't brainwash you. I never saw any instances of any prisoner trying to indoctrinate another into accepting the Communist way of thinking.

In December 1951 the North Koreans disbanded Camp Twelve. They told us we were going to be repatriated, and they had a big banquet for us. They gave us some wine, apples, and other good food. The next day they told us to gather up all our belongings and that we would be taken across the river on boats and be on our way to Panmunjom. A group of over a hundred officers joined us from some other camp, and then all of us went down to the river to wait for the boats, but the boats never came. So the next day they loaded everybody on trucks, but I didn't get to go. Jack Caraveau was so sick that he couldn't be moved. I volunteered to stay back with Jack because we were from the same division and we were the last ones to be captured, as far as I knew. I figured that it was only fair that the other guys get repatriated before us. There was a Capt. Hugh Farler who was also too sick to move, and a Lieutenant Doherty stayed behind with him. The rest of the guys got on trucks and left, and the camp was deserted. I don't know exactly the date, but it was in early December 1951. We thought, "Well they're going to get repatriated," but the next day the planes were still flying. Somebody brought us a little bit of food, but there were no guards. We moved into what used to be the kitchen because there was a lot of firewood there. We burned it all day trying to keep warm, but we didn't get much food.

There were just the four of us there. Captain Farler was delirious and didn't know where he was. Caraveau was coughing and was in bad shape. Days went by and there was still nothing. We had nobody to talk to. Whoever brought us our food couldn't speak English, so we didn't have the faintest idea what was going on. But the planes were still flying, and we could still see dogfights, so we knew that war was not over. Captain Farler died, and we buried him in a peanut patch. Then one day a couple of fancy American jeeps came whirling in there. They were all painted up, with leopard-skin seat covers. A North Korean general popped out with a couple of female aides all dressed in their spick-and-span uniforms. He looked around the compound and came over to where we were. It was Gen. Nam Il, the chief North Korean negotiator during the truce talks. Evidently what happened was the peace

234

talks had broken off, and I guess he just came over to see what was left of Camp Twelve. I didn't think of these things at the time, but I put it all together later. He just looked at the three of us, got in his jeep, and took off. Then a few days later they loaded the three of us on a truck and headed north. We were strafed by a Marine Corsair on the way, but we arrived in Camp Five on New Year's Eve—and that started the next couple of years.

I was put in solitary in Camp Five. I was acting crazy just to harass the Chinese. It was warm this one evening, and I didn't want to stay in this hot little hut. So I built a bench outside the hut. I was lying there, looking up at the sky, when this old Chinese guard came by and said, "Sleepo. Sleepo." I didn't pay any attention to him so he went away. Fifteen minutes later he came back and again said, "Sleepo, Sleepo." I still ignored him. He got ticked and ran off to get the sergeant of the guard. The sergeant of the guard came and said, "Chikami, you sleepo." I mumbled something. Twenty minutes later they got an English-speaking instructor who had been sleeping. He asked me, "Chikami, why you not going to sleep?"

I tell him, "I can't sleep."

He asked, "Why, why? Regulations you go to sleep."

I said, "No, I lost my dog."

He said, "Your dog?"

I said, "Yeah."

He said, "You don't have a dog."

I said, "No, it's gone."

So he got mad and took me up to headquarters. By now it was about midnight, and they got the chief instructor out of bed and he was mad. "Chikami," he said. "Why don't you go to sleep?"

I said, "I lost my dog."

And he said, "You don't have a dog."

I said, "You're right. He's gone."

And he said, "Where did you get the dog?"

I said, "The Turks gave me a dog."

He says, "The Turks don't have a dog."

I said, "No, they gave the dog to me."

He was getting really mad, and he prided himself on knowing a little slang so he said, "Chikami. Let's call a spade a spade."

So I said, "Oh, you want to play cards?"

Oh man, he blew up. He yapped, yapped, yapped in Chinese, and three guards came in, grabbed me, and hustled me out. I still only had summer shorts on. They hustled me up on top of this high hill to a mud hut they called solitary and put me in it. It wasn't funny because it was two or three o'clock in the morning, it had got cold, and I had no blanket. The next day they brought me up a little food and water. For about two or three days they didn't say anything to me. Finally they brought me some more clothes and a blanket. I took the blanket and made a hammock out of it and attached it to these beams. Every time I saw the guard come I would jump into my hammock and swing back and forth like I'm enjoying myself. The guard would get mad and tell me to get out, but I would ignore him. Finally, he came in and cut it down with his bayonet. I didn't know what to do, but I found a little hole in the back wall. I poked my finger through it, which allowed me to look down at the Yalu River. All of a sudden I see another eyeball on the other side. It's the Chinese guard and we're looking at each other. I poked my finger in farther and he pulled back. Then he poked his finger at me, so we're playing this little game. I tried to grab his finger, but I could only get the very tip because the wall was pretty thick. Then I'm looking through the hole and wondering, "What the hell is he doing?" All of a sudden he peed on me. He peed in the hole and right into my eye. I mean, hey, I can't even rinse it out because there's no water. Burned the heck out of my eye and he was laughing.

They let me outside this hut once a day for exercise, and when they did I'd shadow box. They had never seen anything like that. They thought, "This guy really is crazy." Then the guys down in the company got together and signed a petition to get me out of solitary and took it to the commander. The Chinese had just begun to let us play a little basketball, and my buddies needed me to play on our basketball team. We had what we called a United Nations squad: a Japanese, a Puerto Rican, and a Turk on the same team. But they still kept me there for two weeks.

Another time we were all assembled, and they were talking about how that morning their technicians in their white coats and masks had been out in the hills collecting specimens of germ warfare. They had these bugs in this dish that was covered by a glass dome. They passed it around so everyone

236

could look at these bugs. This one red-haired kid, who was a real rebel, lifted up the lid and popped one of the bugs in his mouth before they could stop him [laughs]. Man, they hustled him out of there. They said they sent him to the hospital. We didn't know where the hell he went, but they kept him away for about a week.

Then there was the fly-killing campaign. In early 1953 my buddy and I were in the exercise yard, and we're watching this Chinese guard. He was swatting flies. Well, we didn't pay too much attention because he was always doing crazy things. But the next day there is another guard doing the same damn thing. He was swatting flies, picking them up, and putting them into a little paper envelope. We asked the Chinese in charge, "Hey what's going on?"

He said, "Well, we have a fly-killing campaign going on in China. We're going to make China the most fly-free country in all of Asia."

The Chinese do things like that. In fact, several years before that they had a starling-killing campaign. They killed all the starlings and then the bugs ate all their grain. So we asked, "Why is he saving the flies?"

He said, "Oh, he gets credit for how many flies he kills."

We asked, "What good are the credits?" In China everybody did certain kinds of work or read so many works of Mao to amass these credits. You would get credit for all kinds of things, and these credits helped you work toward getting a Mao Zedong Badge. So they were saving the flies to get credits. One of our guys asked, "Why can't we kill flies?" The Chinese in charge thought about it and said, "I'll let you know."

A couple of days later the Chinese made an announcement at one of the formations: "We understand that some of the prisoners desire to join our fly-killing campaign. Anybody can participate on a voluntary basis. And as an incentive for you to join our campaign we'll give you one factory-made Chinese cigarette for every 200 flies. Anybody who wants to join the campaign raise their hands and we'll issue flyswatters." A whole bunch of people raised their hands and soon everybody was swatting flies. They're all out by the slit trench of the damn latrine swatting flies. Some guys pooled their flies and turned them in when they got 200. They did get a cigarette so the Chinese were living up to their end of the deal. Some of us played poker for flies: "Hey, I'll call you three flies and raise you two." This one guy unraveled the yarn from a sock and fashioned a fly trap. The flies would fly in but then didn't know how to get out. He put it over the slit trench and the first day he caught over 200 flies. I mean just like that he caught a whole mess of them. He turned them in and got his cigarettes. So the next thing you know everybody is trying to make a damn fly trap, but nobody is as good as this guy, and they don't work. This was the only time I almost got into a fight. I went out to the slit trench to do my business. There are six slots and a fly trap over everyone of them. So I picked one up and somebody yells, "Chikami, what the hell are you doing?"

I said, "What the hell does it look like I'm going to do?"

So he says, "Well, move somebody else's trap."

The Chinese nurse had the evening duty of counting these flies, but so many flies were being turned in they couldn't keep up. It was taking up too much time so the Chinese said, "Well, we can't continue this so we're going to find a different way. We're going to weigh them." They got a very fine scale to weigh the flies, but, of course, they cheated a little. It probably now took about 300 flies to get one cigarette, but that's better than nothing. And we're still getting this mass production. This was strictly a capitalistic idea, and the Chinese hated that, but they couldn't do anything because they had made the deal. Sometimes the Chinese would forget to pick up the flies at night and get them in the morning. But by then the flies had dehydrated and didn't weigh nearly as much as they did the day before. So all the GI s were trying to figure out how to keep them fresh. They were putting in little pieces of damp cloth to keep in the humidity so the flies would weigh more. It got ridiculous. My old friend "Sake" Cameron was out there still swatting flies. He had a piece of old goat skin that he covered with excrement and it stunk. He got a little branch and was popping all these big green flies. He was an expert flyswatter. He could hit them and make them pop over dead without crushing them. I asked him, "Sake, how come you're still swatting flies?"

He says, "Come over to my place and I'll show you something." So I went over to his hut and he's got a little bench with all his green flies on it. He had been on work detail and had found these old toothpaste tubes made of aluminum foil. He'd cut a little sliver of that aluminum foil and then pushed it up into the abdomen of the fly. Ten of his flies weighed more that 200 normal flies. He'd mix them up a little bit. The Chinese could never figure out how come his flies weighed so much more than anybody else's. We did crazy things like this to produce a little entertainment and to break the boredom.

238

I know there was a lot of criticism of us prisoners after we were repatriated, but I think a lot of this negative reaction was because of the McCarthy era. I know Colonel Liles pretty well. In fact, I went to visit him last year and I stayed at his home. You're caught between a rock and a hard spot. He was the ranking man in Camp Twelve. Well, what do you do in order to get better food and better medical treatment for the men? You have to decide if you are going to make a broadcast but keep it toned down so you're not blatantly accusing the United States of something. You have to bargain. You're in a tough, no-win situation. No matter what you do there are going to be some POWs who are going to say you're rotten, that you're no damn good. Others will realize you're in a position where you have to decide how much you are willing to cooperate with the enemy to get food, shelter, and care for your men. Take my situation. I was in charge of just a small group. The Chinese gave me the supplies and cigarettes to divide among the guys. How do you divide everything equally right down to the last thing? Apples are not always the same size. Somebody is always going to be unhappy. There is just no way to satisfy everyone.

Gen. William Dean got the Medal of Honor for doing something he never should have. He was stalking a tank. What the hell is a general doing chasing a tank? He ought to be looking after his men. That to me was ridiculous. He also wrote a letter that was turned into propaganda, but he was never singled out. Some of the Air Force POWs wrote propaganda letters admitting to germ warfare and made speeches that were far more serious than anything Colonel Liles or Colonel Fleming did.

Colonel Liles is a humble man, and that thing ruined his whole career. It's sad because I don't think he did anything wrong. He was simply trying to save his men. Yet, there were other enlisted men who really hated him for no reason other than what they had heard. We were all victims of circumstance. Being captured is nothing to be proud of, but I'm not ashamed of it because I was wounded. Yet some of these guys get carried away and think they were really heroes. The real heroes are those who never came home.

When the Freedom of Information Act passed, I sent for my POW file. I couldn't believe what was in it. If I had known, I would not have stayed in the service. They kept investigating me after I got back even though I was still in the service. And it wasn't just me. I'm sure that almost all ex-prisoners of war were watched for at least three years. I didn't know this until I got my file, and I saw they had censored who I wrote to, and who I got letters from while I was in the service. There were accusations from some people I didn't even know. Some corporal reported that Chikami was a big, mean, son of a bitch in camp, and if you didn't agree with him, he would beat the hell out of you. Where did these guys get these ideas? He also said he saw Chikami sign a good conduct pass, and that I had given up because I thought the war was going to end, and that I didn't want to get hurt. The CIC sent two people up into the mountains of Tennessee with a court recorder to take down word for word what this guy said. That was the most ridiculous thing I ever heard. At the time my ex-company commander was still living so all they had to do was contact him. He saw me get shot, he was the one who left me behind. He was later awarded the Distinguished Service Cross, although we had lost over 50 percent of our company the day I was captured. My platoon sergeant at the time threw his rifle away and ran right by me, and he got a Silver Star. I can't say I lost all respect for medals because some were given to the right people, but there were so many that were given to the wrong people and for the wrong reasons.

The worst thing in my file was from a master sergeant I didn't even know. He said that in Camp Five I tried to give the impression of being anti-Communist, but that in my heart I actually leaned toward Communism. He reported he had seen me many a night in Chinese headquarters in earnest conversation with camp officials. The only time I went to headquarters at night was when they threw me into solitary because I wouldn't go to sleep. I couldn't believe these guys. One part of the report said, "Chikami should be notified that he is being investigated." But then another part stated, "No, we can't let him know because this is a national security matter." I was eventually cleared of all allegations, but to think that it even happened, and that all that money was spent investigating us.

Source: Carlson, Lewis H. *Remembered Prisoners of a Forgotten War.* New York: St. Martin's Press, 2002.

"Our Mistakes in Korea" by Brigadier General S.L.A. Marshall (Retired)

General S.L.A. Marshall was a veteran of both World Wars, serving as chief historian for the European Theater of Operations during World War II. General Marshall was in Korea at the time of the Chinese attack, serving as an infantry operations analyst with the Eighth Army. In this article, which originally appeared in the magazine Atlantic Monthly *in September 1953, he offers his perspective on U.S. participation in the war.*

1

Whatever need be said in disparagement of our three years of fighting operations in Korea, it may at least be claimed for them that they possessed the virtue of a rare consistency. Under one Administration they were begun with an air of excessive expectation based upon estimates which were inspired by wishful optimism. Under a second Administration, they are promising to lapse into uneasy quiet amid illusions that are no less remarkable than those which encouraged the initial decision.

Now, looking backward from this time of precarious truce, it can be seen that the ends are no different from the middle. From first to last the failure to budget the expenses of the Korean War, as if keeping them from sight would make the experience less painful, has been symptomatic of a national ailment. We have been reaching for something just around the corner without first moving to the intersection.

In the first summer, we plunged on a sure thing, though the axiom has it that in war nothing is sure. We said we did it because there was no alternative to precipitate action; the future of collective security was at stake, and aggression left unchecked would soon ring the world with fire.

So went the reasoning. But let's look at the record. The decision to intervene was unanimous in the political and military councils of government. But no move toward even partial mobilization accompanied it. The reserves were not called. An ammunition build-up was not programmed, though in some types the stocks were nil. For three months thereafter the Defense Secretary continued to hack at our fighting resources. Relations between State and the Pentagon remained as cold as if they represented opposite sides in a war.

It is said that the original planners mistakenly calculated that they were dealing with a gook army and an essentially craven people who would collapse as soon as mobile men and modern weapons blew a hot breath their way. But the play didn't follow the lines as written.

Initially two American divisions were sent from Japan along with a token air force and a hope that nothing more would be needed. It proved not enough, and so a third was sent along, to be rocked back on its heels. Belatedly a fourth division had been alerted in the United States. Moving into the battle along the Naktong line, its weight was still insufficient to alter the balance.

When at last, in late summer, two additional divisions were landed behind the enemy lines at Inchon, the show, in so far as American field strength was concerned, was all but complete. One more division was added in the hour when the seemingly shattered Communist enemy was being pursued to the Yalu River. Strategy was then at its wishful best; it was wishing out of existence a Red Chinese Army which was already over the border.

So there were seven American divisions to reap the disappointment of the wish and to know the shock of defeat when Communist China, with many times the fighting power of North Korea, entered the war. There were still seven in the following spring. By then the heroic Eighth Army, having been driven from North Korea, was already on the rebound. It was considered the appropriate time for the Joint Chiefs of Staff and others in high place to pass the word that the war was a strategic and tactical stalemate. Concern for Europe influenced the decision; Europe was rated the "decisive" area; so additional American divisions were sent there. This was by way of saying that to stop aggression and make collective security work, it is better to give over a battle which could be won for the sake of one which, under existing conditions, would certainly be lost.

Under both Administrations American policy continued to be guided on the estimates of that hour. At the time of the truce there were still seven American divisions in Korea. There were also 16 ROK divisions, a British Commonwealth division, a Turkish brigade, and numerous stout battalions from other nations.

But when they manned their fire trenches, there was about one fighting man to every 40 yards of distance. Along the general front they were outnumbered by the enemy three to one. The works they held were eggshell thin compared with the depth of the Chinese entrenchments. They consisted really of one line of bunkered trenches slashed through the ridgetops from coast to coast with an occasional half-organized backstop position somewhat to the rear. The Communist defensive zone was entrenched for 20,000 yards back, four times the depth of World War I systems. Their diggings were engineered to provide maximum protection against atomic attack. Ours were not.

So, as forces stand, the war could be properly described as a tactical stalemate. We had the power and they had the push and the people. For two years the situation remained in equipoise mainly because we were motorized and had a tremendous advantage in air and artillery. There had never been sufficient infantry either to do an adequate job of sealing a defensive front or of composing a strategic reserve so that the Eighth Army could really function as an army, using one corps as a maneuver wing. Instead of that, it could meet offensive opportunities only by inching battalions forward.

The UN side, and in particular the United States, which was the major power holding the command seat, accepted a drawn war as inevitable simply out of unwillingness to raise a sufficient infantry. An additional four solid divisions—meaning approximately 60,000 men—might have made all the difference.

But no such augmentation was ever requested and no one arose to ask why not. It is a tender subject in the United States, this one of how many men should be sent to a rifle line where death ever presses close. Too many Americans grow emotional about it, and too few Congressmen are willing to look it in the eye. But the chance for victory rides on having the sufficient number; and when either political or economic considerations finally limit purely military requirements, we ask, if not for stalemate, then for defeat.

Even so, the deliberate political design by which two Administrations treated the Korean War as if it were an insoluble military problem served to achieve one major object. It confused the American public and, confusing it, dulled its memory.

But our confusion is like a low back pain: the hurt is not less because the doctors say there is nothing wrong with the patient.

2

In the second summer of the war, the great illusion was that since we had acknowledged stalemate, the Communists must also see that the game was tied and would be hurting just as hard for a truce. As negotiations began, spokesmen for the Joint Chiefs said privately that the fighting would probably end within three weeks—that it might take as long as six weeks but, on the other hand, could come within six days. President Truman radiated the

243

same optimism. He and the Chiefs seem not to have read of Brest Litovsk [a 1918 peace treaty between Russia and Germany and Austria-Hungary that ended Russian involvement in World War I] or to have known that Mao had praised Communist tactics there as the perfect model for any future negotiation. So again things didn't happen as wished, and some of the by-products of the excessive hope put an additional load on national action.

A limited troop rotation policy was already in effect, having been mothered by necessity. The initial forces had been kept too long and pushed too hard; not to have afforded them relief would have been inexcusable.

But rotation, as it came in full flower under the seeming promise of a quick truce, was a glorified game of musical chairs. Though the fighting pressure had eased, a contract was made with the combat soldier that he would do less than one year in Korea. Provided a truce came forth, there was no great jeopardy in the contract. But if the enemy used the table to prolong the war and harry the United States, it meant that the administrative load among the fighting units would be so greatly increased as to leave little time for training. It meant also that the American divisions of the Eighth Army would henceforth be a half-seasoned body of fighting men barred by regulations from becoming any better than that.

That is the reality. Stuck with its own brainchild, the Army praised rotation as one of the miracles of the Korean War, a bulwark to fighting morale and a conserver of our human material. Analyzed in the field, where men were fighting, it proved to be none of these things.

No doubt something is added to the fighter's morale by the knowledge that in a certain month he will turn home again, provided he lives that long. But what is gained is more than offset by the fact that he never develops any great sense of unity with his company. Reporting to the front for the first time, he joins four or five men in a bunker, and his association with them is likely to be the only feel that he gets of his unit during his first month in combat, or until the unit goes into reserve. By the time he makes a few buddies among the trained men, they are gone on their way. Then, despite his own brief schooling in the front line, he must break in the newly arriving strangers.

Rotation is also a killer of men rather than a saver. There are never enough experienced men to fill the rugged assignments and let the new hands break in gradually. Because of the personnel pinch, men frequently are called on to join a patrol into enemy country their first night in line. Their greenness sometimes proves fatal to the whole group. Such is the turnover that Americans have no chance to develop skill in patrolling. In scouting quality, diversification of maneuver, and catlike caution, they are rarely a match for the Chinese.

Rotation has also furthered that degradation of the Army which is partly the consequence of slide-rule methods in the Pentagon and penny-wise economy in the Bureau of the Budget. Men are not paid what they're worth and are not acknowledged the dignity which they have won under fire. In Korea, companies were commanded by lieutenants, and platoons were frequently led by privates and corporals, with no immediate chance for promotion.

Recently a case study was made in one division of the turnover during a 30-day period. It was perhaps not too significant that of the 1200 replacements incoming, the quota of noncommissioned officers had less than 10 per cent of the grades needed for a body of that number. But it was rather startling to discover that of the 1800 outgoing veterans who had done their time, the quota was still only 40 per cent of what it should have been.

A brigadier of artillery put it this way: "The trouble with rotation isn't that we haven't made it work, but that someone in Washington will get the idea that it's good."

3

During the third summer, the illusion that a truce would arrive on winged feet still hung on. The new hope which came to bloom beside it was that by building a still stronger ROK Army we would shortly find an easy exit from our Korean venture.

The history of this effort, and in particular the tardiness of the decision, shows conclusively that it was inspired by dreams of liquidating our commitments and getting back to the old rocking chair rather than by the hope for military victory.

During the first year of mobile war, South Korea as a potential reservoir of military help to us was virtually ignored, and that was the time when the help was most needed. Americans "choggied" their own supply up the ridge trails to join the fire fight, and wore themselves out in so doing, though there were thousands of Korean backs ready to do the pioneer work. The organization of the Korean Service Corps, which now has a regiment with each of our divisions, came along later. It has been a splendid help.

In that year there were only two competent ROK divisions equipped with organic artillery and a reasonable complement of other heavy weapons. The others got along as best they could without systematized heavy fire support, and it is a wonder that any survived. Yet the Army of the United States did not so much as send one headquarters battery to Korea to initiate a training establishment for ROK artillerymen so that there would be ready men when the guns became available. The word in Washington at that time was that the policy-makers feared to build up the ROK Army lest Syngman Rhee become uncontrollable. Whether that is the true explanation, or the neglect of the force was due to pure sluggishness, is perhaps beyond proof.

But it was not until the leash had been pulled on General Van Fleet's forward operations and talk of truce filled the air that the ROK build-up started. The army is now proceeding toward 20-division organization with an over-all strength of 600,000. There is little fat in the administrative rear, and most of its strength is squeezed toward the fighting components. Here, of course, is the great paradox of the situation. The modern ROK Army was born on the battlefield out of a stricken nation, which had nothing to give but raw manpower. Deprived of our economic help, the Republic could not keep its present army for 60 days.

To rear a modern and well-rounded military establishment and, behind this façade, then to attempt to make a backward nation catch up with the present, while assisting in the revitalizing of its economy, is quite a reversal of the normal processes of history. It is a unique experiment. It is expensive; and to the American who still thinks that military power in any form is a parasite upon the political body, it seems an unnecessary waste of his money and an outrage against Korea's underprivileged people.

Rhee was audacious in expecting us to support 20 ROK divisions, which is more than we had in our own establishment. But Rhee saw perhaps more clearly than we that he would continue to face the Chinese.

That carries us along to the great illusion of the current summer—the wishful hope that soon after the signing of a truce the Communist Chinese will fold their tents, mount their camels, and steal away. Is there any reason in it or is it just another butterfly thought?

Following World War II, the term "vacuum area" was coined to describe the war-ravaged country which, stripped of police power and means of livelihood, became dependent on outside help if it was to survive in nationhood.

Greece was such a place for a time. So were the other Balkans. We went to Greece's rescue. Russia filled the vacuum elsewhere in the peninsula and in Central Europe and never thereafter loosed its grip.

Yet, with this recent example before us, we have failed to envisage the over-all political condition that will obtain in the Korean peninsula now that the truce is signed. Since South Korea is, for the time being, invalided and dependent on us largely for military supply and what is needed to keep life in a now surplus population, we more or less vaguely see that for some years ahead we shall have to fill the vacuum, serving as backer, banker, and supplier. Either that or South Korea, left a hopeless derelict, will be salvaged by Communist neighbors.

But where our thinking falls short—and this applies to our policy-makers—is in our failure to consider that North Korea, economically, politically, and militarily, is a worse wreck than the territory south of the 38th Parallel and that this vacuum is certain to be filled by a major power.

Communist China permitted General Nam Il of North Korea to front as chief delegate at Panmunjom. It was an act of political tact in marked contrast with our policy of keeping the South Korean delegate at the bottom of the totem pole. Behind Nam Il's impeccable front, however, lies only the shattered façade of a puppet state which has never known independence and is now too ill to experiment toward it. Of the more than a million Communists manning the front in Korea, not more than 50,000 of the combat element was North Korean. The interior police power is under supervision by the Chinese. The people till their land to keep the Chinese army fed, and subsist on what is left. Their heavy industry is in ruins; their commerce is limited to the traffic in war materials.

Briefly pictured, here is a situation from which the troops of Red China cannot possibly withdraw. For if that were to be done, a chaotic and, despondent people would embrace the help and faith offered from the Free World. All that now gives North Korea a semblance of unity is the military operations of Red China which the North Koreans now serve.

Red China did not enter the war with the object of throwing over her own prestige and sacrificing her power position at the last moment. To expect such stupid generosity of her is almost criminal folly. The Chinese aim is to defeat the United States and UN coalition, and possibly, beyond that, to expand her territory. So when our statesmen express the pious hope that in a "reconciliation period" which follows a truce, Red China can be persuaded to withdraw, they are blind to fundamental political realities. Red China can't withdraw; nor can water flow uphill.

Korea is a strategically profitless area for the United States, of no use as a defensive base, a springboard to nowhere, a sinkhole for our military power. We don't belong there.

But because of that, to think now of how we can stage an extrication before we have taken any measure of what the post-truce struggle might become, is only to extend the wayward course we have already traveled. It is a time for steadiness, waiting and seeing, and a rugged realism in our appreciation of the situation instead of the pipe-dreaming which has mocked the effort thus far. The retention of a strong American garrison in Korea during the period ahead while the Republic is growing up to its armed establishment might well mean the saving of Southeast Asia and even help to cool off Red China.

Quite a few things enter into the prevention of world war and the preserving of peace. It's infinitely helpful when the strongest power acts both willing and resolute.

Source: Marshall, S.L.A. "Our Mistakes in Korea." *Atlantic Monthly*, September 1953.

SOURCES FOR FURTHER STUDY

Blair, Clay. *The Forgotten War: America in Korea, 1950-1953*. Annapolis, MD: Naval Institute Press, 1987. Widely recognized as the most authoritative and comprehensive work on the Korean War, the book is highly detailed in its day-by-day account of military activity and policy decisions.

Carlson, Lewis. *Remembered Prisoners of a Forgotten War*. New York: St. Martin's Press, 2002. A compilation of oral histories, POWs' personal memoirs (both previously published and unpublished), and analyses of common perceptions of the Korean War POW experience.

Goldstein, Donald M., and Harry J. Maihafer. *The Korean War: The Story and Photographs*. Washington, DC: Brassey's, 2000. A photographic history of the war, with text amply illustrated with photographs that tell the broader story of the war.

Isserman, Maurice. *Korean War*. New York: Facts on File, 2003. A succinct overview of the Korean War, designed for the young adult audience.

Paschall, Rod. *Witness to War: Korea*. New York: Berkley Publishing Group, 1995. A narrative of the Korean War that weaves together accounts based on original source material from a wide range of participants, including foot soldiers, generals, chiefs of state, guerrillas, and more.

Ridgway, Matthew B. *The Korean War*. Garden City, NY: Doubleday, 1967. General Ridgway's personal memoir of his involvement in the Korean War. His narrative avoids military jargon or detail and offers the unique perspective of a commander faced with a difficult assignment.

Truman Presidential Museum & Library. Independence, MO. Online at www.trumanlibrary.org. An excellent source of primary documents relating to the Korean War, including United Nations resolutions, presidential statements, President Truman's diaries, oral histories, and photos.

BIBLIOGRAPHY

Books and Periodicals

Acheson, Dean. *Present at the Creation*. New York: Norton, 1969.

Alexander, Bevin R. *Korea: The First War We Lost*. New York: Hippocrene, 1986.

Allen, Richard C. *Korea's Syngman Rhee: An Unauthorized Portrait*. Rutland, VT: Charles E. Tuttle Company, 1960.

Appleman, Roy E. *Disaster in Korea: The Chinese Confront MacArthur*. College Station: Texas A&M University Press, 1989.

Appleman, Roy E. *South to the Naktong, North to the Yalu: United States Army in the Korean War*. Washington, DC: Office of the Chief of Military History, 1961.

Bateman, Robert. *No Gun Ri: A Military History of the Korean War Incident*. Mechanicsburg, PA: Stackpole Books, 2002.

Benson, Sonia G. *Korean War: Almanac and Primary Sources*. Farmington Hills, MI: UXL, 2001.

Blair, Clay. *The Forgotten War: America in Korea, 1950-1953*. Annapolis, MD: Naval Institute Press, 1987.

Bongard, David L., and Ken Stringer. *Harper Encyclopedia of Military Biography*. New York: HarperCollins, 1992.

Bradley, Omar N., and Clay Blair. *A General's Life*. New York: Simon & Schuster, 1983.

Clark, Mark W. *From the Danube to the Yalu*. New York: Harper & Brothers, 1954.

Carlson, Lewis. *Remembered Prisoners of a Forgotten War*. New York: St. Martin's Press, 2002.

Cumings, Bruce. *Korea's Place in the Sun: A Modern History*. New York: W.W. Norton, 1997.

Cumings, Bruce. *North Korea: Another Country*. New York: The New Press, 2004.

Dean, William. *General Dean's Story*. As told to William L. Worden. New York: Viking, 1954.

Dobbs, Michael. "War and Remembrance: Truth and Other Casualties of No Gun Ri." *Washington Post*, May 21, 2000.

Eisenhower, Dwight D. *Mandate for Change, 1953-1956*. Garden City, NY: Doubleday, 1963.

Ferrell, Robert H. *Harry S. Truman: A Life*. Columbia: University of Missouri Press, 1994.

Foot, Rosemary. *The Wrong War: American Policy and the Dimensions of the Korean Conflict*. Ithaca, NY: Cornell University Press, 1985.

Foreign Relations of the United States, Vol. VII. Washington, DC: Office of Chief of Military History, 1950.

Frankel, Benjamin, ed. *The Cold War, 1945-1991.* Farmington Hills, MI: Gale Research, 1992.

Galloway, Joseph L. "Doubts about a Korean 'Massacre.'" *U.S. News & World Report,* May 22, 2000.

Goldstein, Donald M., and Harry J. Maihafer. *The Korean War.* Washington, DC: Brassey's, 2000.

Gugeler, Russell A. *Combat Actions in Korea.* Army Historical Series. Washington, DC: Center of Military History, United States Army, U.S. Government Printing Office, 1987.

Halberstam, David. *The Fifties.* New York: Villard Books, 1993.

Halliday, Jon, and Bruce Cumings. *Korea: The Unknown War.* New York: Pantheon, 1988.

Hamby, Alonzo L. *Man of the People: A Life of Harry S. Truman.* New York: Oxford University Press, 1995.

Hanley, Charles J., Sang-Hun Choe, and Martha Mendoza. *The Bridge at No Gun Ri: A Hidden Nightmare from The Korean War.* New York: Henry Holt and Company, 2001.

Heinl, Robert Debs, Jr. *Victory at High Tide: The Inchon-Seoul Campaign.* Philadelphia: J. B. Lippincott, 1968.

Higgins, Marguerite. *War in Korea: The Report of a Woman Combat Correspondent.* Garden City, NY: Doubleday, 1951.

Hoare, James, and Susan Pares. *Conflict in Korea: An Encyclopedia.* Santa Barbara, CA: ABC-CLIO, 1999.

Hoyt, Edwin P. *The Day the Chinese Attacked: Korea, 1950, The Story of the Failure of America's China Policy.* New York: McGraw-Hill, 1990.

Isserman, Maurice. *Korean War.* New York: Facts on File, 2003.

Kaufman, Burton I. *The Korean War: Challenges in Crisis, Credibility, and Command.* Philadelphia: Temple University Press, 1986.

Marshall, S.L.A. "Our Mistakes in Korea." *Atlantic Monthly,* September 1953.

Millett, Allan R. "A Reader's Guide to the Korean War." *Journal of Military History,* July 1997.

Mitchell, George C. *Matthew B. Ridgway: Soldier, Statesman, Scholar, Citizen.* Mechanicsburg, PA: Stackpole Books, 2002.

Nahm, Andrew C. *Korea, Tradition and Transformation: A History of the Korean People.* Elizabeth, NJ: Hollym International, 1988.

Paik Sun Yup. *From Pusan to Panmunjom: Wartime Memoirs of the Republic of Korea's First Four-Star General.* Dulles, VA: Brassey's, 1992.

Paschall, Rod. *Witness to War: Korea.* New York: Berkley Publishing Group, 1995.

Perret, Geoffrey. *Old Soldiers Never Die: The Life of Douglas MacArthur.* New York: Random House, 1996.

Ridgway, Matthew B. *The Korean War.* Garden City, NY: Doubleday, 1967.

Sandler, Stanley, ed. *The Korean War: An Encyclopedia.* New York: Garland Publishing, Inc., 1995.

Sandler, Stanley. *The Korean War: No Victors, No Vanquished*. Lexington: University Press of Kentucky, 1999.

Schneider, Carl J., and Dorothy Schneider. *World War II: An Eyewitness History*. New York: Facts on File, 2003.

Spurr, Russell. *Enter the Dragon: China's Undeclared War against the U.S. in Korea, 1950-1951*. New York: Henry Holt, 1988.

Suh, Dae-Sook. *Kim Il Sung: The North Korean Leader*. New York: Columbia University Press, 1988.

Summers, Harry G., Jr. "The Korean War: A Fresh Perspective." *Military History*, June 2000.

Toland, John. *In Mortal Combat: Korea, 1950-1953*. New York: William Morrow and Company, Inc., 1991.

Truman, Harry S. *Memoirs*. 2 vols. Garden City, NY: Doubleday, 1955-1956.

Truman, Harry S. Papers of Harry S. Truman: Post-Presidential Files. Harry S. Truman Library, Independence, MO.

Tucker, Spencer C. *Encyclopedia of the Korean War: A Political, Social, and Military History*. 3 vols. Santa Barbara, CA: ABC-CLIO, 2000.

Westover, John G. *Combat Support in Korea*. U.S. Army in Action Series. Washington, DC: Center of Military History, United States Army, U.S. Government Printing Office, n.d.

Zeinert, Karen. *McCarthy and the Fear of Communism*. Berkeley Heights, NJ: Enslow, 1998.

Zellers, Larry. *In Enemy Hands: A Prisoner in North Korea*. Lexington: University Press of Kentucky, 1991.

Online

Central Intelligence Agency. "Intelligence Memorandum No. 302: Consequences of the Korean Incident," July 8, 1950, and "Intelligence Memorandum No. 304: Effects of a Voluntary Withdrawal of US Forces from Korea," July 10, 1950. http://www.cia.gov/csi/books/coldwaryrs/5563bod4.pdf .

National Park Service, U.S. Department of the Interior. "Korean War Veterans Memorial." http://www.nps.gov/kowa *and* http://www.nps.gov/kwvm/home.htm.

Pace, Frank, Jr. Interview by Jerry N. Hess, January 22, 1972-February 25, 1972. Independence, MO: Harry S. Truman Library. http://www.trumanlibrary.org/oralhist/pacefj.htm.

Truman Presidential Museum and Library. "Conflict and Consequence: The Korean War and Its Unsettled Legacy." http://www.trumanlibrary.org/whistlestop/study_collections/korea/large/index.htm.

Truman, Harry S. "Radio Report to the American People on Korea and on U.S. Policy in the Far East," 04/11/51. Truman Public Papers, Truman Library. http://www.trumanlibrary.org/ publicpapers/index.php?pid=290&st=&st1=

Truman, Harry S. "Special Message to the Congress on Greece and Turkey: The Truman Doctrine," 3/12/47. Truman Public Papers, Truman Library. http://www.trumanlibrary.org/ publicpapers/index.php?pid=2189&st=truman+doctrine&st1=

Truman, Harry S. "Statement by the President on the Situation in Korea," 06/27/50. Truman Public Papers, Truman Library. http://www.trumanlibrary.org/publicpapers/index.php?pid=800&st=&st1=

United Nations. Security Council Resolution, June 25, 1950. http://www.un.org.

United Nations. Security Council Resolution, June 27, 1950. http://www.un.org.

U.S. Constitution, art. 1, sec. 8. http://www.ourdocuments.gov/doc.php?doc=9&page=transcript.

U.S. Department of Defense. "Commemorating the Korean War."http://www.defenselink.mil/specials/koreanwar.

U.S. Department of Defense. "United States of America Korean War Commemoration." http://korea50.army.mil.

U.S. National Security Agency. "NSA Korean War Commemoration." http://www.nsa.gov/korea/index.cfm.

DVD and VHS

Battle for Korea. VHS. PBS Home Video, 2001.

Korean War: Fire and Ice. VHS, 4 vols. History Channel, 1999.

PHOTO CREDITS

Cover photo: Bert Hardy/Getty Images.

Chapter 1: DOD/Time Life Pictures/Getty Images (p. 12).

Chapter 2: National Archives/NLR-PHOCO-A-48223659(69) (p. 16); AP/Wide World Photos (p. 18).

Chapter 3: Library of Congress (p. 31); George Skadding/Time Life Pictures/Getty Images (p. 33); AP/Wide World Photos (p. 35); Carl Mydans/Time Life Pictures/Getty Images (p. 36).

Chapter 4: AP/Wide World Photos (p. 43); U.S. Army/Hulton Archive/Getty Images (p. 45); Haygood Magee/Getty Images (p. 48).

Chapter 5: Hulton Archive/Getty Images (p. 53); National Archives/NWDNS-111-SC-348438 (p. 58); Bert Hardy/Getty Images (p. 60); National Archives/ NWDNS-111-SC-348594 (p. 61); National Archives/NWDNS-80-G-420027 (p. 62).

Chapter 6: National Archives/NWDNS-80-G-420027 (p. 67); AP/Wide World Photos (p. 70); U.S. Army/Time Life Pictures/Getty Images (p. 71); AP/Wide World Photos (p. 72).

Chapter 7: National Archives/NWDNS 127-N-A6759 (p. 77); National Archives/NWDNS-80-G-422112 (p. 79); National Archives/NWDNS-342-AF-82607AC (p. 81); National Archives/NWDNS-111-SC-356309 (p. 84); National Archives/NSDNS-306-FS-259(21) (p. 86).

Chapter 8: U.S. Army Signal Corps/courtesy MacArthur Foundation (p. 88); National Archives/NWDNS-111-SC-365348 (p. 89); National Archives/NWDNS-80-G-429691 (p. 91); National Archives/NWDNS-80-G-429691 (p. 92); Hulton Archive/Getty Images (p. 97).

Chapter 9: National Archives/NWDNS-306-PS-51(10303) (p. 103); U.S. Army/courtesy Dwight D. Eisenhower Library (p. 107); National Archives/NWDNS-342-AF-84421AC (p. 109); AP/Wide World Photos (p. 111).

Chapter 10: Hulton Archive/Getty Images (p. 114); National Archives/NWDNS-111-SC-351359 (p. 115); National Archives/NWDNS-111-SC-347020 (p. 117); National Archives/NWDNS-306-PS-51 (p. 127).

Chapter 11: Time Life Pictures/Getty Images (p. 131); National Archives/NWDNS-127-N-A5426 (p. 135).

INDEX

(ill.) denotes illustration